AF573656

Hugh Stoneman

THE MASTERS' MASTER

Hugh Stoneman

THE MASTERS' MASTER

THE ART FUND HUGH STONEMAN ARCHIVE

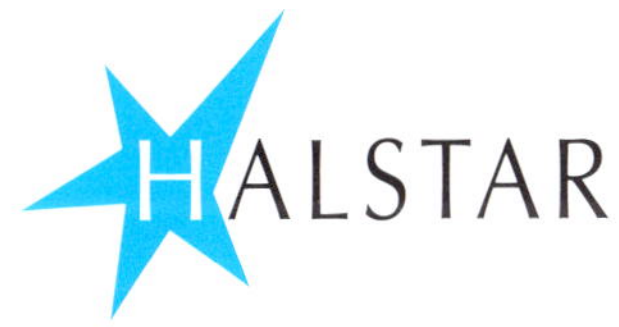

First published in Great Britain in 2009

With contributions from: Donna Williams, Sara Lee, Natalie Rigby, Charles Booth-Clibborn, Mike Tooby, Alex Hooper, Fiona MacCarthy, Linda and Georgia Stoneman, Suzanna Haynes

Photography: Steve Tanner. Studio photographs Linda Stoneman

British Library Cataloguing-in-Publication Data
A CIP record for this title is available from the British Library

ISBN 978 1 906690 21 2

HALSTAR
Halsgrove House,
Ryelands Industrial Estate,
Bagley Road, Wellington, Somerset TA21 9PZ
Tel: 01823 653777 Fax: 01823 216796
email: sales@halsgrove.com

An imprint of Halstar Ltd, part of the Halsgrove Group of companies
Information on all Halsgrove titles is available at: www.halsgrove.com

Printed and bound by Grafiche Flaminia, Italy

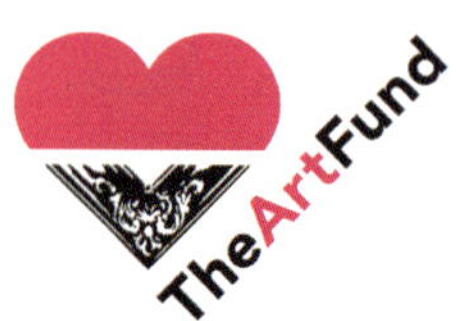

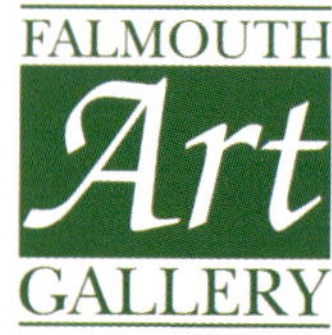

S

STONEMAN GALLERY

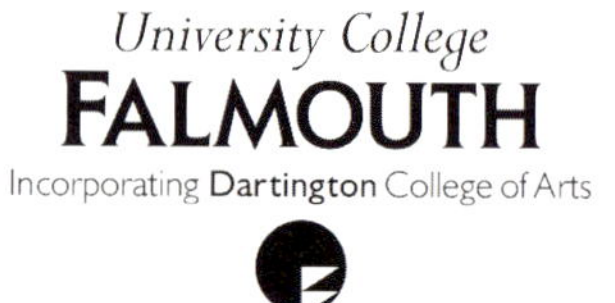

www.artfund.org
www.falmouthartgallery.com
www.stonemanpublications.co.uk

Acknowledgements

FALMOUTH ART GALLERY would like to thank Linda, Daniel and Georgia Stoneman and family for their generosity and help. We would also like to thank Simon Butler and Sharon O'Inn of Halsgrove, Carole Makeham and the many artists who worked with Hugh Stoneman for supporting this publication.

A great many people and organisations assisted with the project, in particular we would like to thank:

The Art Fund, Peter Barclay, Dr Wendy Baron OBE, David Barrie, The Anthony Benjamin Estate, Clojo Bedingham, Michael and Linda Bickford, K. Blake, The Sandra Blow Estate, Polly Bolitho-Dymond, Charles Booth-Clibborn, Tamsin Bough, Sophie Bowness, Marina Bradbury, Harriet Bradshaw, The British Library, Lizzy Brookes, Piers Browne, Rachael Browning, Christopher Le Brun, Tanera Bryden, Amy Bullocke, Louise Burrows, Shannon Butler, Simon Butler, Richard Calvocoressi CBE, Seamus Carey, Chris Carter, Megan Chapman, Martin Clark, Pat and Steve Collinson, Rhys Conion, Professor Michael Craig-Martin RA CBE, Alan Cristea Gallery, Mary Crockett, Suzanne Crook, Joshua Crowle, Cecily Cuff, Maureen Davies, Pam Dodds, Jilly Easterby, Becky Edwards, Geoffrey Evans, Falmouth School, Falmouth Town Council, Arwen Fitch, Laura Fleming, Glen Freestone, Anthony Frost, Dr Francesca Geens, Issy Goode, Lucy Grisse, Felix Griffiths, John Grimble, The *Guardian*, Dee Hall, Ellie Hardman, Richard Harold, Amanda Harris, Sophie Harrison, Annabel Hawken, Helston Community College, The Barbara Hepworth Estate, David Heseltine, Sir Geoffrey and Lady Carol Holland, Josephine House, John Howard, Sara Hughes, Lyndsey Ingram, Timo Jaakkola, Peter Jordan, Rachael Kantaris, Meera Karan, Louise Krogsriis, Dr David Landau CBE, Sara Lee, Billie Lee-Smith, James Lingwood, Little Parc Owles Trust, Professor Alan Livingston CBE, Christopher Lloyd CVO, MJ Long, Etienne Lullin, Jo Lumber, Fiona MacCarthy, Andrew Macdonald, Carole Makeham, Magnum Photos, Jonathan Marsden LVO FSA, Sarah-Jane Marsden, Danny Mason, Mullion School, Helen Munro-Berry, The Museum of Modern Art New York, Catherine Naylor, Debbie Orford, Sally Osman, Mark Osterfield, Jemima Owen-Jones, Zella Packer, Paragon Press, Nancy Patterson, Emmie Payne, Penryn College, Sarah Philp, Matthew Pickett, Joanne Pilcher, Simon Polglase, Courtney Porter, Sandra Powlette, Joe Rainbow, Bianca Rees, Professor Lord Renfrew of Kaimsthorn FBA FSA, Richard Saltoun, Charles Sebag-Montefiore FCA FSA, Florian-Oliver Simm, Avril Stansfield, Timothy Stevens OBE, Dr Deborah Swallow, Tate St Ives, Tate St Ives Members, John Tonkin, Mike Tooby, Christian Topf Design, Megan Turner, University College Falmouth, Professor William Vaughan, David Verey CBE, Tony Waddington, Elizabeth Waddling, The Hon Felicity Waley-Cohen, The family of Naomi Weaver, Pat Webster, Susanna Webster, Petrouilla Silver Weschke, The Estate of Karl Weschke, Jeremy Whittaker, Glyn Winchester, Sophie Wright, Paul Zuckerman.

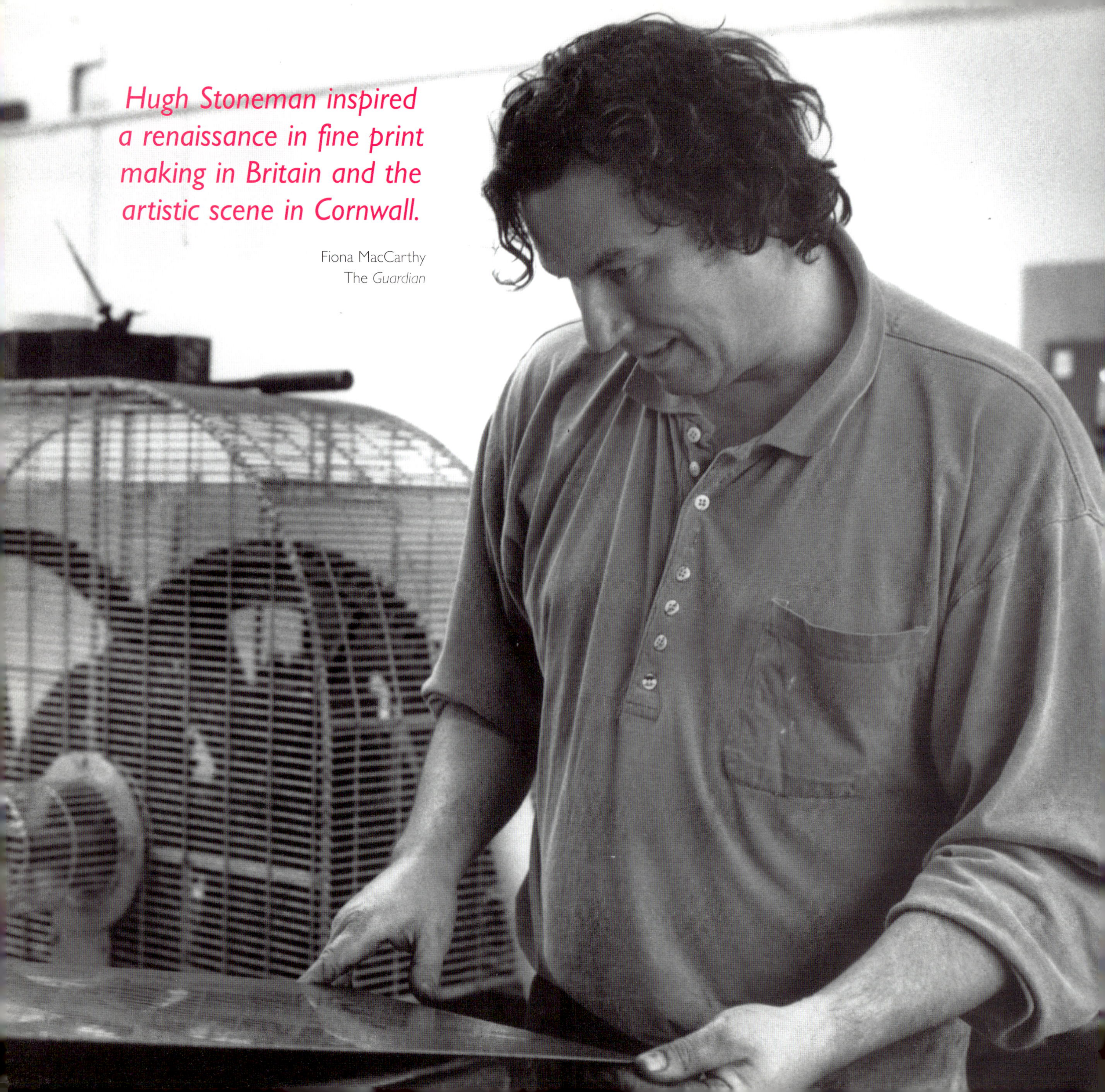

Hugh Stoneman inspired a renaissance in fine print making in Britain and the artistic scene in Cornwall.

Fiona MacCarthy
The *Guardian*

The Art Fund Hugh Stoneman Archive at Falmouth Art Gallery

PROFESSOR ALAN LIVINGSTON CBE introduced Linda Stoneman to Falmouth Art Gallery staff because he felt it would be helpful for us to be aware of the astonishing range of work produced by Linda's late husband, Hugh Stoneman, during his career as a Master Printer.

We knew of his outstanding skills through the excellent exhibition held at Tate St Ives from 26 January to 11 May 2008. However, at that time, we didn't appreciate that the work on show there was just the tip of a very large and impressive iceberg.

Thanks to Alan Livingston's meeting we were invited by Linda to see Hugh's archive of prints produced for major contemporary artists. Our visit was like entering an Aladdin's cave of contemporary art. A thought occurred – could it be possible for Falmouth Art Gallery to acquire this amazing archive as a unique resource for future generations?

With some trepidation the idea was proposed to Linda. She was instantly enthusiastic and, after discussing it with her family, she generously agreed to sell the archive of 99 master prints to Falmouth. The price agreed, £30,000, was kind and very sympathetic to a small, Cornish public art gallery. It was dramatically below the current market value. Indeed, Linda was generously giving us the opportunity of acquiring an important collection of some of the greatest international artists of the second half of the 20th century for a sum equivalent of purchasing an oil painting by a second tier Victorian artist.

There was a slight problem – Falmouth Art Gallery did not have £30,000! We felt that if we could get a representative of a funding body to actually see the whole archive they would find it irresistible. We approached The Art Fund, who had supported the gallery in acquiring Trevor Bell's masterpiece, 'Five Bar', an awe-inspiring abstract he painted in Florida after witnessing the launch of Apollo 17, the first night-time launch of a space mission. They had also assisted us with funding to acquire historic works by John Opie RA, Sir Frank Brangwyn RA, Charles Napier Hemy RA RWS and Henry Scott Tuke RA RWS.

We telephoned Dr Francesca Geens, Head of Grants at The Art Fund, and informed her of the archive and the difficulty in getting all of it to London. As always she was extremely helpful. A short period of time elapsed before she rang to announce that The Art Fund's then Director, David Barrie, would come to Cornwall to see the archive.

The Art Fund cannot possibly fund all the worthwhile requests it receives for important works of art. We watched David Barrie study the 99 prints in the archive and hoped that he was impressed.

Due to exceptional circumstances we applied for a 100% grant and took a cross-section of the archive up to London for consideration by the panel of Art Fund Trustees and advisors. Behind closed doors David Barrie informed the committee of his visit and his views of the whole archive.

After a short but nervous wait we received the fantastic news that committee had approved our application: The Art Fund Hugh Stoneman Archive was to be purchased and housed at Falmouth Art Gallery. There was great celebration because the archive transformed the already impressive Falmouth Art Gallery print collection. In one swoop this acquisition enabled Falmouth to boast one of the most important print collections outside of London.

Brian Stewart
Director
Falmouth Art Gallery

The Masters' Master –
The Art Fund Hugh Stoneman Archive

HUGH STONEMAN (1947–2005) was one of the greatest Master Printers of the 20th century. His career spanned three decades in which he worked closely in a unique dialogue with major international painters, photographers, sculptors and ceramicists.

A combination of hard work, discipline and a natural flair for the complex techniques of printmaking placed him at the very top of his field. Hugh's outstanding skills allowed him to focus clearly on texture and image, rather than being distracted by the process. His talent enabled him to take contemporary printmaking to new heights.

It was for this reason that The Art Fund purchased the exceptional archive of artists' prints that Hugh Stoneman made throughout his career. This archive was presented to Falmouth Art Gallery, which houses one of the most important print collections outside of London with Old Master engravings and woodcuts by Dürer, Rembrandt, Claude and Piranesi through to contemporary works by Matisse, Picasso, Warhol, Sir Peter Blake, Francis Bacon, Merlyn Evans and Patrick Caulfield. Through The Art Fund the gallery has also acquired the Mrs Naomi G. Weaver Gift featuring works by Eduardo Chillida, Prunella Clough, Raoul Dufy, Mary Fedden, Barry Flanagan, Henry Moore, Edvard Munch, Barbara Rae and Pierre Auguste Renoir.

The Art Fund Hugh Stoneman Archive is exceptional because it features a range of work by a single Master Printer working in collaboration with international artists. It is a rare resource indeed, providing a unique opportunity for scholars, students, artists and printmakers to study a representative selection of this Master Printmaker's career.

The archive of 99 prints includes significant pieces by Hugh's long-term collaborators Ian McKeever RA, Sir Terry Frost RA, Adam Lowe and Arturo Di Stefano; several outstanding examples of photogravure by Eve Arnold, Fay Godwin and Linda McCartney; and many important prints by artists such as Sandra Blow RA, Eileen Cooper RA, Patrick Heron, John Hoyland RA and Kurt Jackson.

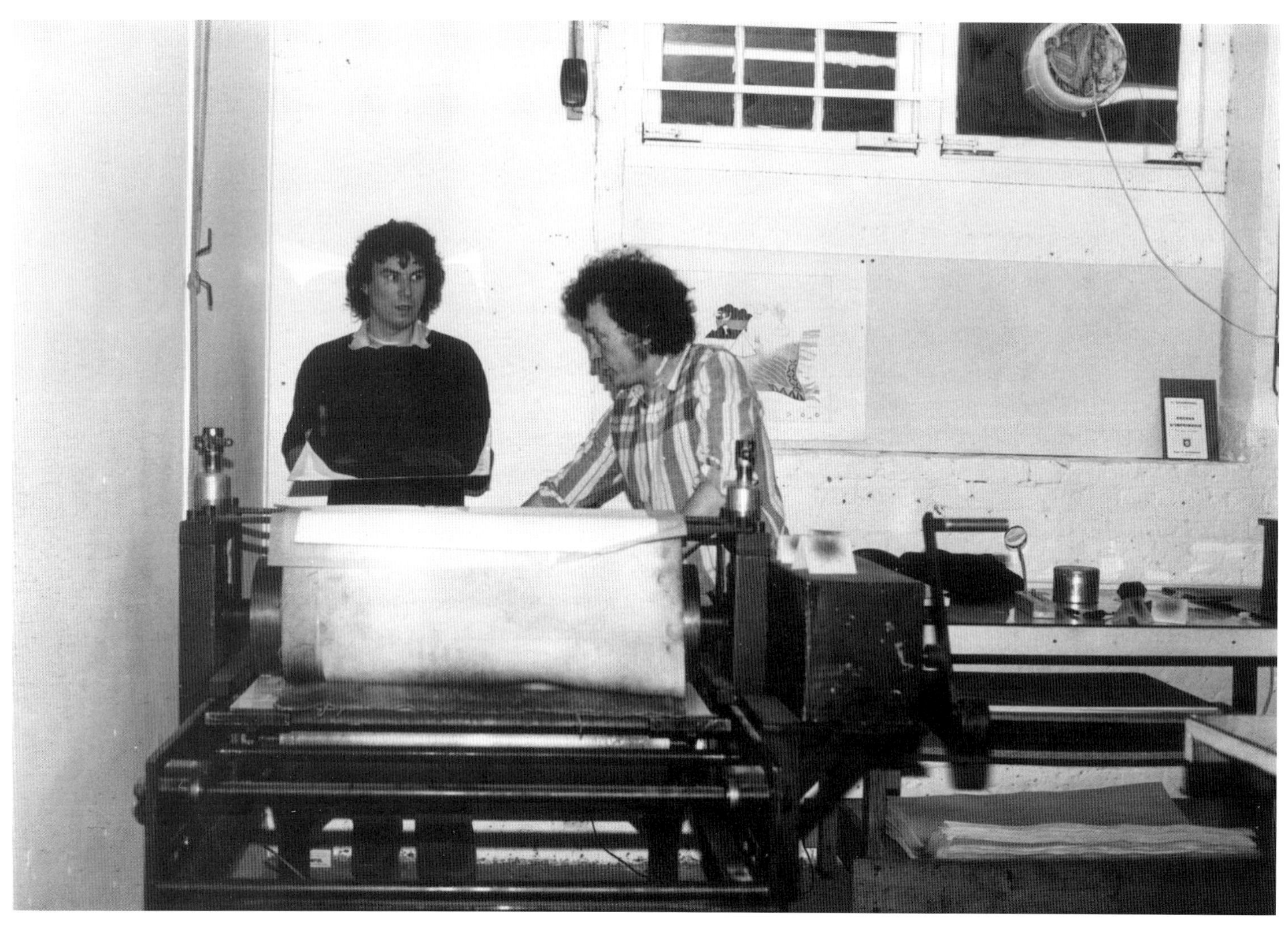

Hugh and Anthony Benjamin in The Print Centre, Covent Garden

Hugh Stoneman was born in Islington, London in 1947. He was educated as a boarder at Blundell's School, Tiverton in Devon, where he excelled at cricket and squash. After abandoning a place at Trinity College, Dublin to read Law, Hugh studied as a painter at Camberwell College of Art, London between 1967 and 1970. After graduating he was still considering architecture as a career, before discovering his talent for printmaking while studying etching in Paris with Stanley William Hayter CBE. Hayter was an important and influential British painter and printmaker, associated with Surrealism and Abstract Expressionism. In Paris, Hayter founded the legendary Atelier 17 studio and he is credited with influencing artists such as Picasso, Giacometti, Miró, Calder, Chagall, Pollock and Rothko. He also worked with the artist and writer Sir Roland Penrose. *Time* magazine described Hayter as the 'greatest innovator of modern etching', so Hugh could not have had a better mentor.

Hugh returned to London to establish his own print studio. The Islington Studio opened in 1972, with his first wife Alyson as a co-director. It provided access to much-needed equipment, advice and help for over 300 artists. This was followed in 1979 by The Print Centre, Covent Garden and The Print Centre, Islington in 1988. Hugh worked on commissioned pieces for publishers and also under the studio imprint Print Centre Publications, gaining a reputation with artists and collectors for his high-quality portfolios. Hugh could offer artists a wide depth of knowledge in etching, photogravure, woodcut, linocut, lithography and letterpress – he was an expert in them all.

The Islington Studio

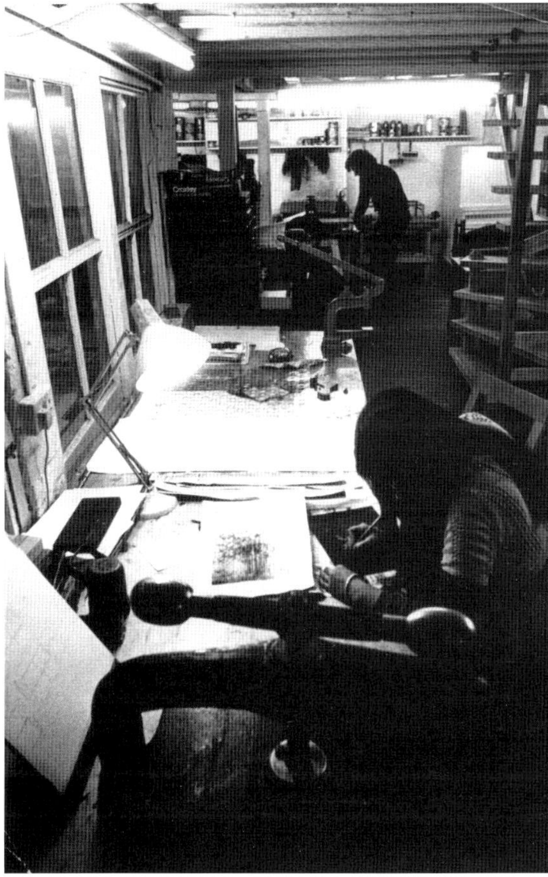

Hugh's links with Cornwall were always strong. He was based first at Newlyn at Dod Procter's former studio and later he bought Orchard Flower Farm, Madron in the early 1980s with his second wife Linda, which was to become the family home – Hugh commuting to his studio in London every week. In 1995 he eventually relocated his business, taking his presses and equipment with him, to a purpose-built print studio alongside his home, Orchard Flower Farm, where he worked for the rest of his life. His intense enthusiasm helped to bring a new artistic energy to a region that was already rich in creativity.

Apart from his printmaking expertise Hugh also lent his support and experience to the Borlase Smart–John Wells Trust, as a Trustee. He supported the Trust's proposal to renovate the historic Porthmeor Studios in St Ives. The studios provide workspace for today's contemporary artists and in the past for major artists such as: Wilhelmina Barns-Graham, Trevor Bell, Francis Bacon, Sandra Blow, Terry Frost, Patrick Heron, Frances Hodgkins and Breon O'Casey.

Chris Hibbert, Manager of the Porthmeor Studios Proposal, commented: *"When I was appointed Hugh's support was invaluable, particularly at crucial times. He was one of the nicest people I have met and this was helpful in uniting people for a common cause."*

Many artists from all over the world travelled down to Cornwall to collaborate with Hugh. They recognised and respected his technical expertise and his intuitive flair for image making. Their total confidence in Hugh provided an opportunity for them to venture into highly creative and productive new areas.

Eileen Cooper RA produced several series of important prints with Hugh, including the multi-block linocut 'Dreamland', which is included in the archive. The print is rich in powerful colour and poignant symbolism. Eileen gained a great deal from their collaboration and reminisced: *"In a playful way Hugh encouraged artists to take ambitious steps within print. He was determined to extend his already formidable knowledge and enjoyed taking artists with him. He always made you feel that you led the way."* Today, Eileen continues to collaborate with Hugh's colleague Sara Lee, an accomplished Master Printer in her own right – together they produce outstanding images.

Hugh began an eighteen-year collaboration with Ian McKeever RA in 1987, creating a large number of high quality print portfolios together, including the extraordinary suite 'Jerusalem'. The images 'Coloured Etching' (1996) and 'Between Space and Time' (1998) are included in the Art Fund archive at Falmouth. Ian maintains that Hugh took him to places he could never have managed on his own. He commented: *"To watch Hugh inking up and then wiping clean a large etching plate was a beautiful sight. He seemed to know instinctively the density of ink required for each proof and how cleanly it should be wiped to find the right print. With broad shoulders, like those of a scrum forward, he would lean into the plate and work. Standing next to him one could feel the intimacy and love he had for the activity. He knew when to be emphatic and when to caress, when to leave in or take out with a single kiss.*

Ian McKeever at Hugh's studio, Madron

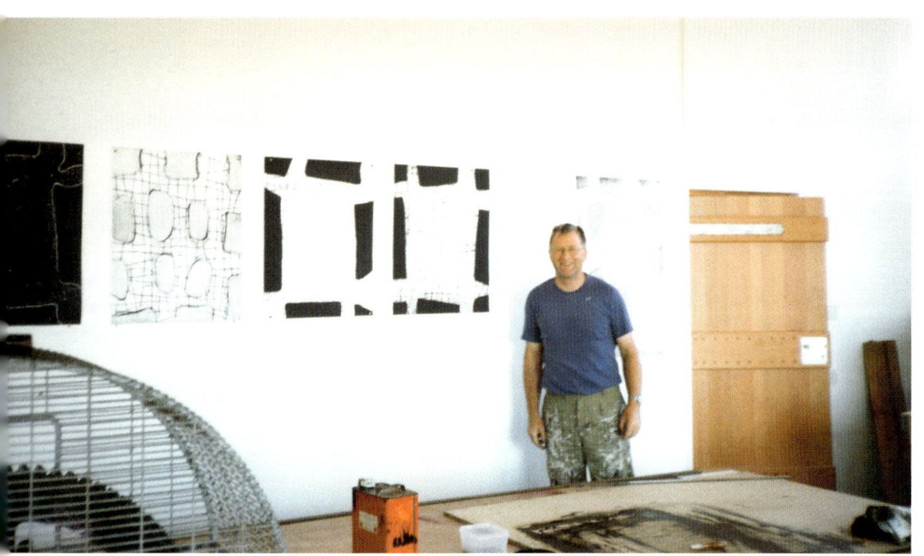

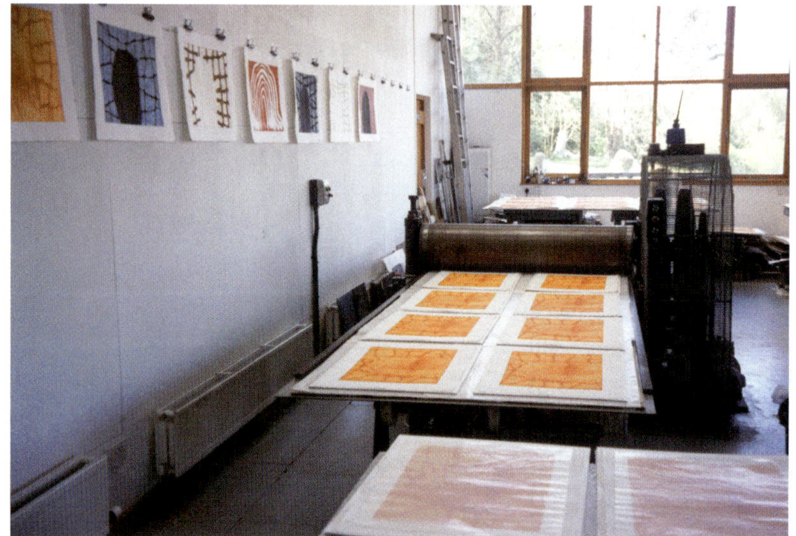

If other printers might ask if a plate needed six or seven minutes in the acid, (as if the artist would know!), Hugh reduced such technicalities to language the artist could understand. 'Black' or a 'tone' he would say with a certain feel to his voice and the gesture of running the flat of his hand across the surface of a plate, as if to suggest the plate could find and reveal its own needed state, and usually it did. More than anything in working with Hugh one had to watch his hands, they were always a pointer and a sign suggesting a way forward."

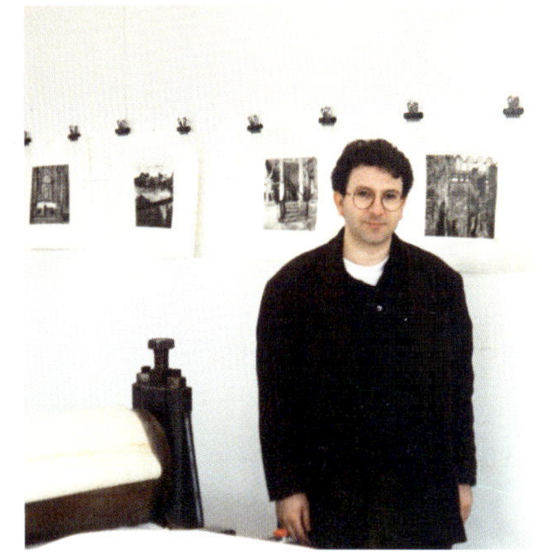

Arturo Di Stefano at Hugh's studio, Madron

Another long-term working relationship was with the artist Adam Lowe, who fed discoveries and ideas from printmaking into his painting. Adam has used printmaking terms as titles for a number of his paintings and prints, such as 'Registration Marks', and 'Digital Prints', and in the case of the atmospheric and moody photogravure etching in the archive, 'Emulsion 3'.

Hugh's collaboration with Arturo Di Stefano was also fruitful. They worked on exciting projects such as the 'Strands', 'Atelier' and 'Smoke' series using a range of techniques including aquatint etching, photogravure and woodcut. The most important example of this collaboration in the archive is the large, predominantly blue, woodcut 'Atelier 3'. It is infused with a haunting presence helped by the grain of Hugh's woodcut. The making of an image for Arturo *"...is like a journey undertaken without a known destination."* To him a painting or print *"can be a portal to memories and feelings that can change the way we view the world to the extent that we are able to see it anew."*

Arturo described working with Hugh to Mike Tooby: *"He was a great facilitator of one's ideas, understanding immediately what the artist was trying to achieve and even, at times, with great sensitivity and intuition, anticipating the artist's intention. He could offer several solutions to any problem or bring about the desired effect and make the image appear effortlessly, as if by magic, gifting it to the artist.*

His studio was a place where you worked hard, set by the example of his unflagging industry, where you could relax into making mistakes, allowing error to be turned into something useful and advantageous. No obstacle could not be surmounted and transformed into a possible means of invention. His work-rate and stamina meant that at the end of a working day, usually beyond the normal run of hours, there would be a whole range of prints on display, from tentative first proofs, to state and trial proofs and so on. A print was something that could be tested to destruction, the results of which provided the ground for more images to be generated in completely unexpected ways."

Another of Hugh's successful collaborations was with the celebrated abstract artist Sir Terry Frost, who lived nearby at Newlyn. Although they had worked together in London, Hugh's move to Cornwall allowed their relationship to blossom. Printmaking was very important to Terry – for him painting and printing were inseparable, with one medium creating ideas for the other. His magnificent 'Orchard Tambourine' series of woodcuts, published by Charles Booth-Clibborn under his imprint the Paragon Press, are among the most important images of Terry's career.

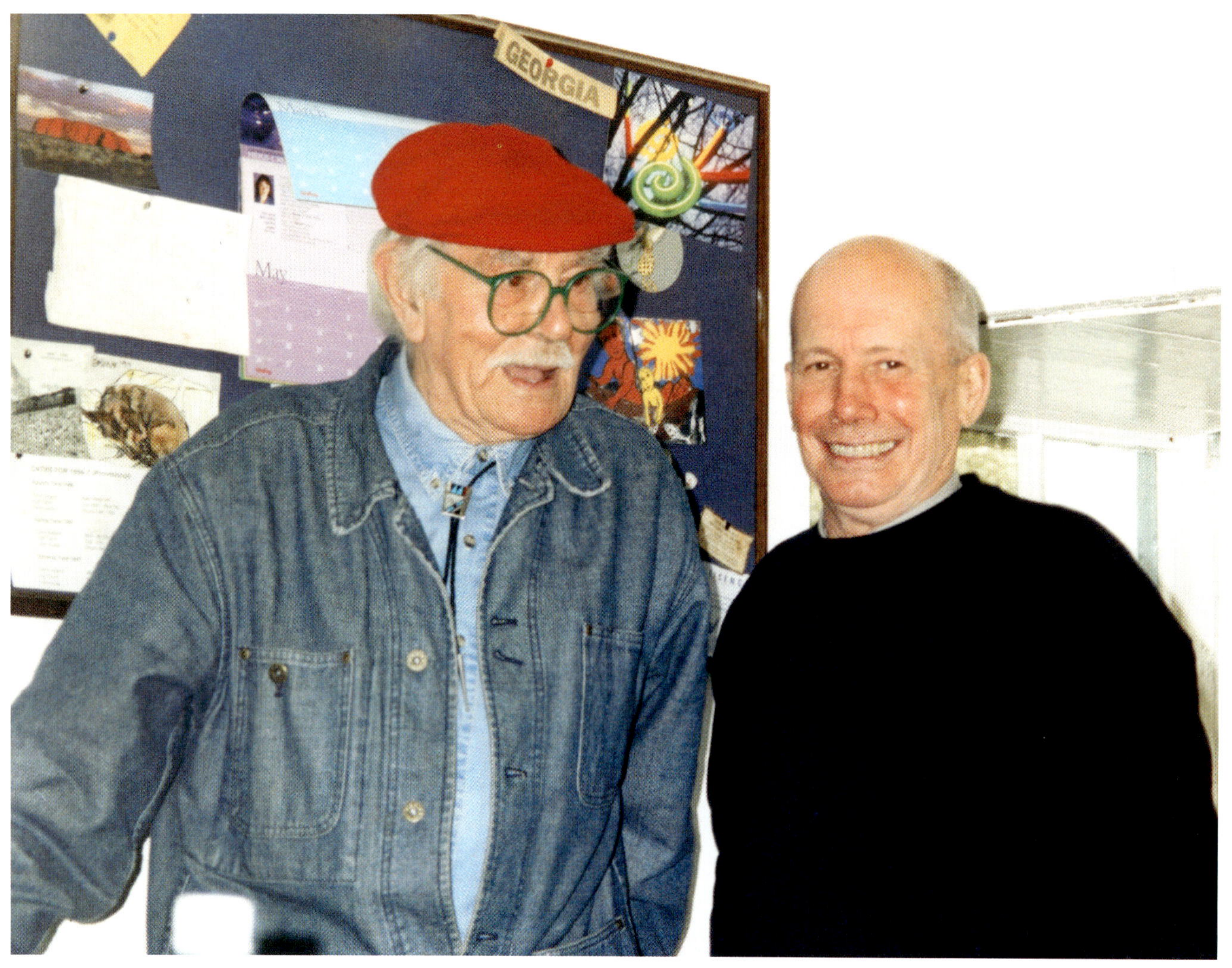

Sir Terry Frost and Richard Smith at Madron

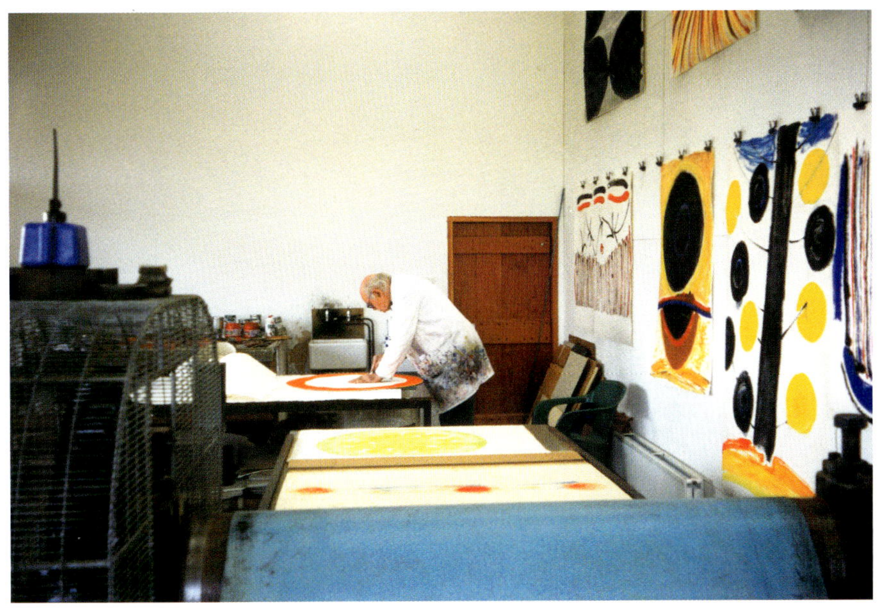

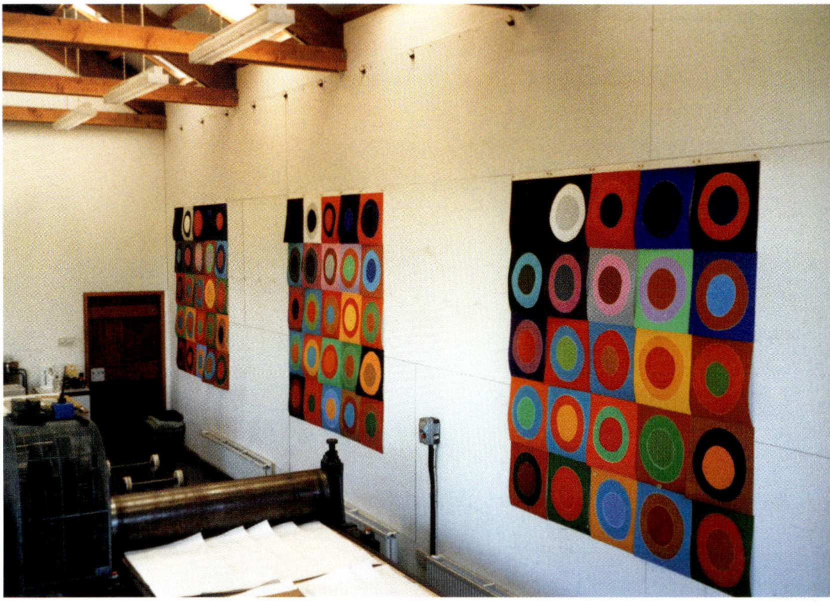

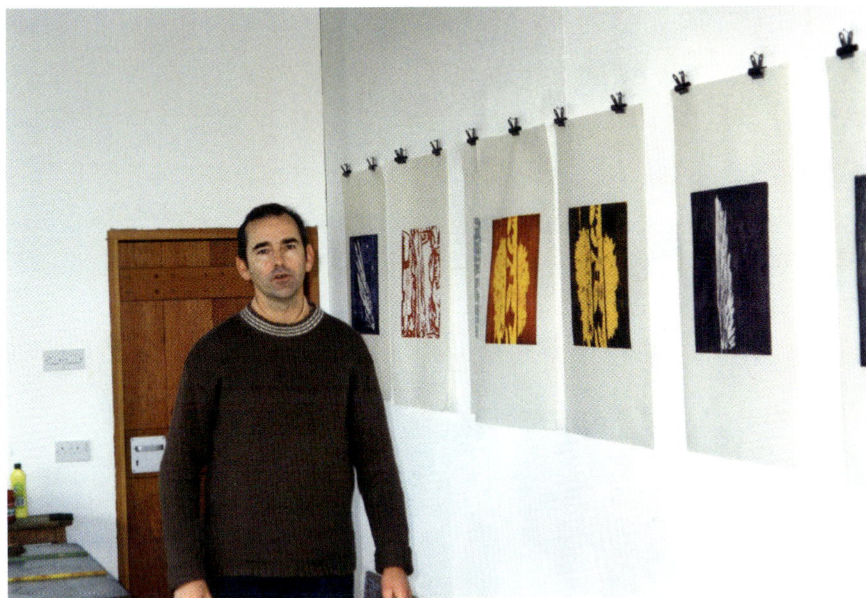

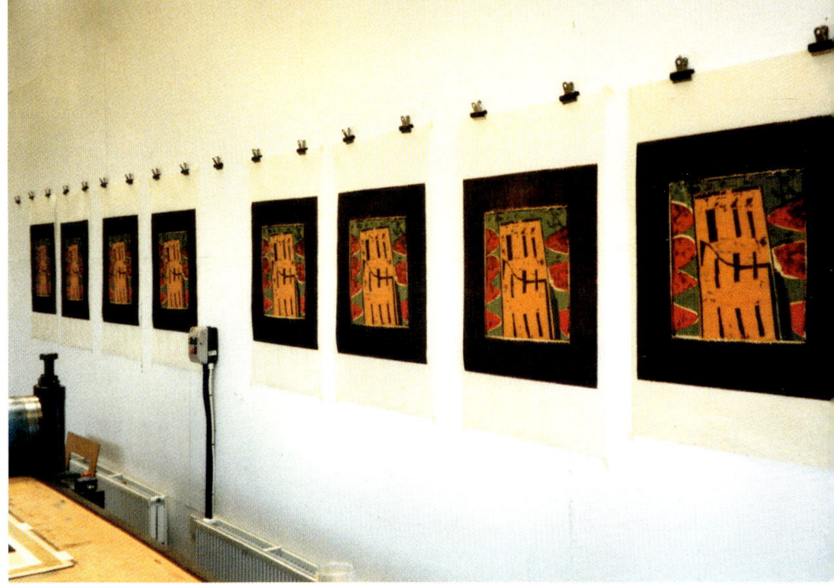

Top: Sir Terry Frost at Madron. Above: Christopher Le Brun at Madron.

The series was inspired by collages Terry had made using leftovers of canvas and card mounts. The blocks were cut by Hugh from quarter-inch plywood using a jigsaw and each colour had to be printed twice in order to achieve the saturation of tone that Terry required. He was delighted with the outcome and acknowledged that without Hugh's exacting standards the images could not have been achieved. The title 'Orchard Tambourine' paid tribute to Hugh who lived at Orchard Flower Farm, while the second part of the title references the percussion instrument, the shape of which is echoed in the composition. Acutely aware of an individual's highly personal response towards colour, Terry was happy for others to arrange the prints in a different order or not even in a square at all. His wish was that the viewer should derive as much enjoyment from the sets as the artist himself in the process of their creation.

The archive also features the triptych 'Timberaine'. The idea for this sprang from a large painting of stripes Terry had recently completed that was inspired by forest tree trunks. Terry referred to the painting as 'a jungle'. He concocted the title from the words 'timber' and 'rainforest'. Working in woodcut allowed Terry to accomplish the quality and clarity of the design that he envisaged, in contrast to his painting, where the edges of the stripes were inevitably softer. Under Hugh's guidance Terry chose a specific grain of wood – ash – to achieve the suitable surface texture. The prints were conceived as monoprints with each triptych having a slightly different appearance. Hugh cut an individual block of ash for each colour stripe.

Another delightful woodcut in the archive is 'Yellow Tower' by Christopher Le Brun RA. The tower has become an important motif in Christopher's work, and his collaboration with Hugh has been particularly successful. Hugh's skilful use of the wood grain creates a rich texture that combines beautifully with Christopher's powerful use of line, colour and shape.

Hugh's studio at Madron

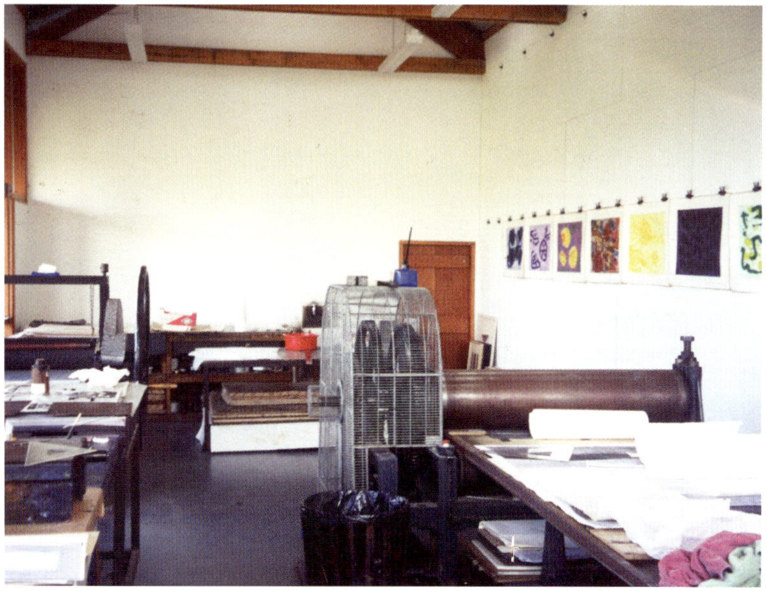

Charles Booth-Clibborn commissioned Hugh to work with Patrick Heron on an extraordinary portfolio of sugarlift etchings entitled 'Brushworks' – the artist's only series of autobiographical prints. Patrick applied the sugar-lift with long Chinese brushes that he used for gouache, showing an innate instinct for the ways the marks on a new plate would interact with those previously made on the other plates for printing each of the colours. Hugh delighted in Patrick's sense of freedom and use of accidental effects. Patrick lived close by at 'Eagles Nest' near Zennor and every Friday between December 1998 and March 1999 Hugh took plates and proofs to him until the final images were complete. The two men would usually start each session by taking a walk before returning to Patrick's studio for refreshment and a discussion of the previous week's proofs. On the day that Patrick happily approved the final proofs he passed away at the age of 79. The Patrick Heron proof in the archive is vibrant and full of youthful energy.

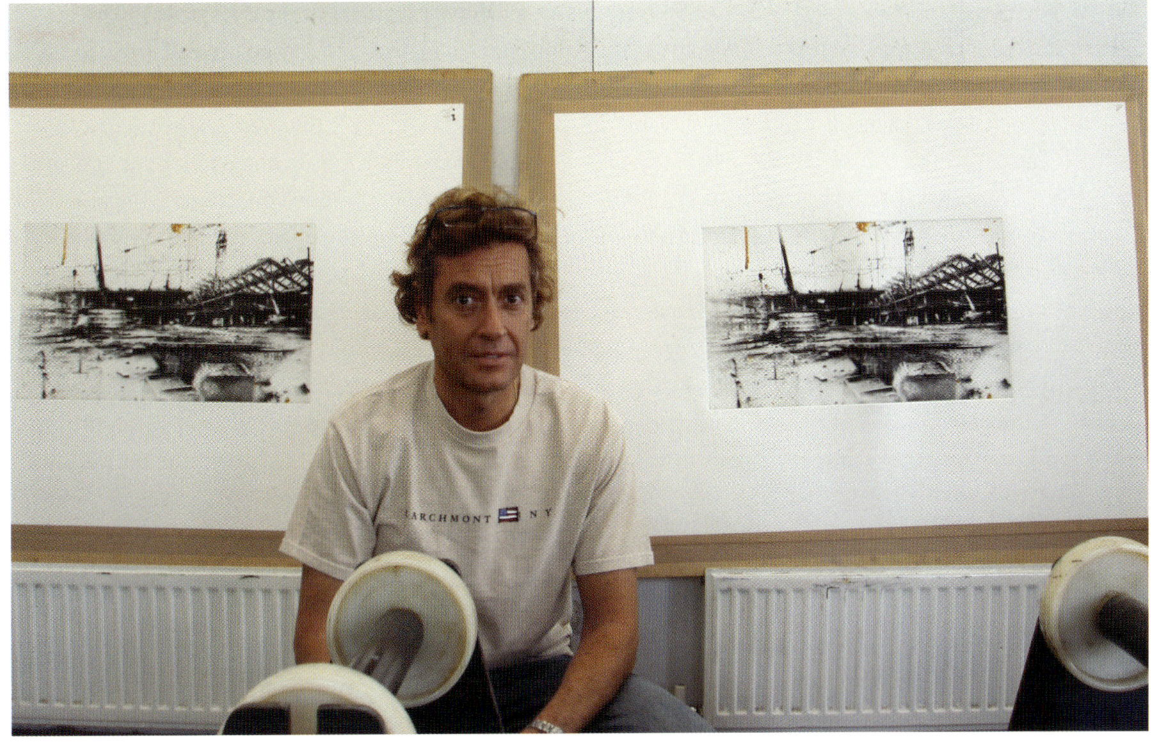

César Galicia at Hugh's studio, Madron

When George Shaw exhibited at the Newlyn Art Gallery in the autumn of 2004 Charles Booth-Clibborn suggested he should contact Hugh. They first worked together on the series 'Twelve Short Walks'. The series was originally called 'Twelve Walks', but George changed the title as a tongue-in-cheek reference to Richard Long's walks across the British Isles.

The drawings for 'Twelve Short Walks' were based on photographs of Tile Hill, situated on the outskirts of Coventry where the artist was brought up. At the time they were drawn he didn't have a studio and was also between houses, so he used a friend's kitchen table to make small drawings based on these familiar images. He was initially thinking of working directly on a plate but Hugh felt that dustgrain gravure would be more suitable for his work.

George explained the process: *"I did a sketch on a piece of paper and then laid the acetate sheet on top and drew on this with acrylic wash and scratched back with scalpels and knives. It always stays as a positive image although it is transferred on to the plate. This was quite important for me."*

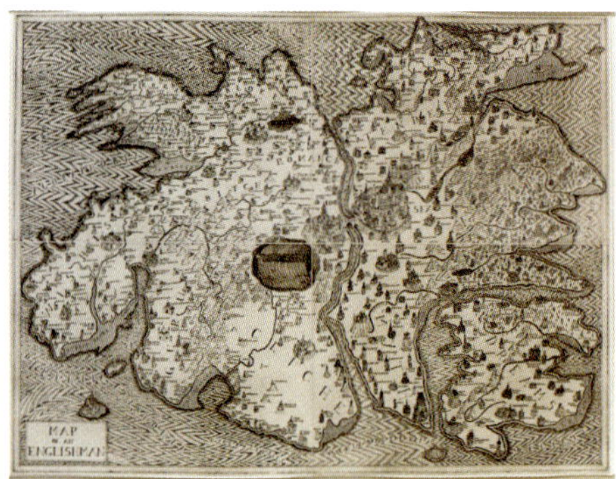

Grayson Perry, Map of an Englishman, dustgrain gravure, 112 x 150cms, The Paragon Press

'Twelve Short Walks' is like a biographical storyboard. The portfolio has all the settings of a film but none of the action. George comments: *"It was almost the moment before somebody shouts action and all of the characters walk on. The mysterious mood emanating from the images is due to the unknown ... You don't know what is in the bushes, you don't know what is round the corner. Generally, it would just be a bitter boy who would just thump you in the face... but it's also the not knowing."*

Charles Booth-Clibborn arranged for Hugh to work with the Turner Prize-winning artist Grayson Perry on the subversive panoramas 'Map of an Englishman' and 'Print for a Politician'. As with George Shaw, Stoneman proposed dustgrain gravure as the perfect technique for the artist's tenderly detailed, visionary narratives. Grayson remarked: *"I just loved the fact that, after working on pottery for years, which is quite hard work – at the end of a day of drawing on pots I have a dent in my finger from the knife I use – but drawing on film is just like dreaming. I can just do it for hours and hours."* Several proofs of the prints were made to achieve a *"blurry look – that was quite important to me. I wanted it to look like a hand-made thing."*

In preparation for the 'Map of an Englishman' Grayson studied antiquarian maps, his favourites being from Holland made during the sixteenth century, and traditional English county maps that can sometimes be seen in country houses. Grayson's interest in mapmaking goes back to his childhood: *"As a kid I had a very developed imaginary world and I used to draw maps of that."*

Although Grayson had made a small sketch of 'Map of an Englishman', he did not make a full size preparatory drawing because *"I enjoy the adventure – the novelty – and it would be killed if I knew exactly what I was going to do. So I actually learn on the job."* The houses in the top third of the print are noticeably smaller than the ones further down. This was not planned beforehand, but Grayson likes the effect: *"It's almost like you have those little poor houses and then, down near the ridge, you have the rich houses."*

The 'Consciousness' lake in the middle of the map was originally meant to show waves blowing across the water. The finished area now resembles a brain – the seat of consciousness itself. For Grayson this was a happy mistake and he liked the associations that came with it. In the top right hand corner Grayson has included well-known art critics who have denigrated his work. In a humorous riposte he has exiled his critics offshore *"stranded on their lonely little islands."*

In order to enhance the print's interest as an object Grayson also designed a special moulding for the frame, which was made to look like old frames in English country houses.

Perhaps Hugh's greatest contribution to contemporary printmaking was in the technique of photogravure. Early in his career a commission to make a portfolio of prints of street scenes of Baghdad photographed during the 1920s and 1950s by the Iraqi politician Kamil Chadirji led him to experiment with this early nineteenth century technique. The process of photogravure involves etching a copper plate using a gelatine transfer and a positive image of a silver print. This creates a distinct texture and, in Hugh's hands, gave tonal images of extraordinary subtlety.

The archive contains Chadirji's 'Pots', which is a clever composition featuring a line of handmade coil pots in the hot sun of Baghdad. The strong shadows cast by the pots create exciting patterns and Hugh was able to emphasise these with the use of subtle tones. The outstanding quality of these photogravures led to other commissions and collaborations, notably from Eve Arnold and Fay Godwin.

Fay recorded the desolate landscapes of the Calder Valley, west of Halifax. These feature the lost lands of Elmet, the last Celtic kingdom to fall to the Angles. The area prospered during the Industrial Revolution, when it was the centre of the textile trade, but this has now faded away. Fay captured the landscape in its moody decline and this has been intensified in the outstanding photogravure prints produced by Hugh, with a starker contrast between light and shade. The graininess from the plate and the soft, heavy paper on which the images were printed add to its romantic melancholy.

The writer and cultural historian Fiona MacCarthy considers Hugh's finest examples of photogravure printing to be the prints he made of Eve Arnold's photographs taken in America during the 1950s and early 1960s. She writes: *"The photogravure process infuses these images with whole new implications, heart-rending overtones of vanished glamour, intimations of tragedy and loss."* Mike Tooby agrees: *"Stoneman's images of Eve Arnold's series of portraits are widely regarded as exemplary in the photogravure printing of monochrome photography."*

The set was published in September 2002 in conjunction with the Eve Arnold exhibition at the Zelda Cheatle Gallery, London. The archive contains the artist's proof set. When the Art Fund presented the archive to Falmouth Art Gallery the national press focused on the iconic image 'Marilyn Monroe playing pool'. It was taken at Reno, Nevada in 1960 during a break from filming on the set of her last completed feature film *The Misfits* – the classic American film written by Arthur Miller and starring screen legends Clarke Gable and Montgomery Clift.

Also popular with the press was the image 'Charlotte Stribling a.k.a. Fabulous', the famous model, waiting backstage for her entrance cue to model clothes designed and made in Harlem. The image was taken at the Abyssinian Baptist Church, Harlem in 1950.

Arguably the most powerful and cleverest image in the series is 'Silvana Mangano, Museum of Modern Art, New York'. The celebrated Italian film star, singer, dancer and model married the film producer Dino De Laurentiis. She is seen with two Brancusi sculptures 'Mlle Pogany' and 'Endless Column' – the latter echoing the shape of Silvana's slim figure.

Rhys Conlon of the Department of Paintings and Sculpture at the Museum of Modern Art, New York informed us that 'Endless Column' didn't become part of their permanent collection until 1983. It is likely that the photograph was taken during the Brancusi sculpture exhibition held there between 7 July and 15 August 1954.

Hugh used photogravure to good effect for the print 'The Head of Henry Moore' by Robert Lyon. This was originally drawn in 1923, when Moore and Lyon were both students at the Royal College of Art, and is the earliest known portrait of the sculptor. In Hugh's skilful hands the photogravure captures all of the delicacy and sensitivity of the original drawing now in the National Portrait Gallery collection.

Among the many international artists Hugh worked with is one of Australia's most admired artists, G.W. Bot. Her birth name is Christine Grishin, but according to Aboriginal belief each member of a clan inherits a totemic relationship with a particular plant or animal of the region. She liked this idea of oneness with the environment and as wombats were prevalent in her area they became her totemic animal. The earliest written reference to a wombat occurs in a French source where it is called 'le grand Wam Bot' – hence her exhibiting name.

G.W. Bot works in Canberra and immerses herself in the depth and intensity of the surrounding landscape, which always informs her highly original compositions. *"I first came to work with Hugh in 1997 during my first exhibition at the Hart Gallery, Islington. The wonderful Pat Gilmour, founding curator of prints at the Tate Gallery, London (1974–1977) and the National Gallery of Australia (1981–1989) here in Canberra, had sent me a list of printers and printmaking workshops that I might work with. I contacted Hugh from Australia. He hand typed me such a beautiful response I knew I had to work with him. The Hart Gallery commissioned a series of drypoints from me which Hugh and I did at Hugh's studio, Madron Hill, together with Mike Ward. 'Tattoo' comes from this series. It is to do with our imprint on the landscape, the puncturing that occurs when we live, work and so often destroy the land that surrounds us. There is also a sense of mystery of the landscape which I felt very strongly in Cornwall and is definitely the case in the Australian bush. It is as if the land is watching and witnessing us as we tattoo it.*

I further worked with Hugh in 1999 and 2001. Hugh and his wife Linda would meet me at the train station in Penzance when I came down from London. Work commenced immediately, preparing plates, inking up and proofing. Not a moment was lost, the hours were long but there was always time for stories, visits to and from Terry Frost and an Australian red wine to end the day. Hugh's input into my journey as an artist will always remain. It was an honour to have known and worked with Hugh."

The year before Hugh died he collaborated on a magnificent etching, 'Winter Wood' with Kurt Jackson, one of Cornwall's most successful and best loved artists. Kurt remembers:

"I was working on my 'Two Woods' project that subsequently toured between Bath's Victoria Art Gallery, St Barbe Museum and Art Gallery in Lymington, and Truro's Royal Cornwall Museum. I was comparing a Cornish wood to another one near Bath, feeling that I had worked enough in paint and wanted to use another medium – I played about with some small etchings in my usual random, chancy way in a damp studio but felt that I needed to work on a larger scale; I needed help and professional advice. I'd heard about Hugh – a well-known and nationally respected printmaker in the area and I'd seen what he had done at Tate St Ives; so he was the obvious person to approach. We chatted and he suggested using photogravure – I could use the technique en plein air – he was excited (like me) – we had plans to do some large seascapes together. I worked on this piece in Skewjack Woods, near Sennen – the most westerly piece of woodland in Britain, I reckon. The drawing and writing happened as I sat in the woods that day. Soon after, Hugh fell ill and the print was actually completed between his visits to hospital. We were never able to attempt the large seascapes."

In the last years of Hugh's working life he became preoccupied with the formidable possibilities of linocut, a development from the woodcuts he made with Terry Frost. Hugh loved the immediacy of the process, its strength and its precision. He used this to wonderful effect in 'Here's Flowers', the sequence of large-scaled, hand-coloured linocuts on Velin Arches Blanc paper that he prepared with Gary Hume RA in 2005. Despite being ill Hugh continued to work on these prints until the week before he died from cancer on 9 December 2005. They were the last prints he signed off.

The printmaker Sara Lee reminisced: *"Hugh was always at his happiest talking about such technicalities as the length of etch, dampness of paper or whether to hand tissue, or just scrim wipe, and was still experimenting and breaking boundaries.*

When asked, Hugh would often describe himself, and those of us lucky enough to work alongside him, as 'backroom boys' – inky fingered printers 'stuck somewhere back in the eighteenth century'. He was referring to the arcane raw materials of the studio space – copper plates, woodblocks, ink, scrim, dampened paper, wool blankets, presses. His unerring modesty and a self-effacing nature made him reluctant to talk about his own role.

Hugh had something of a conjuror about him: his commitment to a project and his total immersion in it were coupled with a light touch. It allowed artists to feel at ease and yet aware that his studio was a place of serious endeavour. With all other work cleared away, his collaborating artists felt that they had his complete attention. His ability to respond intuitively at each stage of the plate-making process, sometimes pursued over several weeks or months, meant that the final images were frequently unexpected.

What appeared to be magic was in reality the result of hours of careful research and preparation. Hugh's day began early, long before anyone else arrived. With the music of his beloved Purcell for company he would begin dampening paper, preparing plates, mixing colour, writing notes on off-cuts of beautiful paper in his illegible hand and setting the studio straight. His mischievous wit and wry humour meant that studio days, with cricket or classical music on the radio, were sane as well as productive. Hugh ran his workshops with generosity, enabling everyone to feel part of the team."

The publisher Charles Booth-Clibbon of Paragon Press commented: *"Hugh was a most civilized, charming and modest man. I shall always associate him with the music of Henry Purcell that he adored. He was a true Englishman and I miss him greatly.'*

Hugh working on a woodcut for Terry Frost at Madron

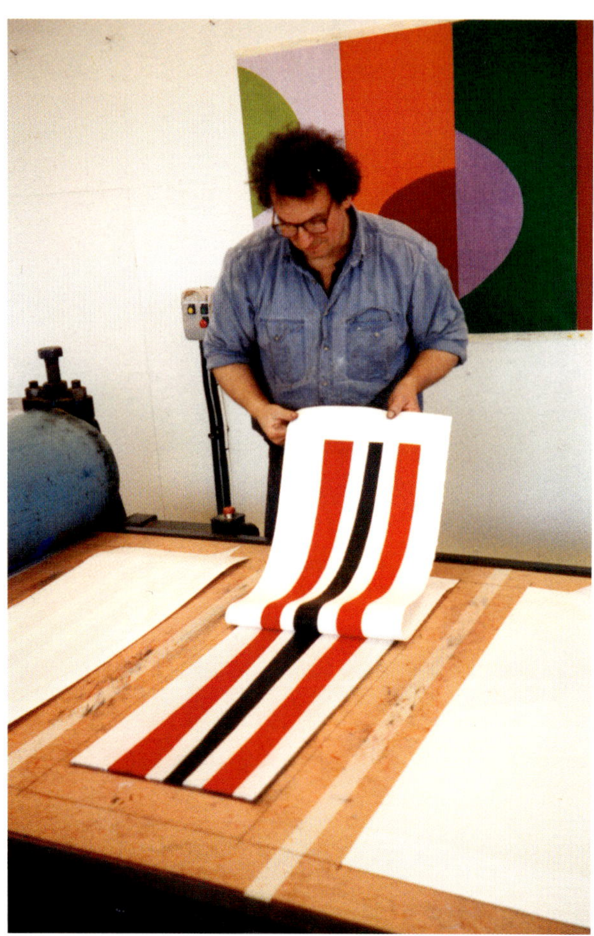

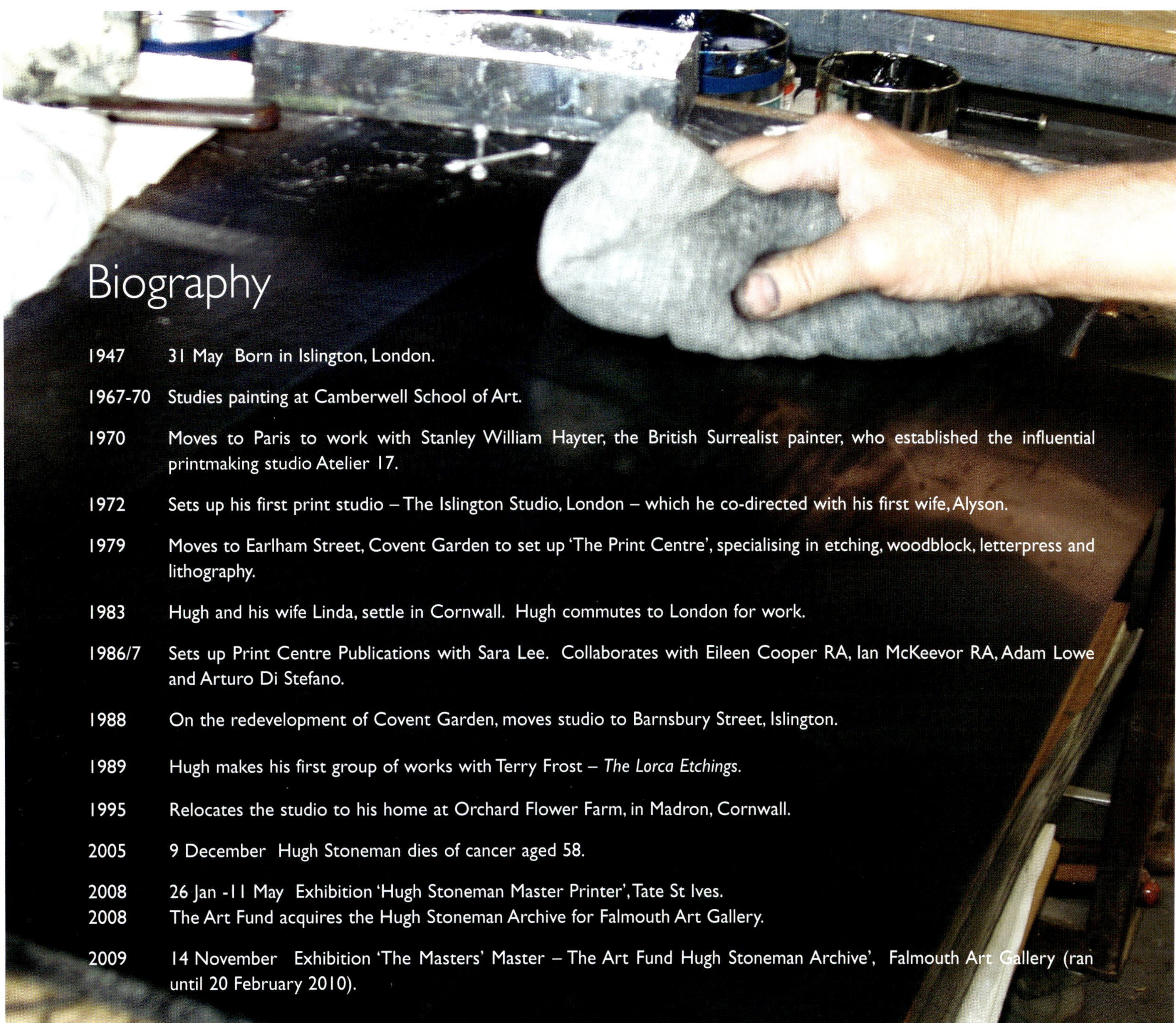

Biography

1947 31 May Born in Islington, London.

1967-70 Studies painting at Camberwell School of Art.

1970 Moves to Paris to work with Stanley William Hayter, the British Surrealist painter, who established the influential printmaking studio Atelier 17.

1972 Sets up his first print studio – The Islington Studio, London – which he co-directed with his first wife, Alyson.

1979 Moves to Earlham Street, Covent Garden to set up 'The Print Centre', specialising in etching, woodblock, letterpress and lithography.

1983 Hugh and his wife Linda, settle in Cornwall. Hugh commutes to London for work.

1986/7 Sets up Print Centre Publications with Sara Lee. Collaborates with Eileen Cooper RA, Ian McKeevor RA, Adam Lowe and Arturo Di Stefano.

1988 On the redevelopment of Covent Garden, moves studio to Barnsbury Street, Islington.

1989 Hugh makes his first group of works with Terry Frost – *The Lorca Etchings*.

1995 Relocates the studio to his home at Orchard Flower Farm, in Madron, Cornwall.

2005 9 December Hugh Stoneman dies of cancer aged 58.

2008 26 Jan - 11 May Exhibition 'Hugh Stoneman Master Printer', Tate St Ives.

2008 The Art Fund acquires the Hugh Stoneman Archive for Falmouth Art Gallery.

2009 14 November Exhibition 'The Masters' Master – The Art Fund Hugh Stoneman Archive', Falmouth Art Gallery (ran until 20 February 2010).

Glossary of Print Terms

Fine Art prints are published in limited numbers in order to maintain quality and exclusivity. The total number of prints is known as the edition. Each print is usually signed by the artist and numbered, conventionally in pencil, below the image on the print margin. This shows the individual number of the print over the total number of the edition (for example 7/20).

Bon à Tirer (B.A.T.)
French meaning 'good to pull' or good to print. In America it is often known as R.T.P. or 'right to print'. This is the final proof signed off by the artist and by the printer, the authorization of which allows the edition to start. During the printing each sheet of the edition is checked against the B.A.T.

Artist's Proof (A/P)
A print signed by the artist. It is customary that the artist has an additional percentage of the limited edition for private use.

Printer's Proof (P/P)
A print signed by the artist specifically for the studio and printers involved in making the edition, usually for their own use.

Hors de Commerce (H.C.)
Literally meaning 'outside commerce' or not for sale. It is a print signed by the artist and is generally for the publisher's use. They are often used for display, publicity or held in the archives.

Monoprint
Meaning 'one print'. A single and unique print is usually made by applying ink directly on to a block or plate and generally run through a press. It can be used to include several 'pulls' taken from the same image, but each time with differences in colour. Any 'family' of techniques may be used for a monoprint.

The intaglio family of techniques
'Intaglio' is Italian for 'incision'. Marks, grooves and hollows below the surface of a metal plate are incised with tools or 'bitten' with acids. The plate is inked and the surface is wiped clean, still leaving ink in the cut areas below the surface. The image is printed by laying a dampened sheet of paper over the plate and running it through a press under pressure. It is this pressure that causes the indentation or 'plate mark' common to

all intaglio techniques. The pressure forces the softened paper into the inked cuts, transferring the image from the plate on to the paper. All intaglio images are reversed when printed. Hugh generally preferred copper for the plates to make his intaglio prints – a method used in commercial printing from the 1700s. Many engravings after the 1820s used for books and for topographic prints replaced copper plates with steel to enable a longer print run. However, copper produces a softer image compared to the harshness of steel engravings. The following are intaglio techniques used by Hugh Stoneman:

Etching

The image is bitten or etched into a metal plate with acid. The plate is covered with an acid-resistant protective layer, known as 'the ground', through which the image is drawn (i.e. scratched revealing the metal underneath). This enables the artist to draw those lines almost as freely as sketching with a pencil on paper, although the image when printed will appear in reverse unless originally drawn in reverse using a mirror. After drawing, the plate is immersed in an acid bath and the exposed copper bitten away creating the hollows, which hold the ink.The first known dated etching was made in 1513. They were originally monochrome, but they can also be printed in colours.

Hard ground etching

A hard acid resistant protective layer made of wax and bitumen is applied to the surface of a heated plate with a roller. When the plate cools the protective layer of ground hardens. The image is drawn through this with a variety of sharp-pointed tools, revealing the copper beneath. It is then immersed in acid, which eats at the revealed metal only. This gives a clean pen-like appearance with crisp lines.

Soft ground etching

A soft acid resistant protective layer made of a sticky wax/bitumen is applied to the plate surface. This remains soft when cold. A sheet of lightweight paper is laid on top and the image is drawn on this. The ground is pulled into the paper revealing the mark on the plate which, when etched, gives a gentler and softer pencil or charcoal-like line and texture. It is especially used for drawn prints.

Aquatint

A traditional etching technique used to introduce tone, rather than line, to an image. Resin dust is sprinkled and allowed to settle on the plate, fused with heat and then etched. The acid bites around each tiny grain of resin, forming pools of tone from fine to dark depending on the length of time the plate is submerged in the acid. By painting out chosen areas with stopping-out varnish, or resist, and re-etching the plate, graduations of tone can be achieved. The method seems to have been discovered in the mid-seventeenth century, then neglected until the mid-eighteenth century. From the 1770s it became an increasingly common technique, in keeping with the growing popularity of watercolours. The name 'aquatint' was adopted because the print was frequently used to imitate the effect of watercolour wash.

Sugarlift

This technique allows the image to be painted directly on to the plate using a saturated sugar solution, which is then covered with a thin bitumen acid resist. When dry the plate is immersed in warm water which floats off the sugarlift and exposes the plate in those areas. The plate is then aquatinted and etched.

Photogravure

A same sized continuous tone (positive) of the image is exposed to photosensitive gelatine tissue. When transferred on to a prepared copper plate, the gelatine acts as a variable acid resist, enabling the print to reproduce graduating tones. This method is particularly suitable for photographs with a period feel, such as those in the archive by Eve Arnold, Kamil Chadirji and Fay Godwin. It is also used with very contemporary images.

Dustgrain gravure

A variation of the photogravure process, where the positive image is usually hand drawn on to acetate and the copper plate is aquatinted during the plate-making process.

Drypoint

The image is drawn directly on to the plate using a sharp tool. The resulting incised line has ridges of metal either side, which gives the characteristic rich blurred line.

Carborundum

An extremely hard abrasive called silicon carbide grit is mixed with acrylic binders and painted on to the surface of a plate. The finished plate is then inked and wiped in the same way as an intaglio plate. Its raised texture typically gives a deep tone, rich colour and strong emboss into the paper. The three prints in the archive by John Hoyland RA use carborundum and photogravure with stunning effect.

Chine collé

A technique in which thin pieces of fine tissue or china paper are stuck to the image during the printing process in order to introduce colour or tone.

The relief family of techniques

This is any form of printing where the image is inked and printed from the raised surface, and where the deep cuts and grooves appear blank on the paper. It is the opposite of intaglio, where the surface remains blank and the cuts and grooves are printed. Like intaglio all relief print images are reversed during the printing process. Hugh Stoneman frequently used woodcut and linocut to good effect.

Woodcut

This is made from a plank or block of wood sawn along the grain and smoothed. The design is cut away and then the raised surface is inked, usually with a roller before being printed, normally through a press. Often the grain of the wood is evident in the final print, and under Hugh's skilful hands becomes an integral part of the design. The strong contrasts, relatively simple lines and textured grain give the medium its unique appeal. An excellent example in the archive is 'Four Circles' by Breon O'Casey.

Linocut

The image is cut away using lino (linoleum) as the block. It is then inked, usually with a roller, before being printed, normally through a press. The soft surface is far easier to work than wood. Unlike wood, lino traditionally gives a flatter, more homogeneous printing surface.

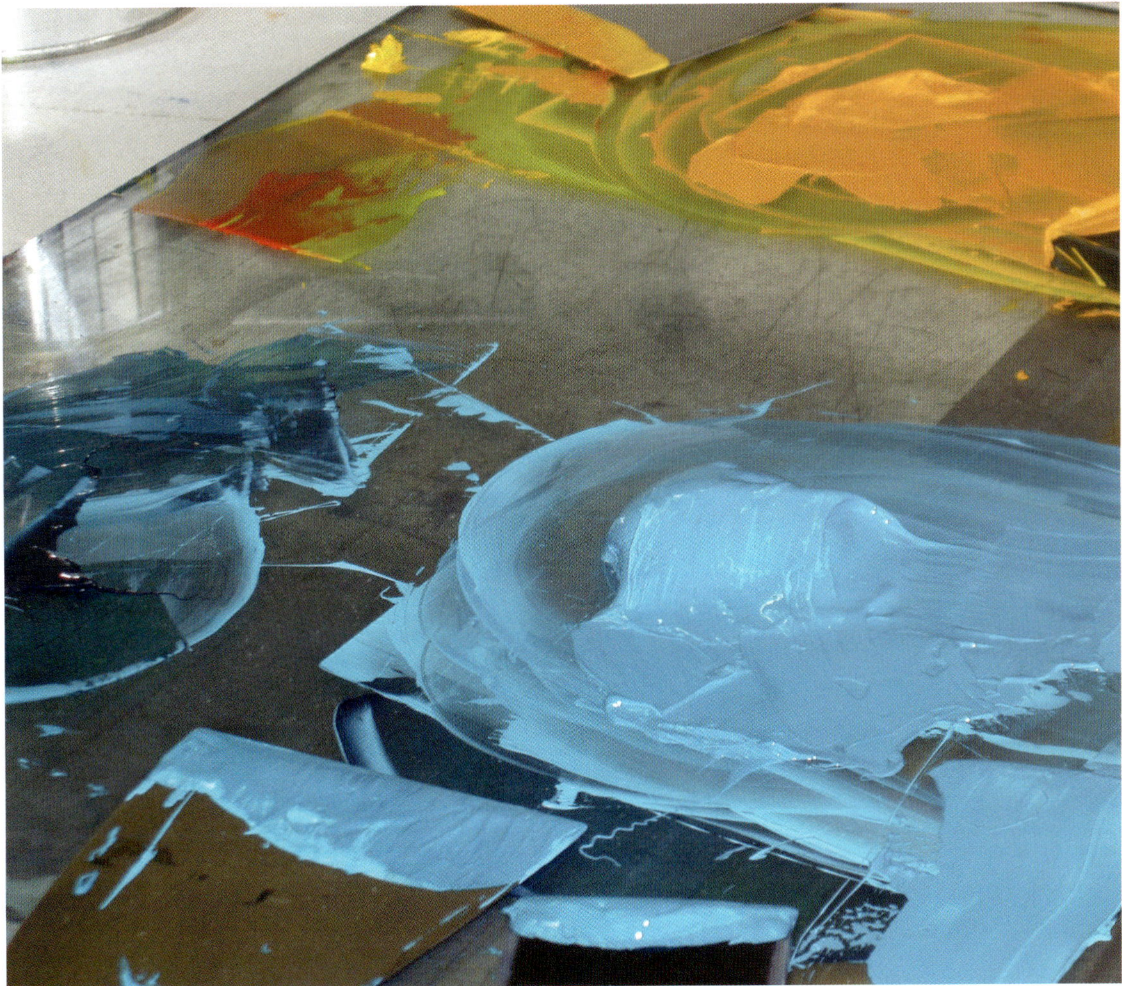

Bibliography

Gascoigne, Bamber: *How to Identify Prints*, Thames & Hudson, 1986 (reprinted 1998)

Gilmore, Pat and McKeever, Ian: *Colour Etching*, Alan Cristea Gallery, London, 1997

Lee, Sara and Tooby, Mike: *Hugh Stoneman Master Printer*, Tate Publishing, 2008

Lee, Sara: 'Master Printer', *Art Quarterly*, Art Fund, Spring 2009, pp. 36–39

Lulin, Etienne and Simm, Florian-Oliver (edited by): *Contemporary Art in Print – the Publications of Charles Booth-Clibborn and His Imprint* The Paragon Press 2001 – 2006, The Paragon Press and Contemporary Editions Limited, 2006

MacCarthy, Fiona: 'Out of the frame', The *Guardian* – Review, 19 January 2008, pp. 12–13

Phillips, Phoebe and Robb, Tom: *Modern and Contemporary Prints – A Practical Guide to Collecting*, Antique Collectors Club, 2004

Printmaking Today, Volume 15, Summer 2006 (with text by Ian McKeever and Arturo Di Stefano)

Tooby, Mike: Hugh Stoneman's obituary, The *Guardian* 3 February 2006

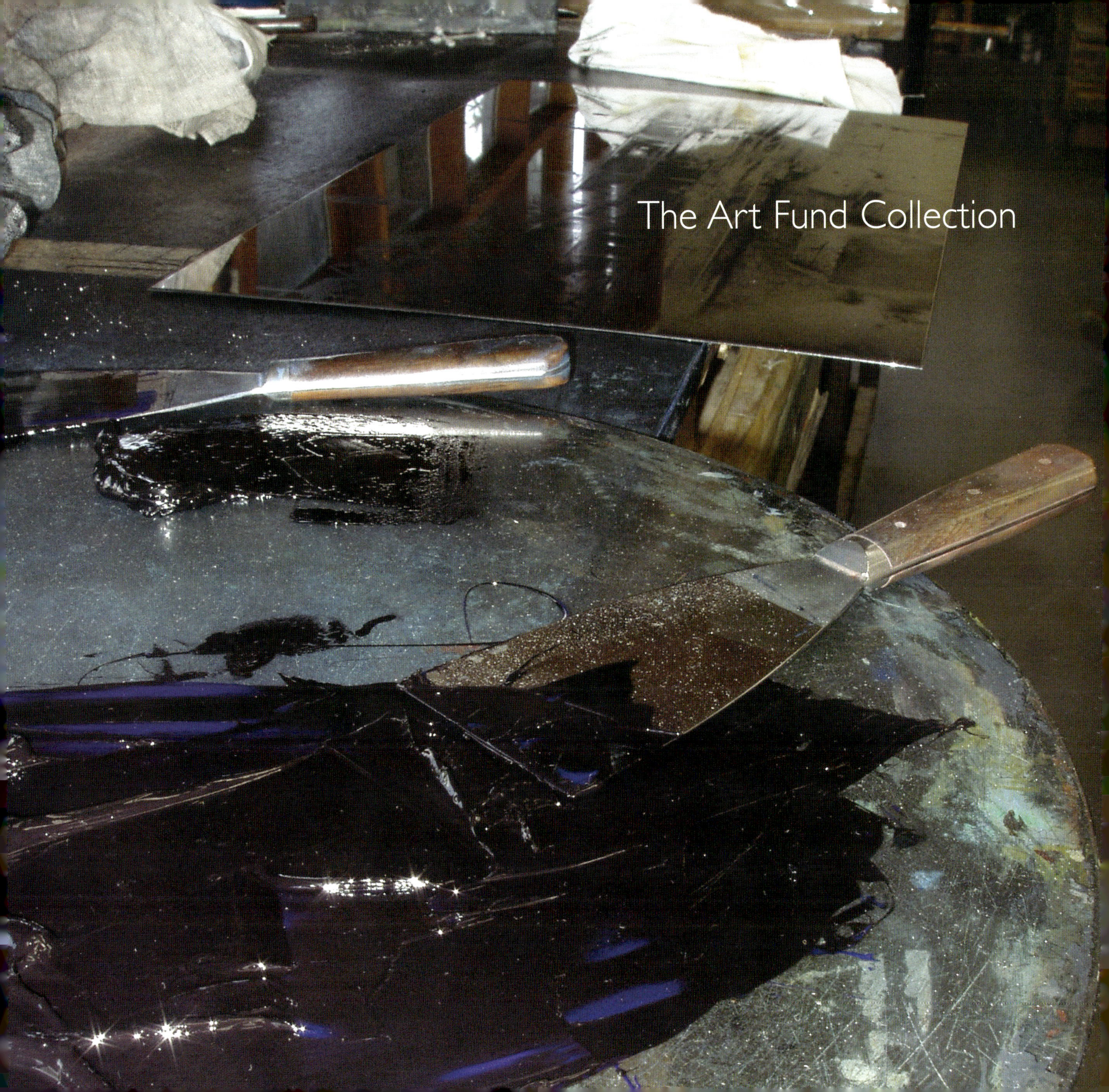

The Art Fund Collection

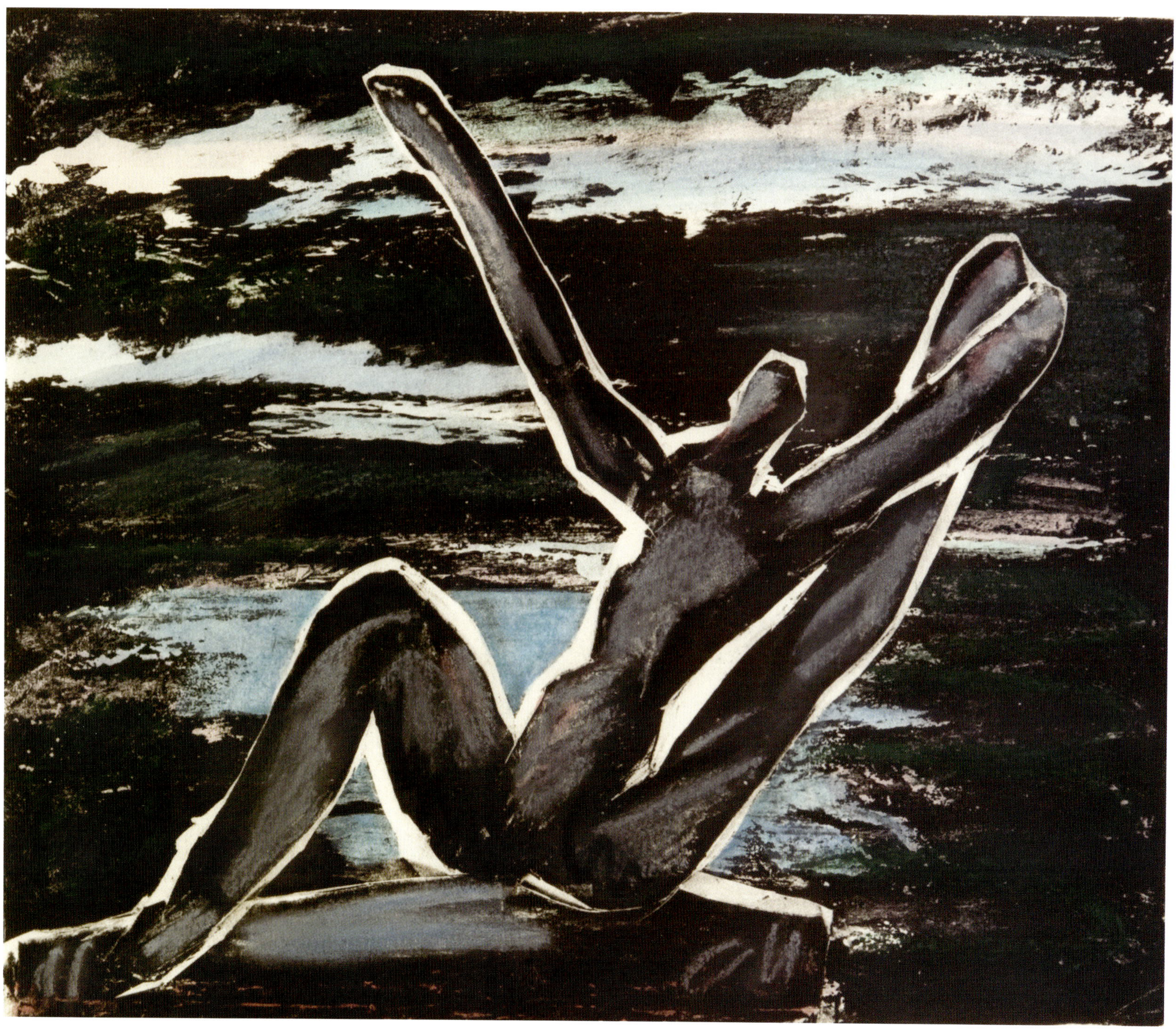

Ivor Abrahams RA (born 1935): 'Arcadia' suite, printer: Hugh Stoneman (1947–2005), publisher: Bernard Jacobson, signed and dated 1990, dustgrain gravure with hand colouring by Catherine Naylor (B.A.T.), 52.5 x 45cms. The Art Fund Hugh Stoneman Archive. Falmouth Art Gallery collection. FAMAG: 2008.26.1

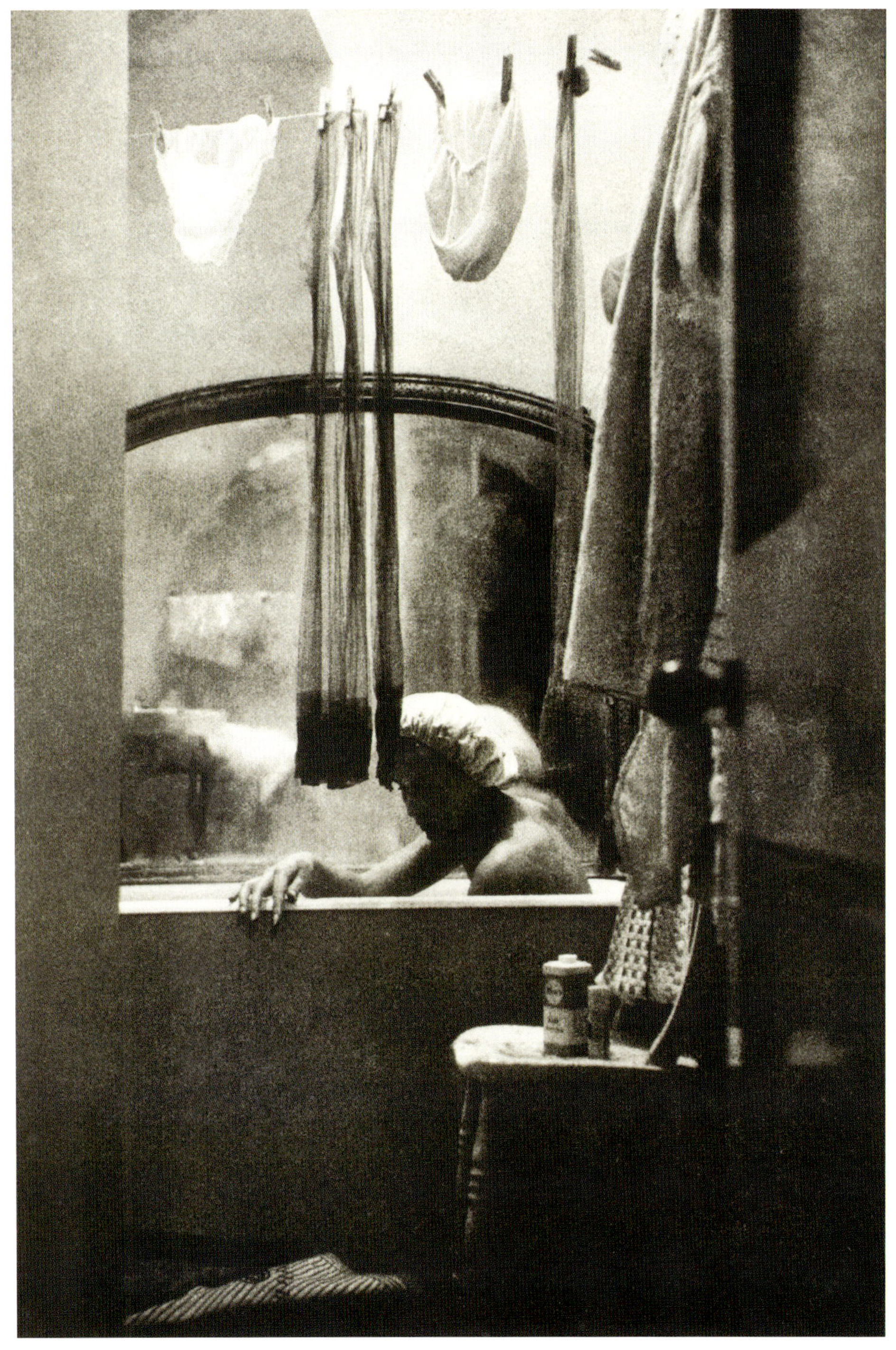

Eve Arnold (born 1912): 'One of four girls who share an apartment', London 1963, printer: Hugh Stoneman (1947–2005), publisher: Hugh & Linda Stoneman with Michael Ward, signed and dated 2002, photogravure etching (artist's proof) published 2002, 35.5 x 25.5cms. The Art Fund Hugh Stoneman Archive. Falmouth Art Gallery collection. © Eve Arnold & Magnum Photos. FAMAG: 2008.26.2

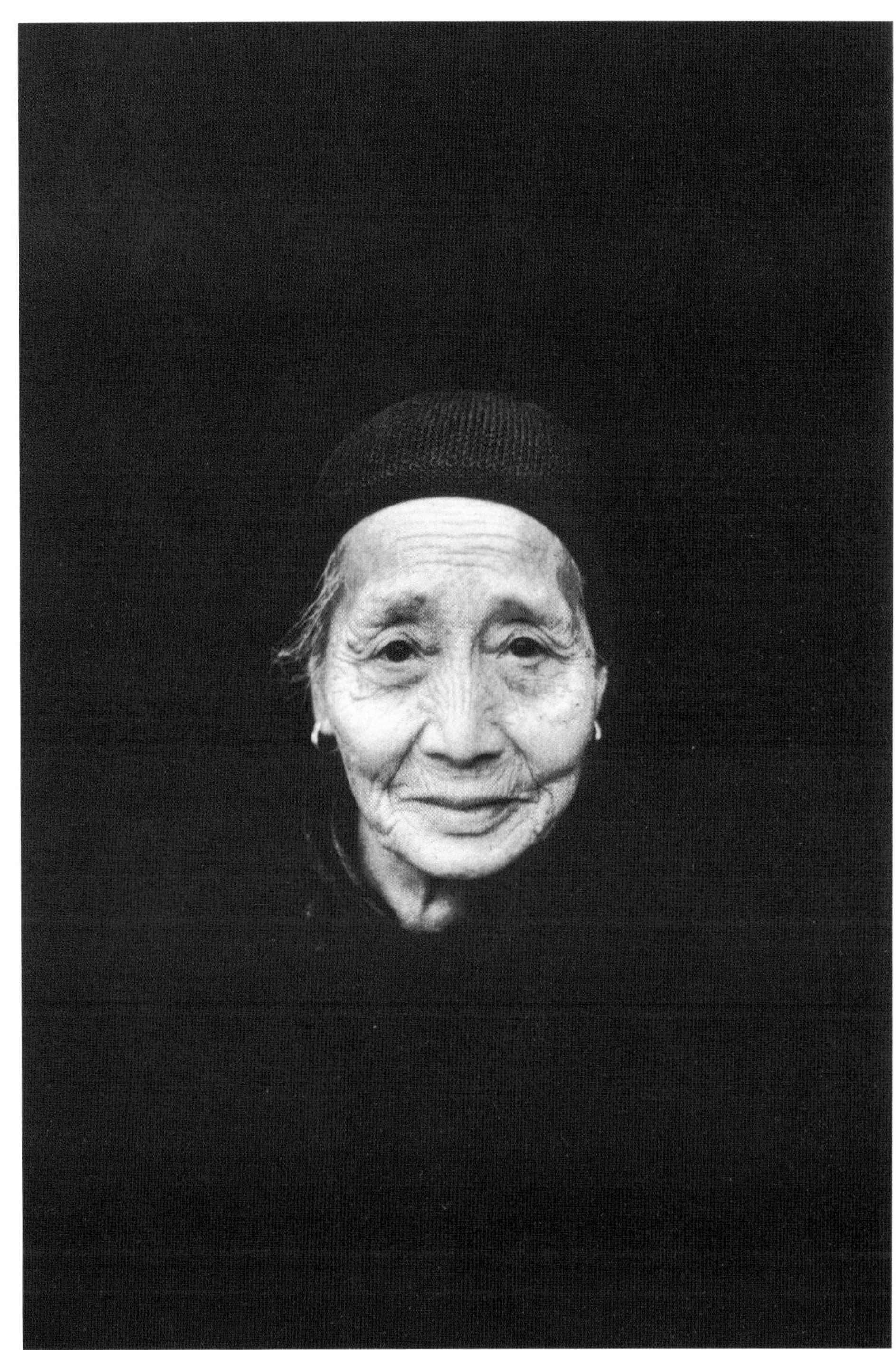

Eve Arnold (born 1912): 'Retired Worker, Guelin, China', 1979, printer: Hugh Stoneman (1947–2005), publisher: Hugh & Linda Stoneman with Michael Ward, signed and dated 2002, photogravure etching (artist's proof) published 2002, 35.5 x 25.5cms. The Art Fund Hugh Stoneman Archive. Falmouth Art Gallery collection. © Eve Arnold & Magnum Photos. FAMAG: 2008.26.3

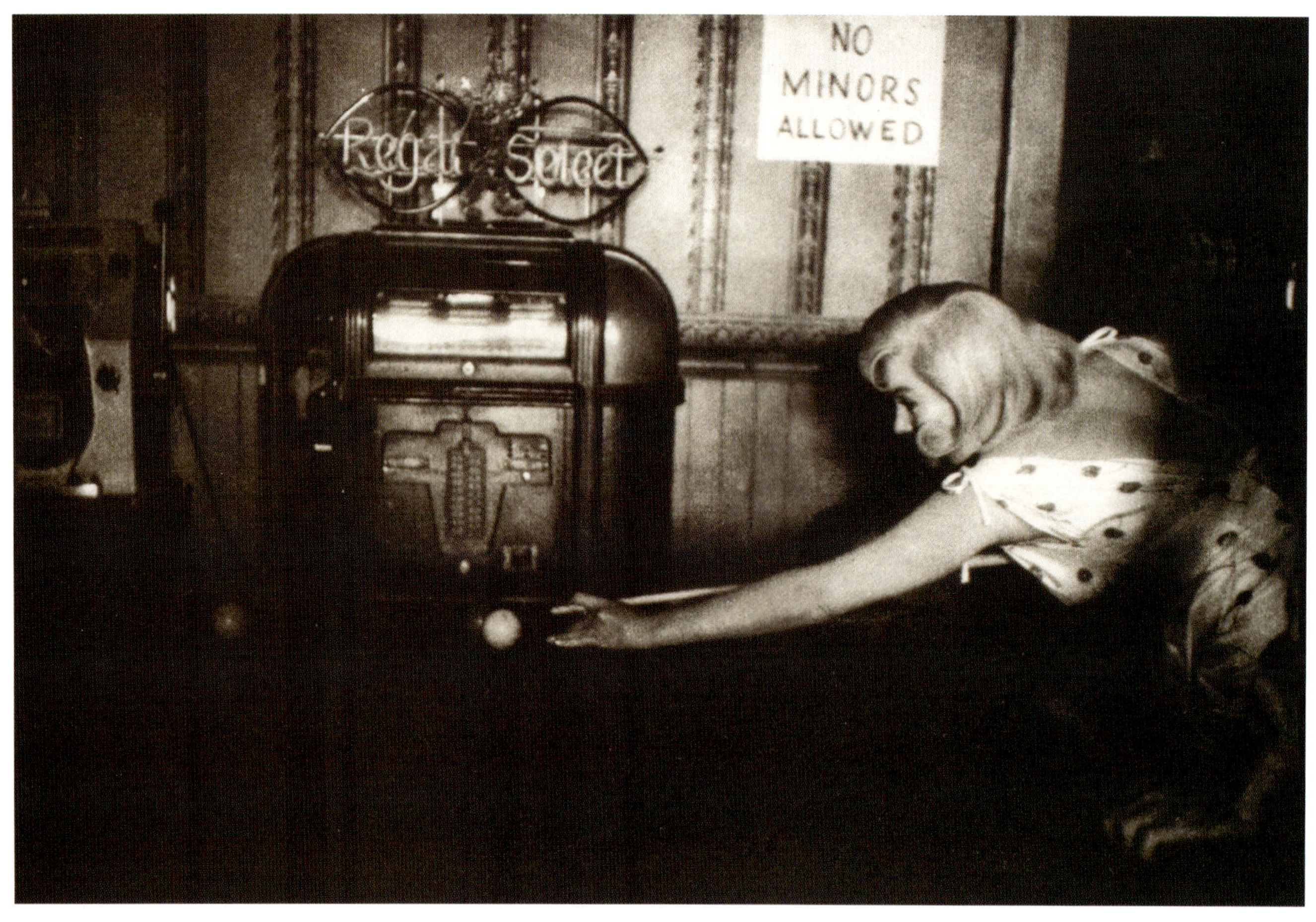

Eve Arnold (born 1912): 'Marilyn Monroe playing pool, Reno, Nevada', 1960, printer: Hugh Stoneman (1947–2005), publisher: Hugh & Linda Stoneman with Michael Ward, signed and dated 2002, photogravure etching (artist's proof) published 2002, 25.5 x 35.5cms. The Art Fund Hugh Stoneman Archive. Falmouth Art Gallery collection. © Eve Arnold & Magnum Photos. FAMAG 2008.26.4

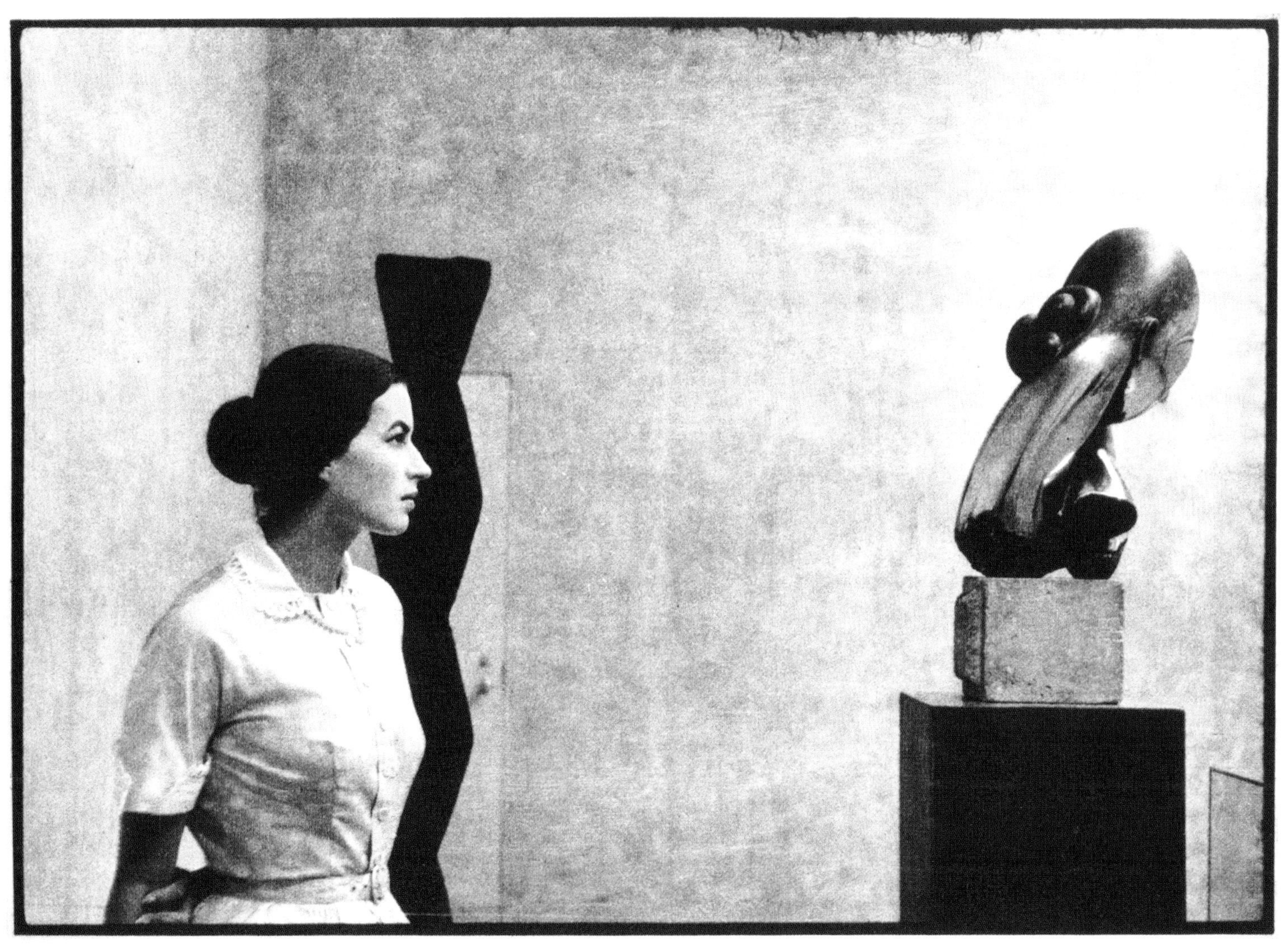

Eve Arnold (born 1912): 'Silvana Mangano, Museum of Modern Art, New York city', 1956, printer: Hugh Stoneman (1947–2005), publisher: Hugh & Linda Stoneman with Michael Ward, signed and dated 2002, photogravure etching (artist's proof) published 2002, 25.5 x 35.5cms. The Art Fund Hugh Stoneman Archive. Falmouth Art Gallery collection. © Eve Arnold & Magnum Photos. FAMAG 2008.26.5

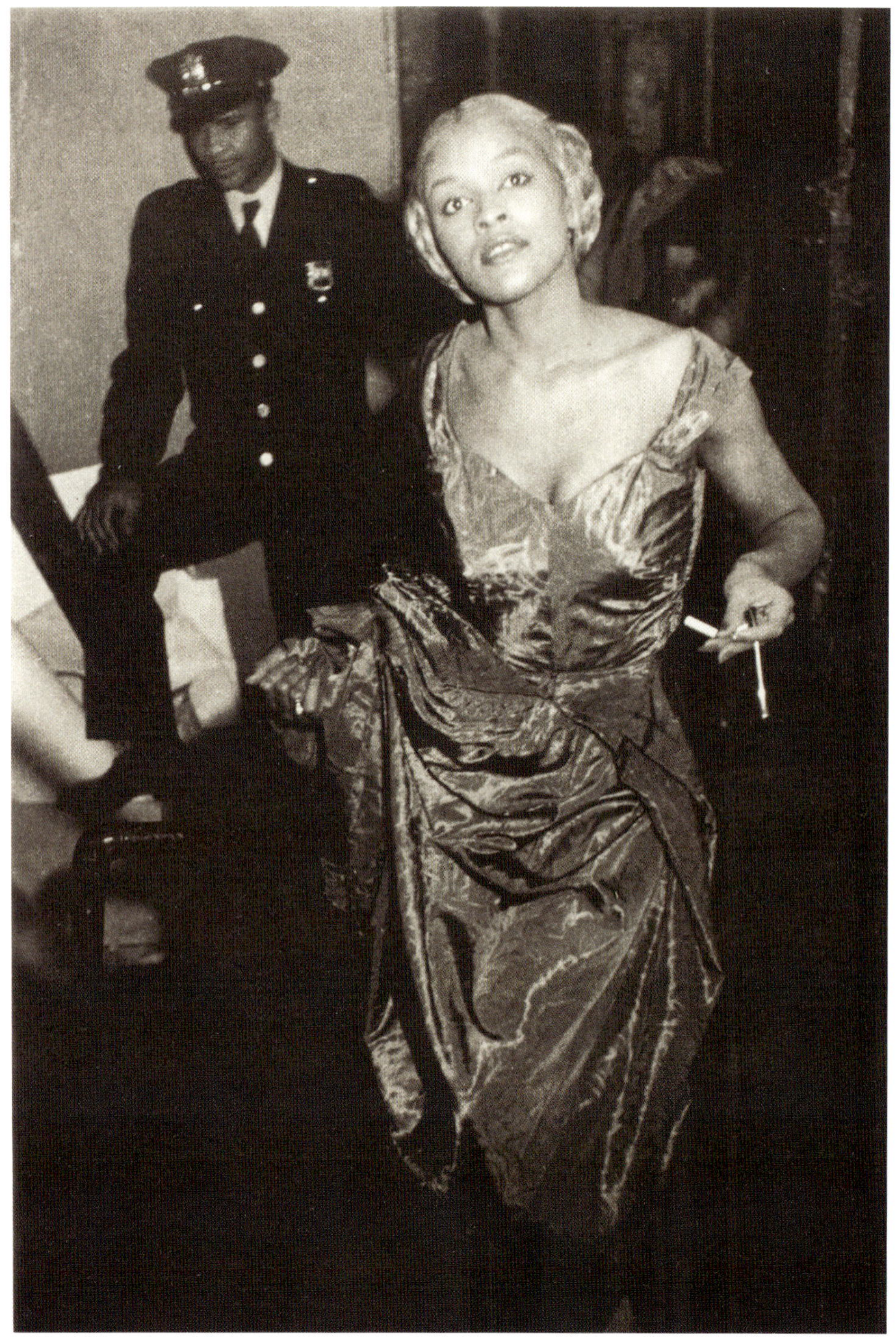

Eve Arnold (born 1912): 'Charlotte Stribling, a.k.a. Fabulous, fashion show, Harlem', 1952, printer: Hugh Stoneman (1947–2005), publisher: Hugh & Linda Stoneman with Michael Ward, signed and dated 2002, photogravure etching (artist's proof) published 2002, 35.5 x 25.5cms. The Art Fund Hugh Stoneman Archive. Falmouth Art Gallery collection. © Eve Arnold & Magnum Photos. FAMAG 2008.26.6

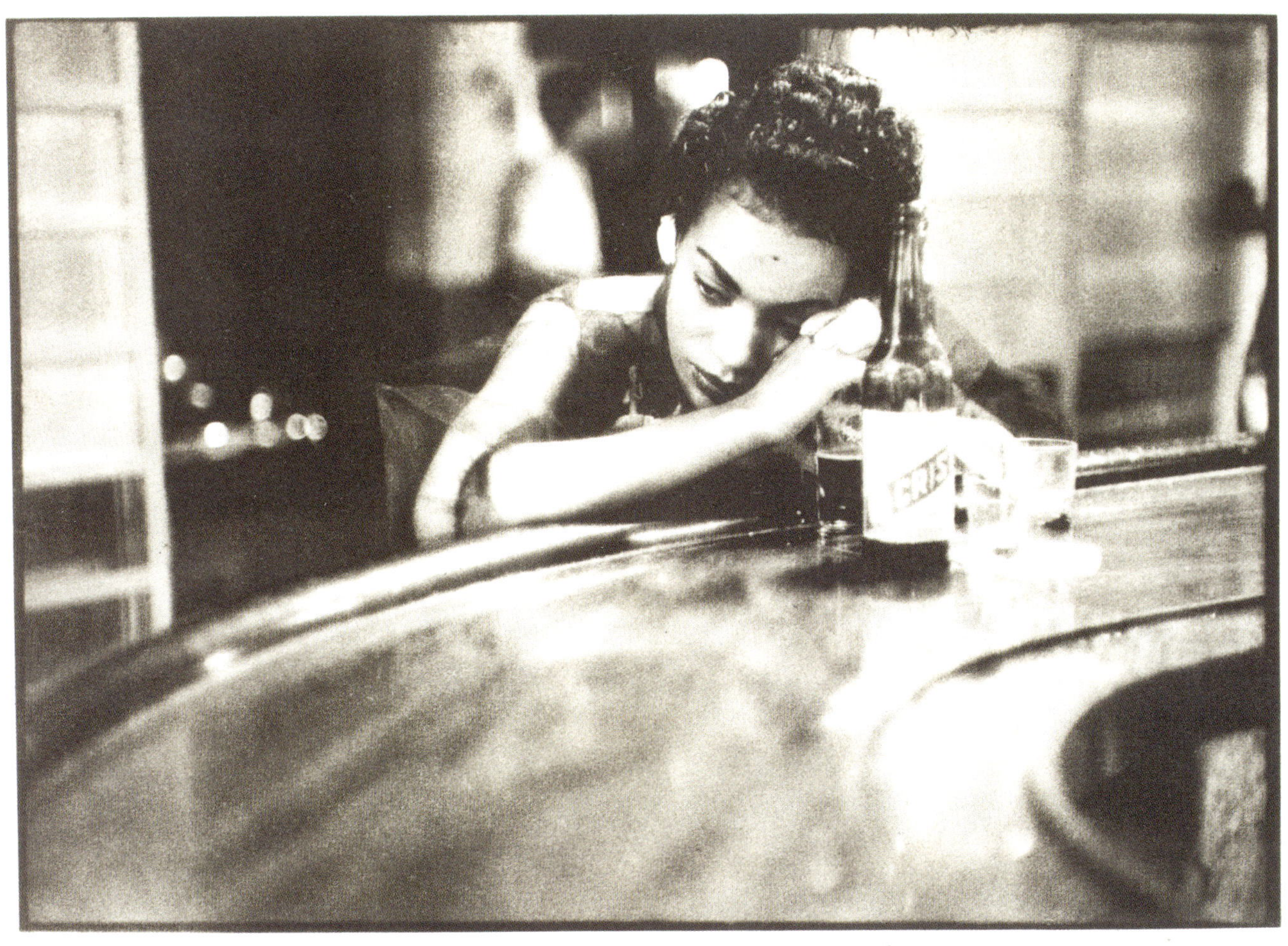

Eve Arnold (born 1912): 'Cuban Bar Girl, Havana', 1954, printer: Hugh Stoneman (1947–2005), publisher: Hugh & Linda Stoneman with Michael Ward, signed and dated 2002, photogravure etching (artist's proof) published 2002, 25 x 35.5cms. The Art Fund Hugh Stoneman Archive. Falmouth Art Gallery collection. © Eve Arnold & Magnum Photos. FAMAG 2008.26.7

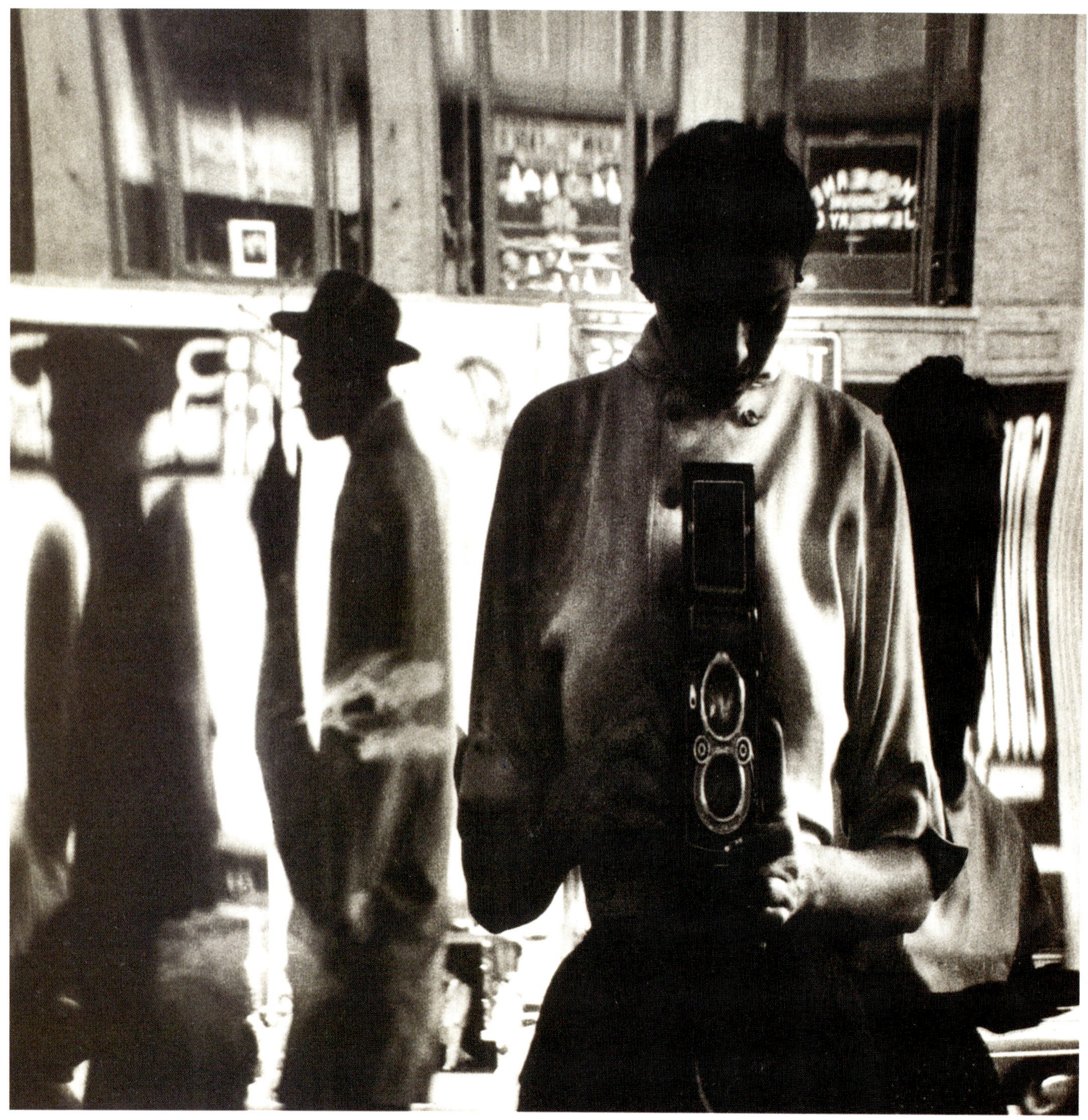

Eve Arnold (born 1912): 'A Self-Portrait in a distorting mirror, 42nd Street, New York', 1950, printer: Hugh Stoneman (1947–2005), publisher: Hugh & Linda Stoneman with Michael Ward, signed and dated 2002, photogravure etching (artist's proof) published 2002, 35.5 x 25.5cms. The Art Fund Hugh Stoneman Archive. Falmouth Art Gallery collection. © Eve Arnold & Magnum Photos. FAMAG 2008.26.8

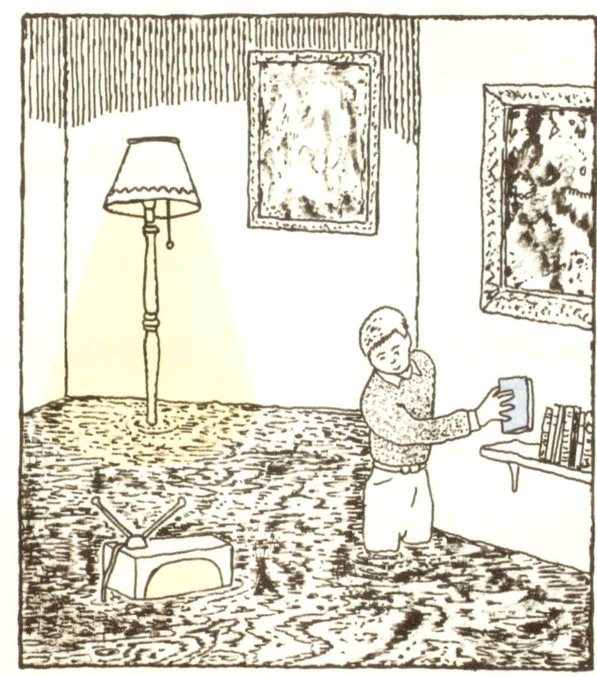

Glen Baxter (born 1944): 'Without Brenda', printer: Hugh Stoneman (1947–2005), signed and dated 1988, photogravure etching (printer's proof), 66 x 50cms. The Art Fund Hugh Stoneman Archive. Falmouth Art Gallery collection. FAMAG 2008.26.9

Anthony Benjamin (1931–2002): 'Strip', printer: Hugh Stoneman (1947–2005), signed and dated Dec. 1974, etching (1st colour proof), 76 x 56cms. The Art Fund Hugh Stoneman Archive. Falmouth Art Gallery collection. FAMAG 2008.26.10

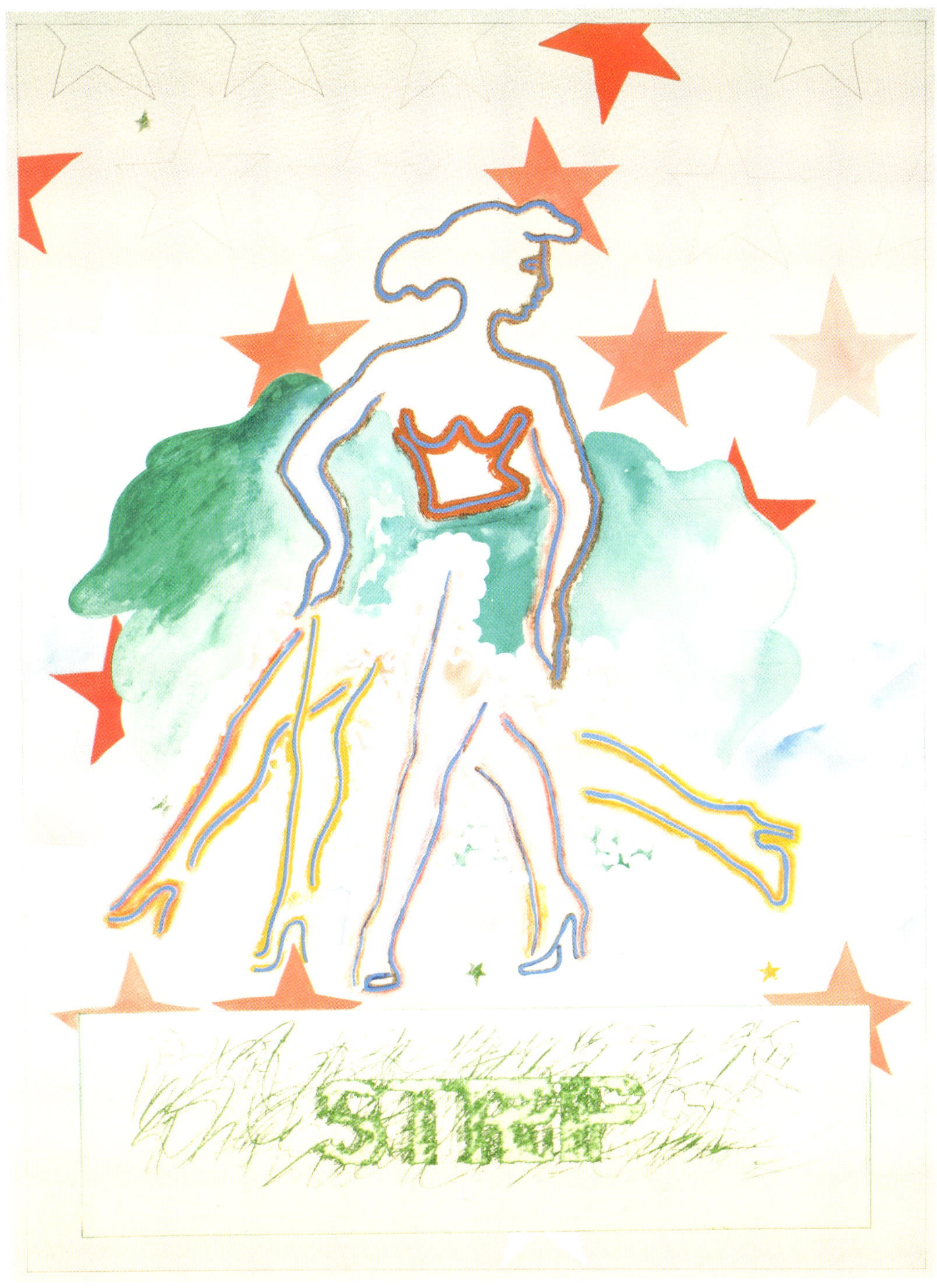

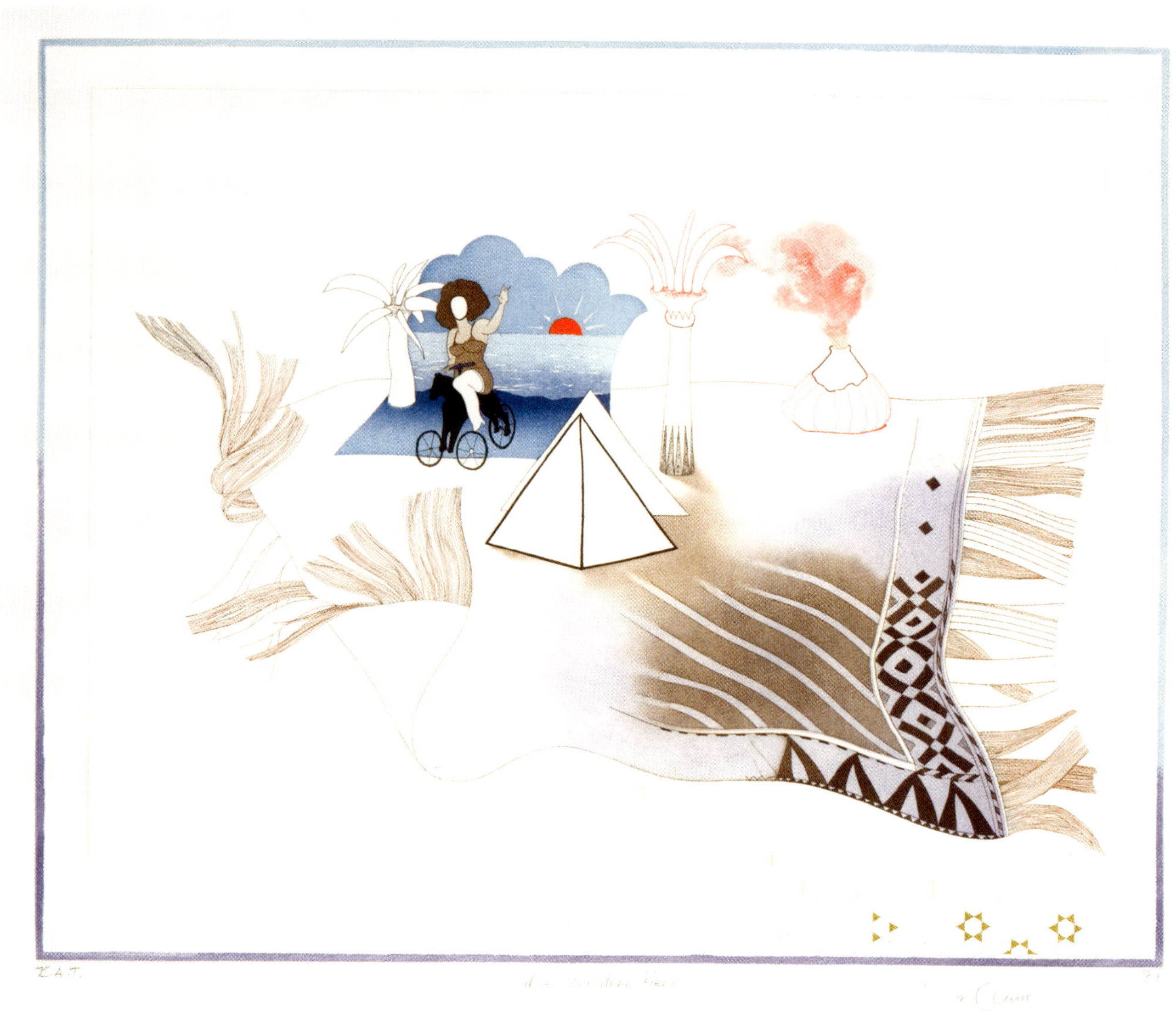

Anthony Benjamin (1931–2002): 'Wish You Were Here', 1977, printer: Hugh Stoneman (1947–2005), signed and dated 1981, etching (B.A.T.), 76 x 57cms. The Art Fund Hugh Stoneman Archive. Falmouth Art Gallery collection. FAMAG 2008.26.11

Anthony Benjamin (1931–2002): 'Domes', printer: Hugh Stoneman (1947–2005), signed and dated 1977, etching (printer's proof), 60.5 x 40cms. The Art Fund Hugh Stoneman Archive. Falmouth Art Gallery collection. FAMAG 2008.26.12

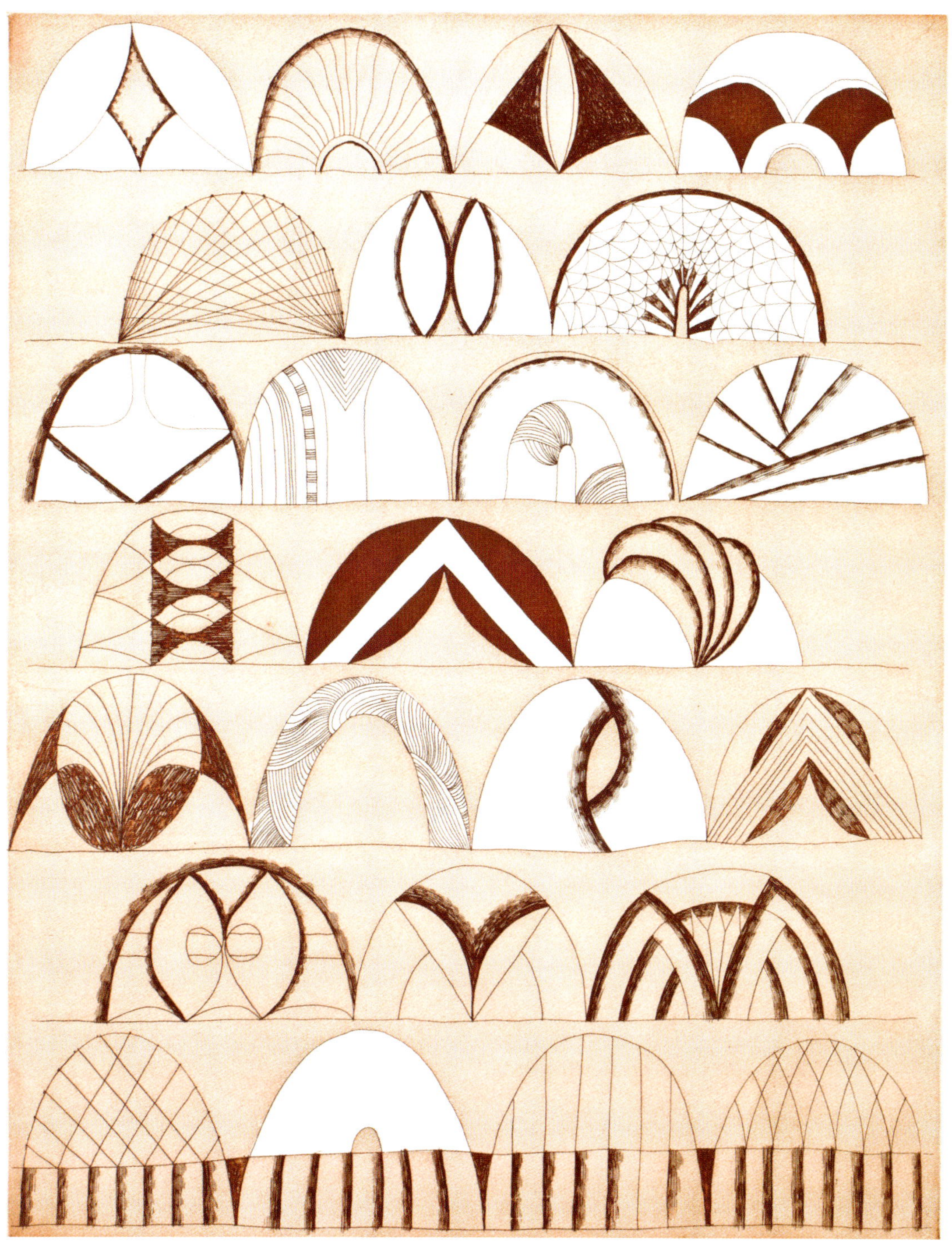

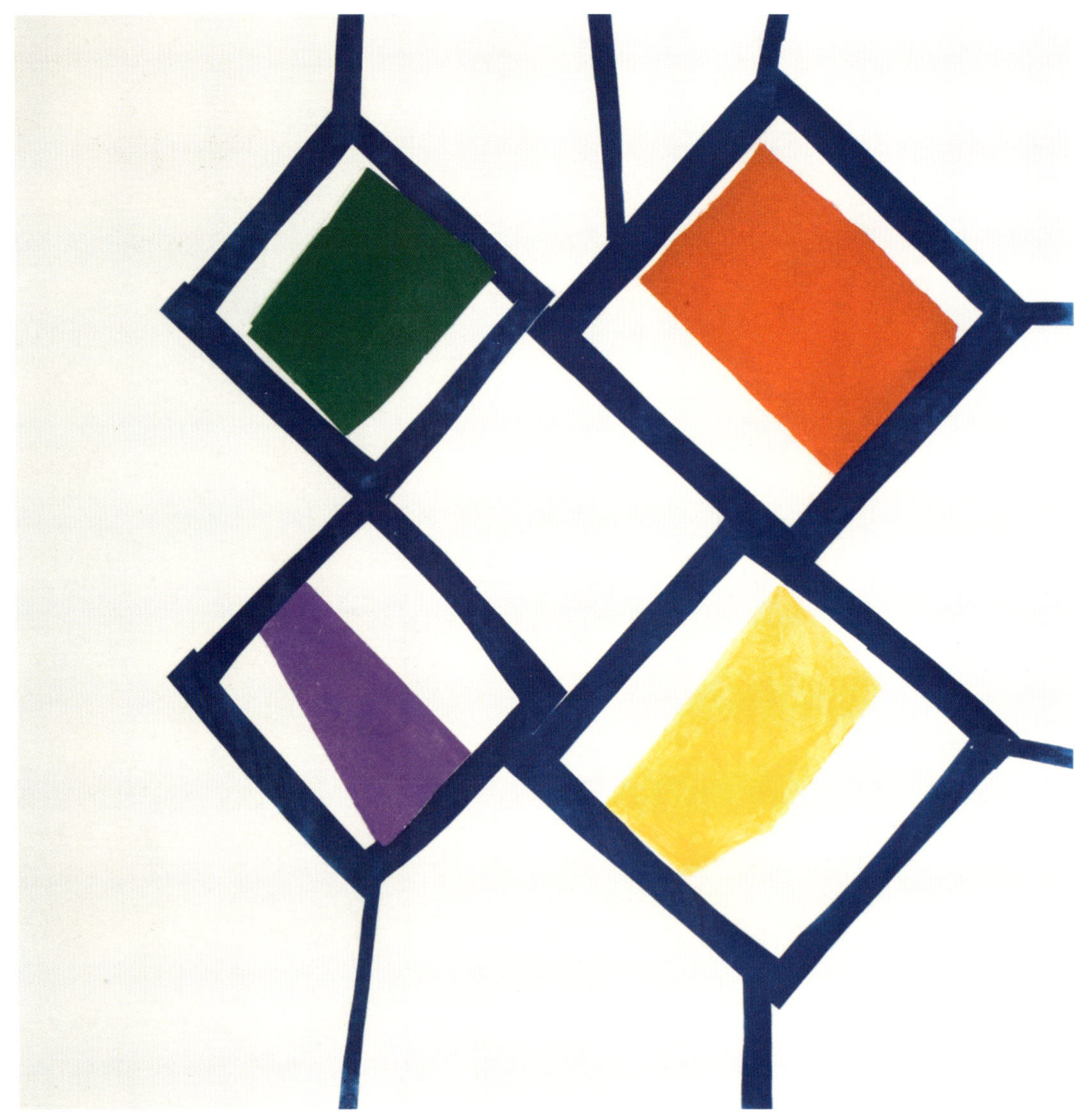

Sandra Blow RA (1925–2006): 'Revolve', printer: Hugh Stoneman (1947–2005), publisher: Linda Stoneman, signed and dated 2003, etching (proof print 1), 77 x 73cms. The Art Fund Hugh Stoneman Archive. Falmouth Art Gallery collection. © The Sandra Blow Estate. FAMAG 2008.26.13

G.W. Bot (born 1954): 'Tattoo', printer: Hugh Stoneman (1947–2005), publisher: The artist, signed and dated 1997, etching (printer's proof), 57.5 x 75cms. The Art Fund Hugh Stoneman Archive. Falmouth Art Gallery collection. FAMAG 2008.26.14

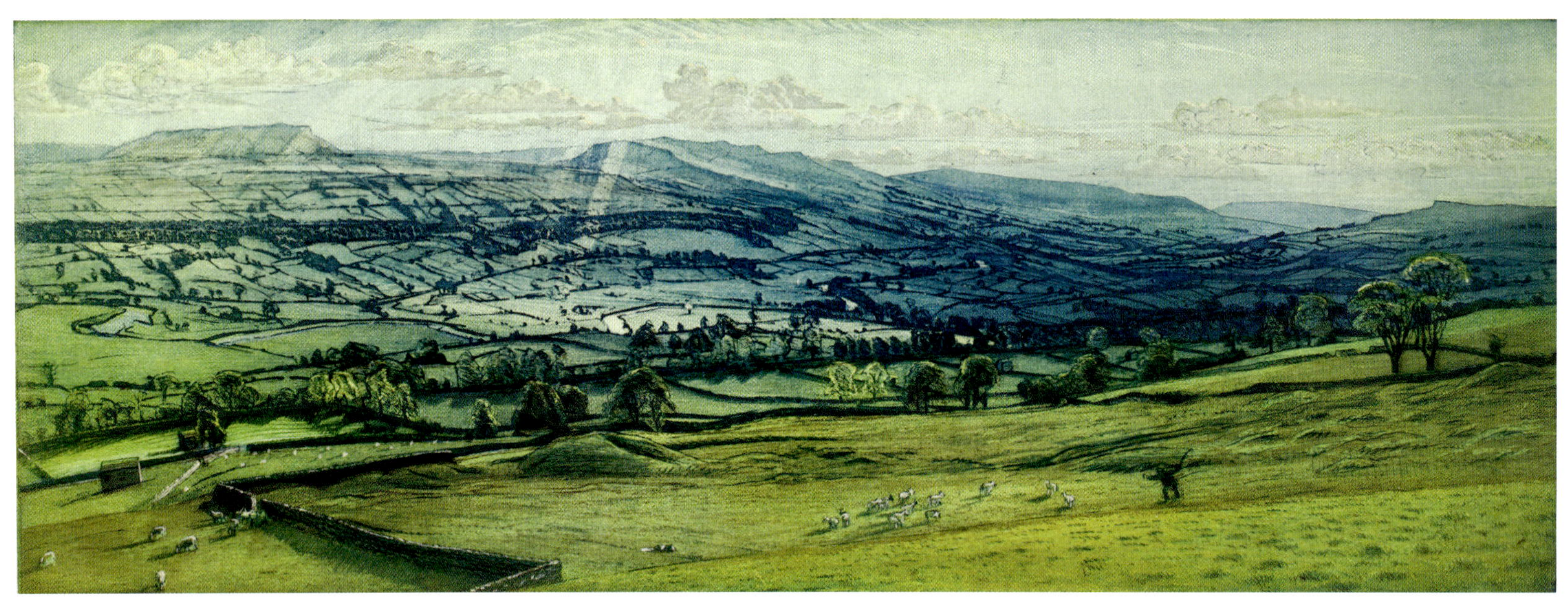

Piers Browne: 'The Ure Valley, Wensleydale', printer: Hugh Stoneman (1947–2005), signed and dated 1981, etching (number 41 of an edition of 100), 76 x 57cms. The Art Fund Hugh Stoneman Archive. Falmouth Art Gallery collection. FAMAG 2008.26.15

Elizabeth Butterworth (born 1949): 'Molluccian Cockatoo', printer: Hugh Stoneman (1947–2005), publisher: The Metropolitan Museum of Art, New York, signed and dated 1986, etching (printer's proof), 68 x 48.5cms. The Art Fund Hugh Stoneman Archive. Falmouth Art Gallery collection. FAMAG 2008.26.16

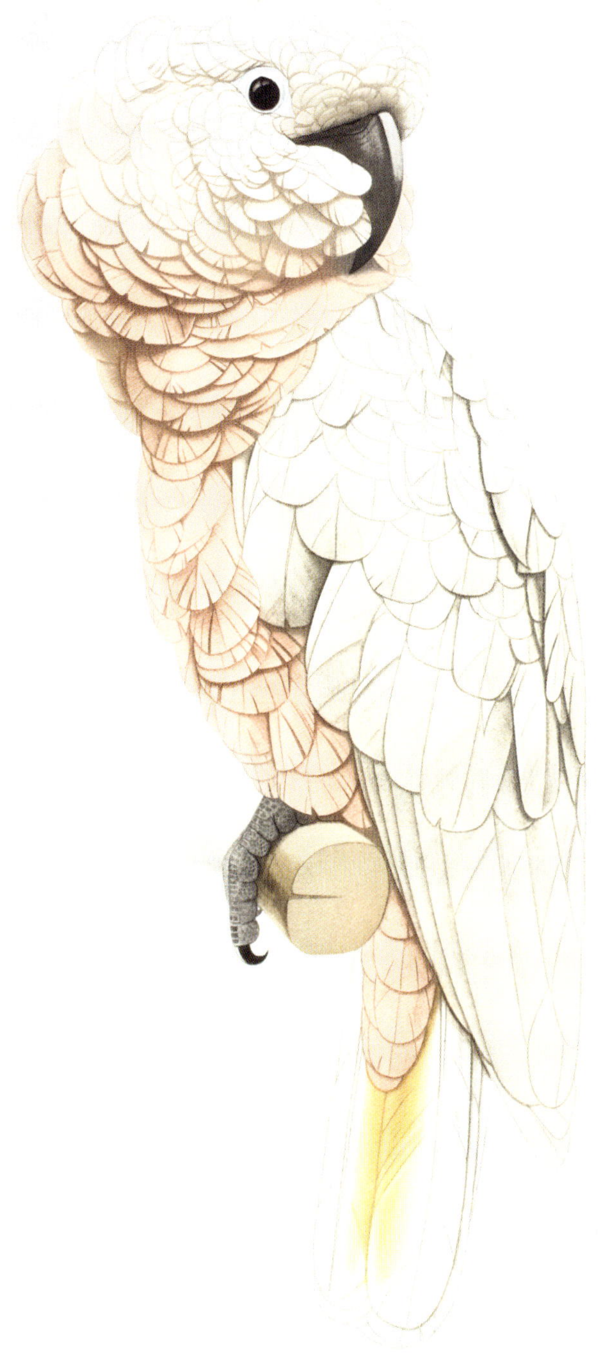

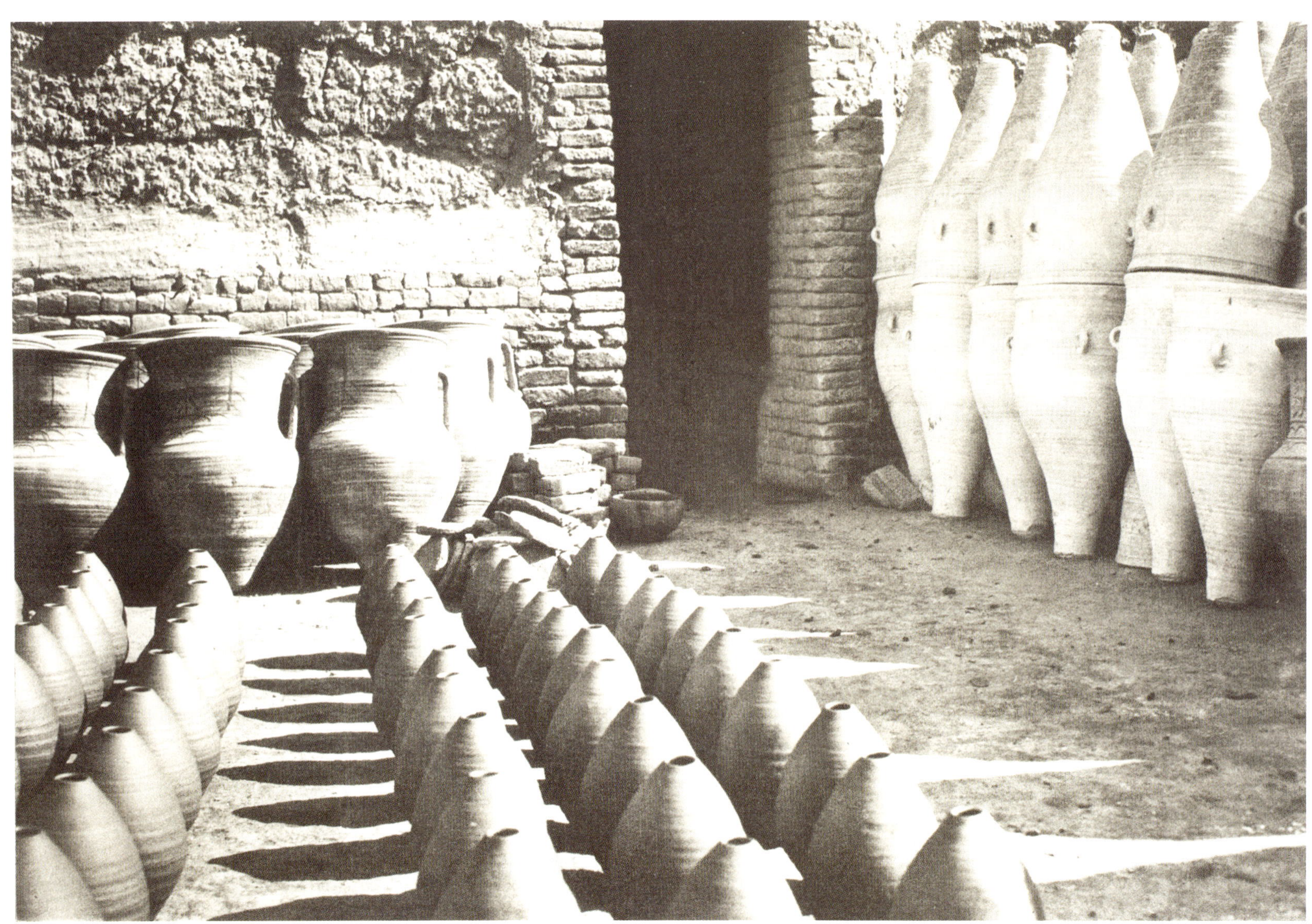

Kamil Chadirji (1897–1968): 'Pots' – from the series 'Eight Etchings from Photographs', printer: Hugh Stoneman (1947–2005), publisher: Rifat Chadirji/LAAM Ltd, photogravure, 36.5 x 43cms. The Art Fund Hugh Stoneman Archive. Falmouth Art Gallery collection. © Rifat Chadirji. FAMAG 2008.26.17

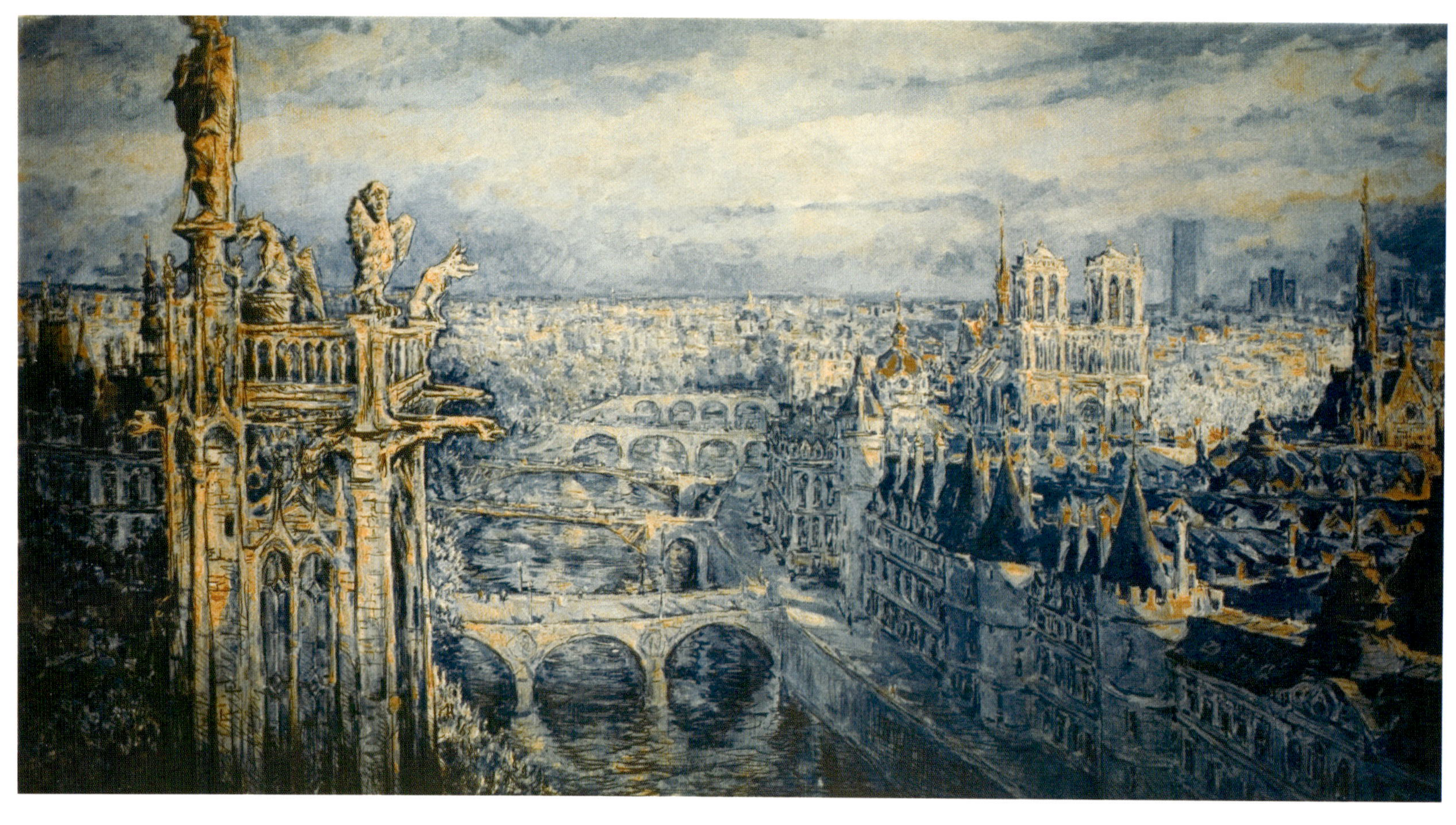

Sergei Chepik (born 1953): 'Paris', printer: Hugh Stoneman (1947–2005), signed and dated 1993, photogravure etching (printer's proof), 55.8 x 85.4cms. The Art Fund Hugh Stoneman Archive. Falmouth Art Gallery collection. FAMAG 2008.26.18

Maurice Cockrill RA (born 1936): 'Heart', printer: Hugh Stoneman (1947–2005), signed and dated 1998, etching (printer's proof 2), 70.9 x 55.3cms. The Art Fund Hugh Stoneman Archive. Falmouth Art Gallery collection. FAMAG 2008.26.19

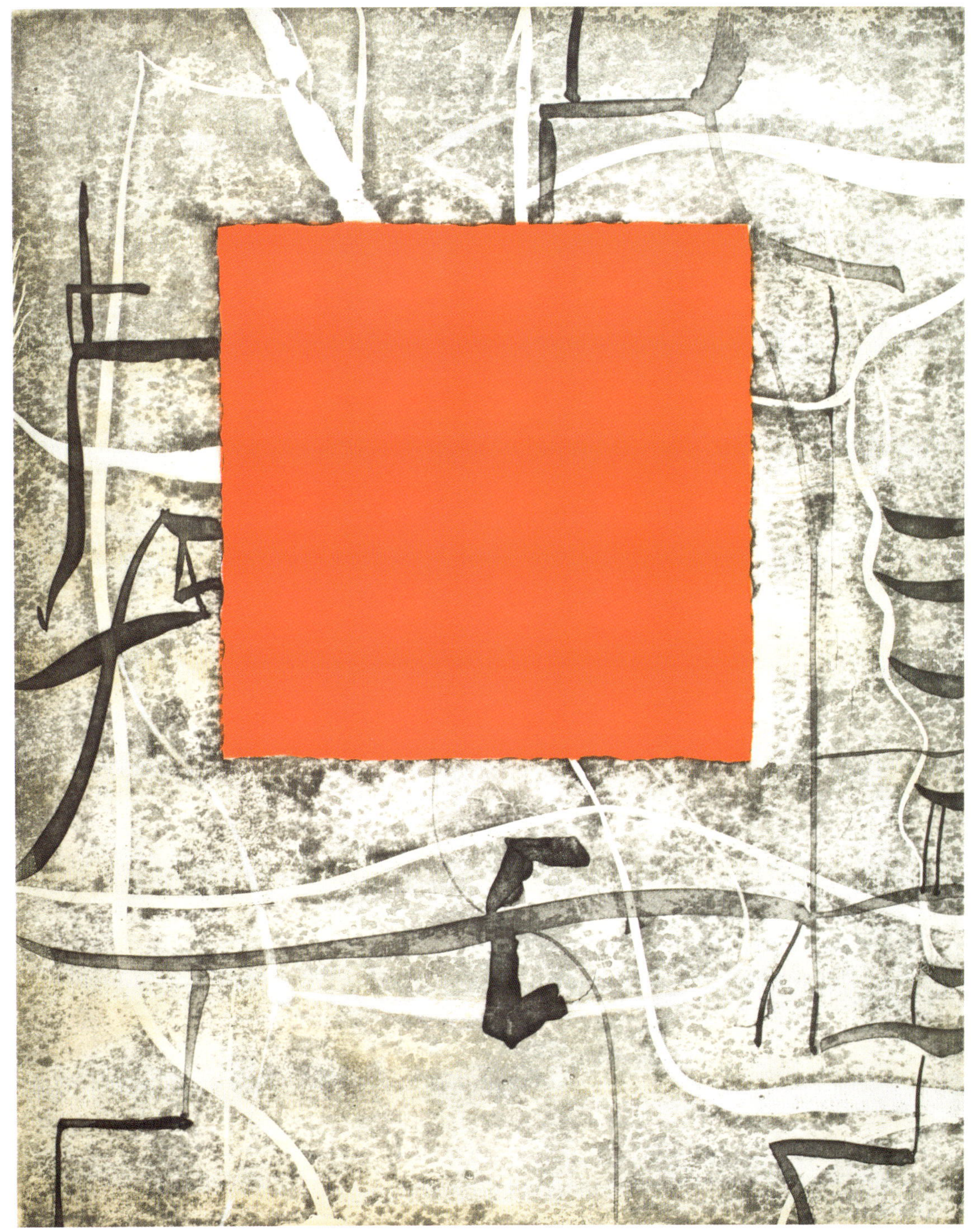

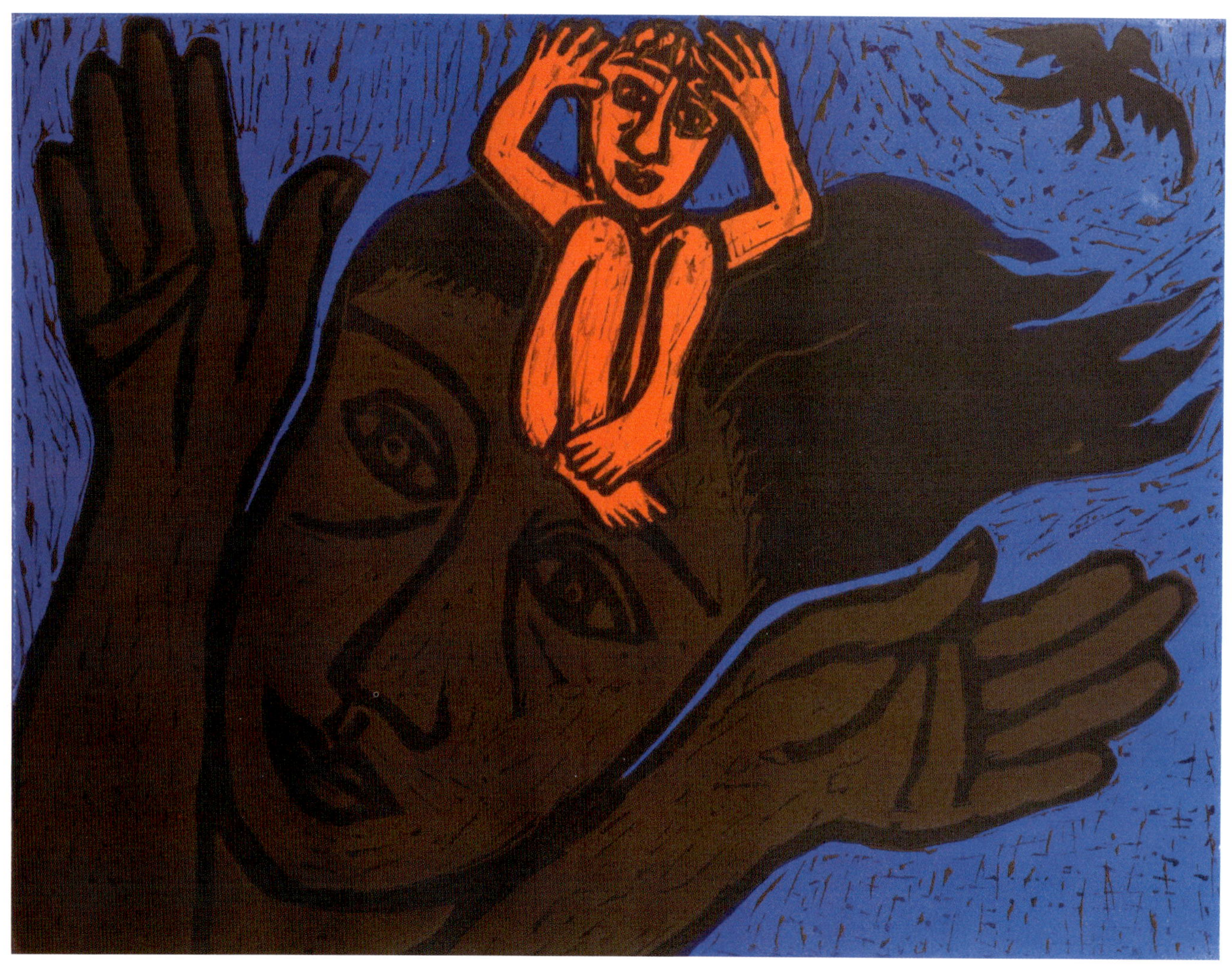

Eileen Cooper RA (born 1953): 'Dreamland' – from the series 'Six Linocuts', 1992, printer: Hugh Stoneman (1947–2005), publisher: Print Centre Publications & Benjamin Rhodes, signed and dated 1992, linocut (printer's proof), 58 x 76cms. The Art Fund Hugh Stoneman Archive. Falmouth Art Gallery collection. FAMAG 2008.26.20

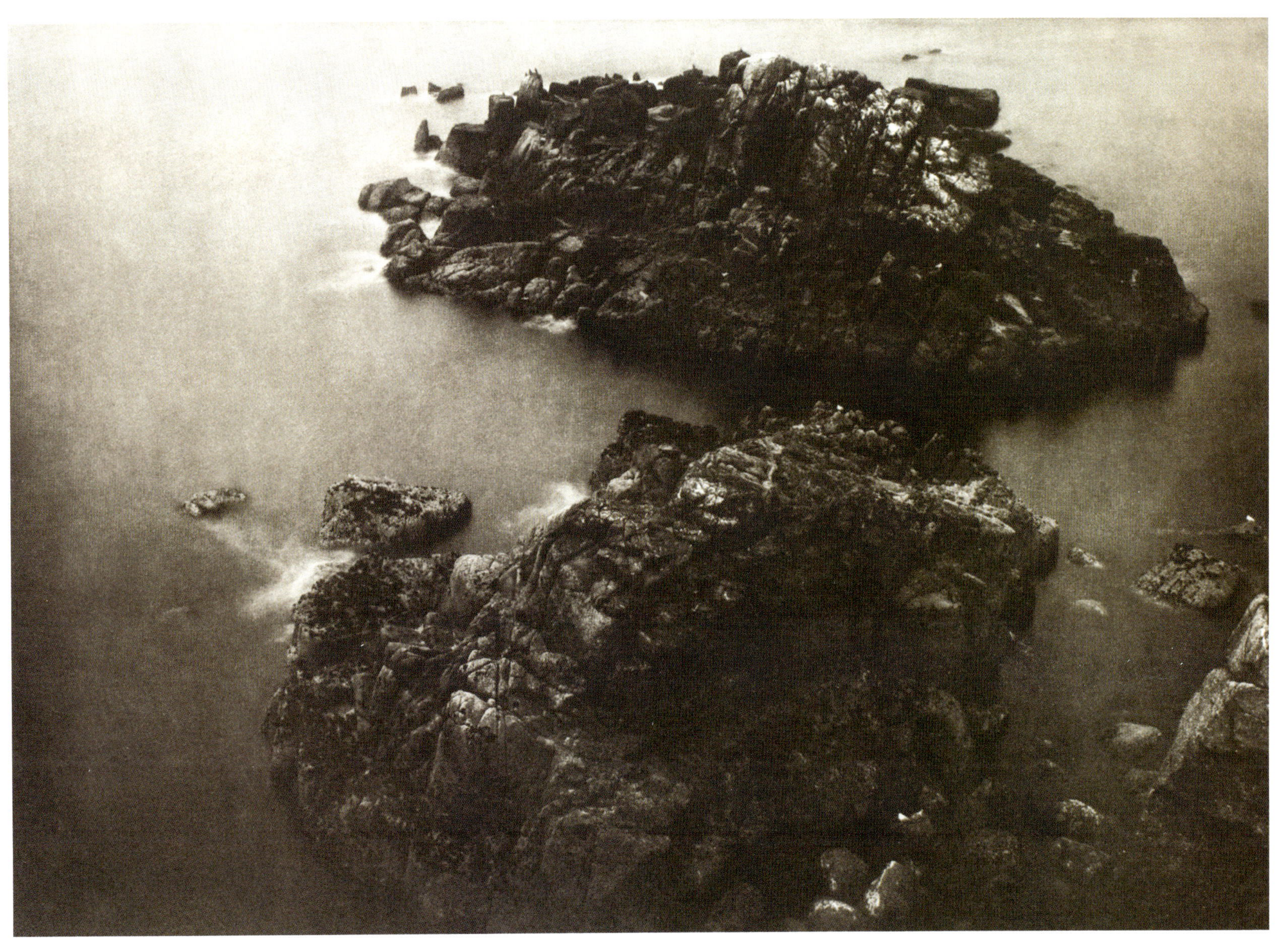

Thomas Joshua Cooper (born 1946): 'Arrival – The total eclipse of the sun farthest south west. The Celtic sea at the world's edge, Lands End, Cornwall', 11 August 1999, printer: Hugh Stoneman (1947–2005), publisher: Michael Hue Williams Fine Art, signed and dated 11.8.1999, photogravure (printer's proof 1), 20.8 x 26.8cms. The Art Fund Hugh Stoneman Archive. Falmouth Art Gallery collection. FAMAG 2008.26.21

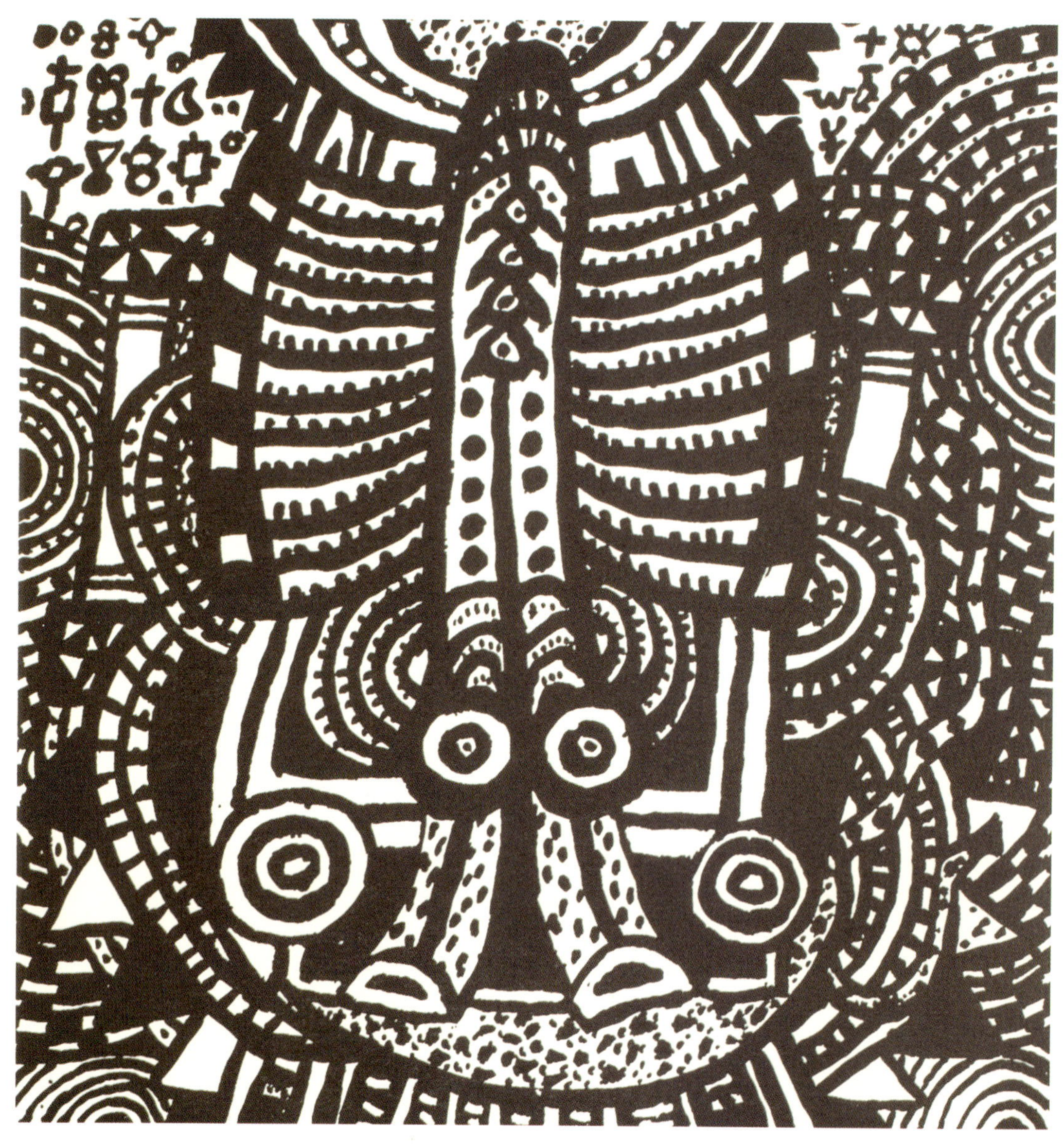

Alan Davie (born 1920): 'Susan's Delight', 2003, printer: Hugh Stoneman (1947–2005), publisher: Tate St Ives, woodcut, 57 x 51cms. The Art Fund Hugh Stoneman Archive. Falmouth Art Gallery collection. FAMAG 2008.26.22

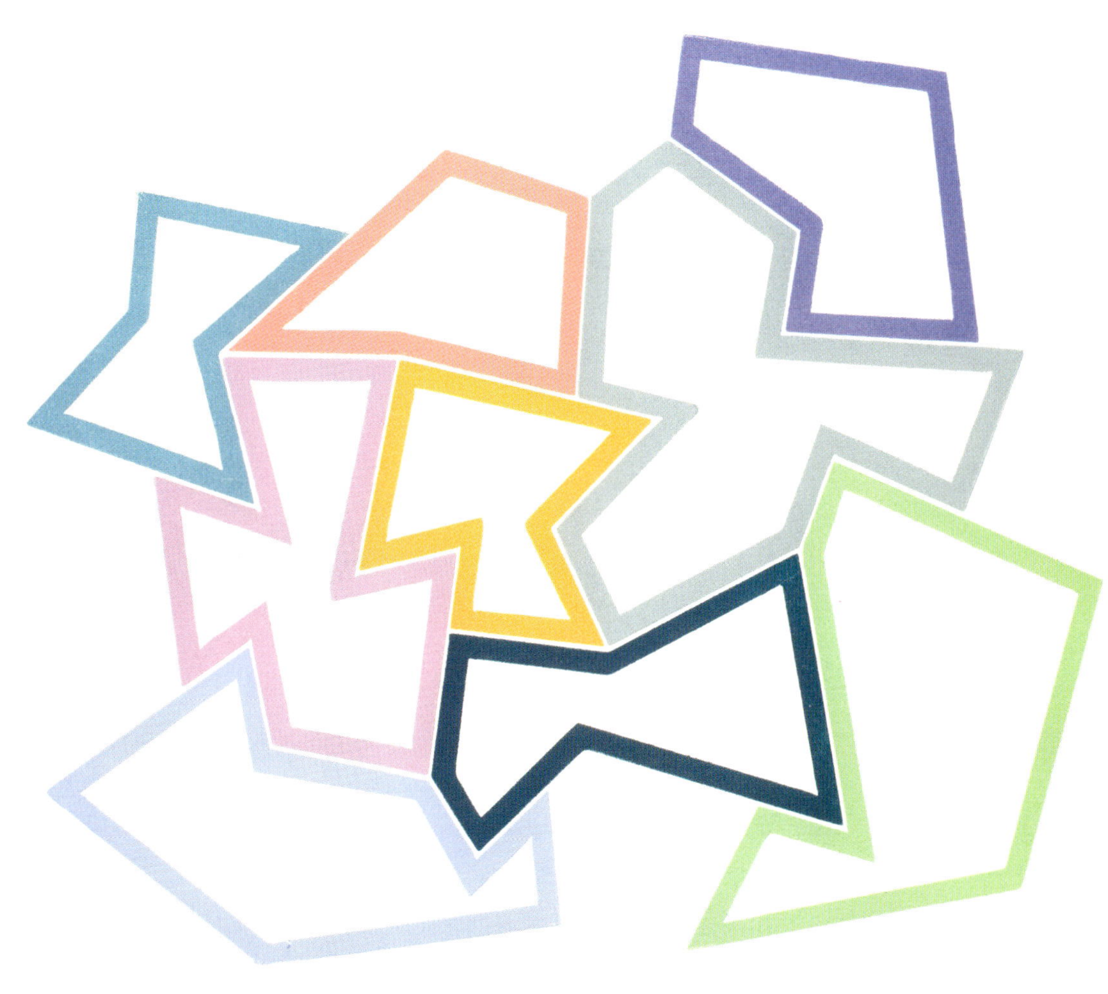

Richard Deacon RA (born 1949): '9 x 9', 2005, printer: Hugh Stoneman (1947–2005), publisher: Tate St Ives, woodcut, 53.5 x 52.5cms. The Art Fund Hugh Stoneman Archive. Falmouth Art Gallery collection. FAMAG 2008.26.23

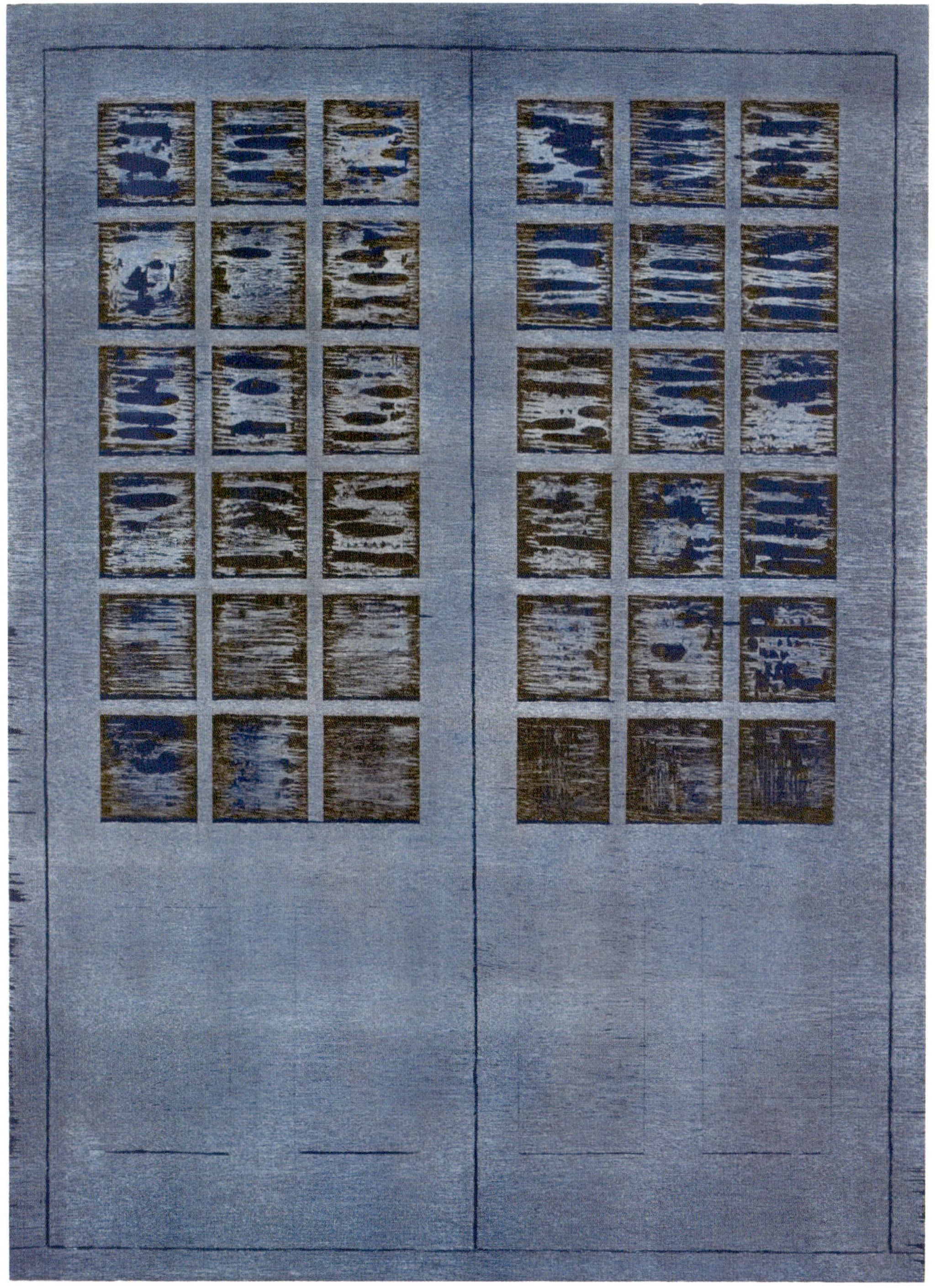

Arturo Di Stefano (born 1955): 'Atelier 3', 2000, printer: Hugh Stoneman (1947–2005), publisher: Purdy Hicks, woodcut, 97.8 x 73cms. The Art Fund Hugh Stoneman Archive. Falmouth Art Gallery collection. FAMAG 2008.26.24

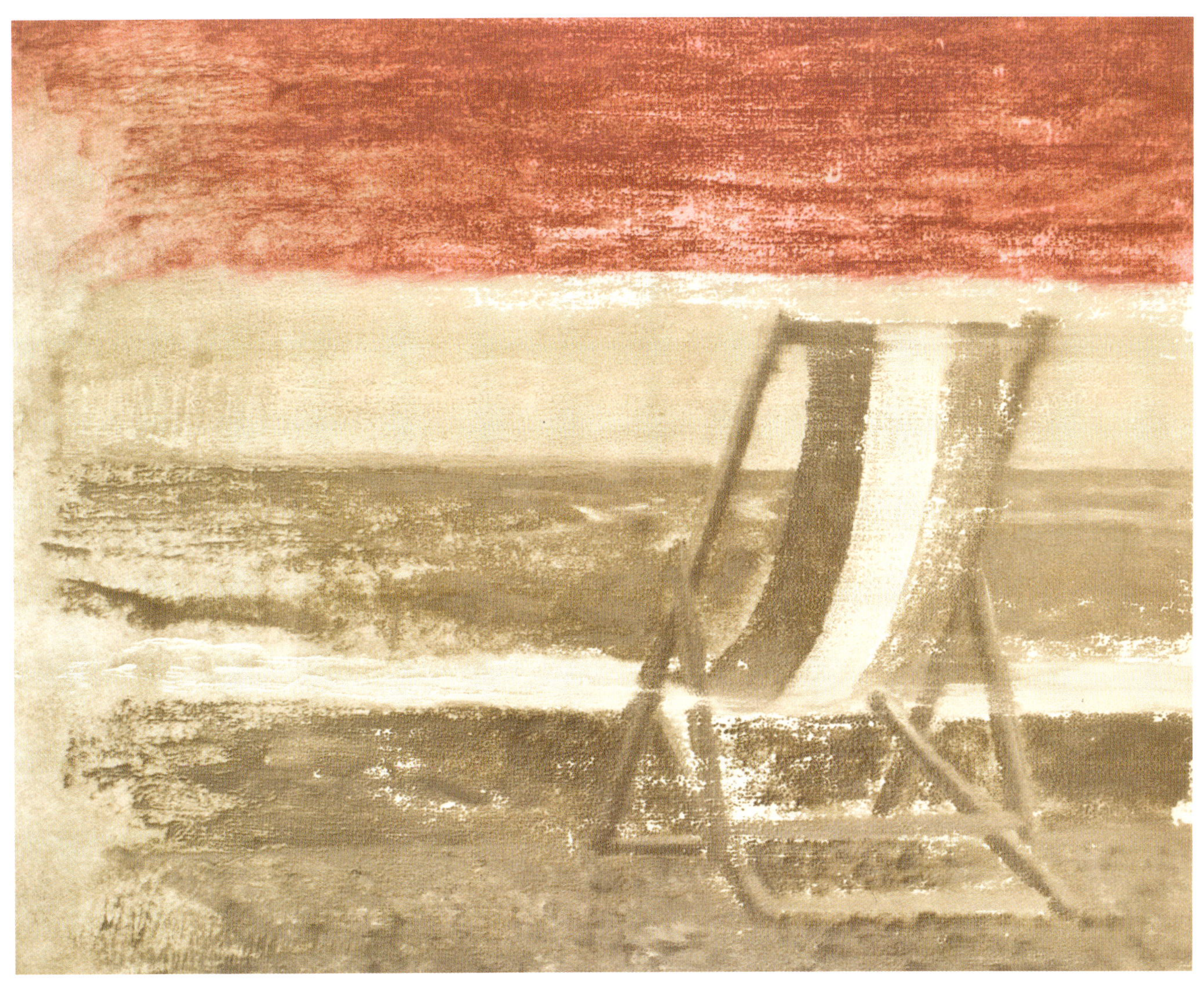

Arturo Di Stefano (born 1955): 'Strands' series, 1998, printer: Hugh Stoneman (1947–2005), publisher: Purdy Hicks, signed and dated 1998, aquatint etching (B.A.T.), 39 x 49.2cms. The Art Fund Hugh Stoneman Archive. Falmouth Art Gallery collection. FAMAG 2008.26.25

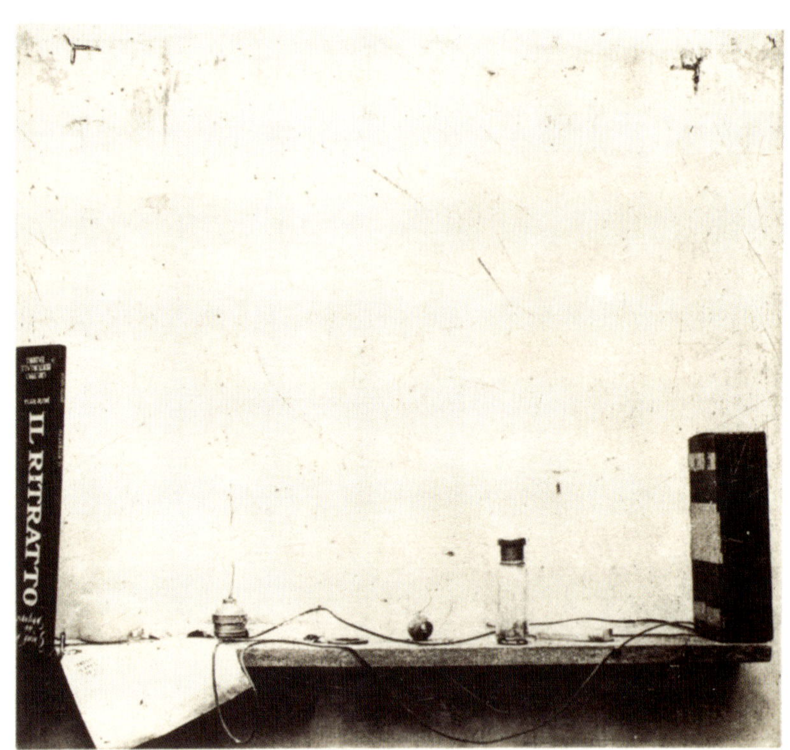
IL RITRATTO

Manuel Franquelo (born 1950): From the series of 14 etchings – 'The Language of Things', printer: Hugh Stoneman (1947–2005), publisher: Estampa digital, signed and dated 2002, dustgrain gravure and etching with chine collé (artist's proof 1), 54 x 58.1cms. The Art Fund Hugh Stoneman Archive. Falmouth Art Gallery collection. FAMAG 2008.26.26

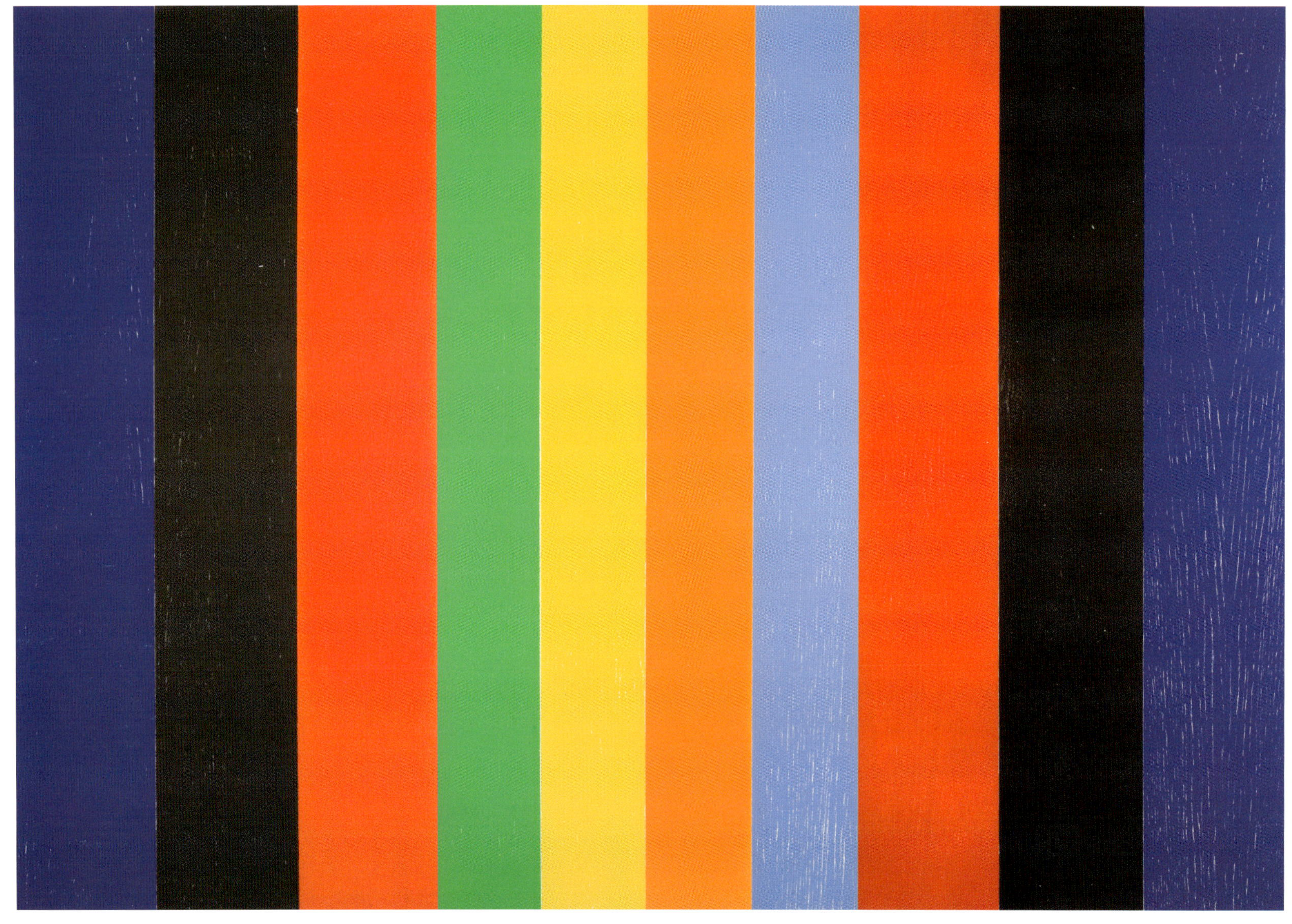

Sir Terry Frost RA (1915–2003): 'Timberaine A,' printer: Hugh Stoneman (1947–2005), publisher: Paragon Press, woodcut, 106 x 150cms. The Art Fund Hugh Stoneman Archive. Falmouth Art Gallery collection. © courtesy of the Estate of Terry Frost. FAMAG 2008.26.27

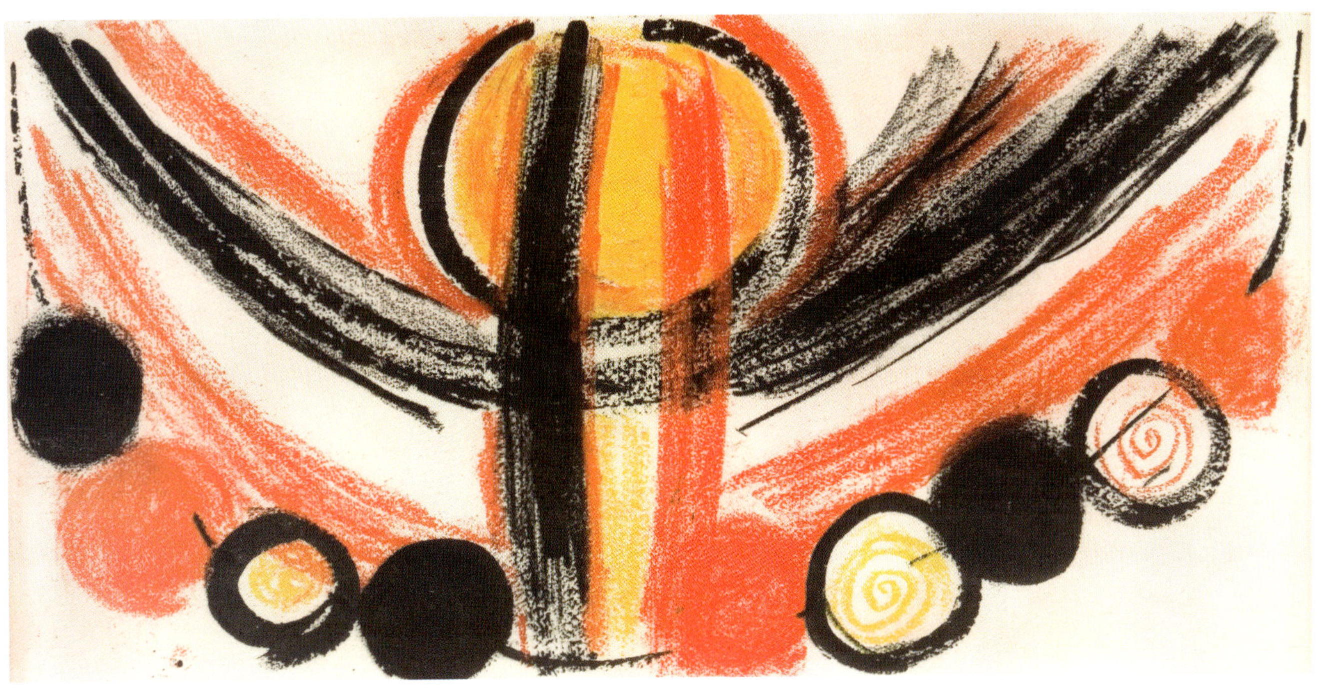

Sir Terry Frost RA (1915–2003): 'Sunbow', printer: Hugh Stoneman (1947–2005), signed and dated 2002, etching (B.A.T.), 30 x 58.5cms. The Art Fund Hugh Stoneman Archive. Falmouth Art Gallery collection. © courtesy of the Estate of Terry Frost. FAMAG 2008.26.28

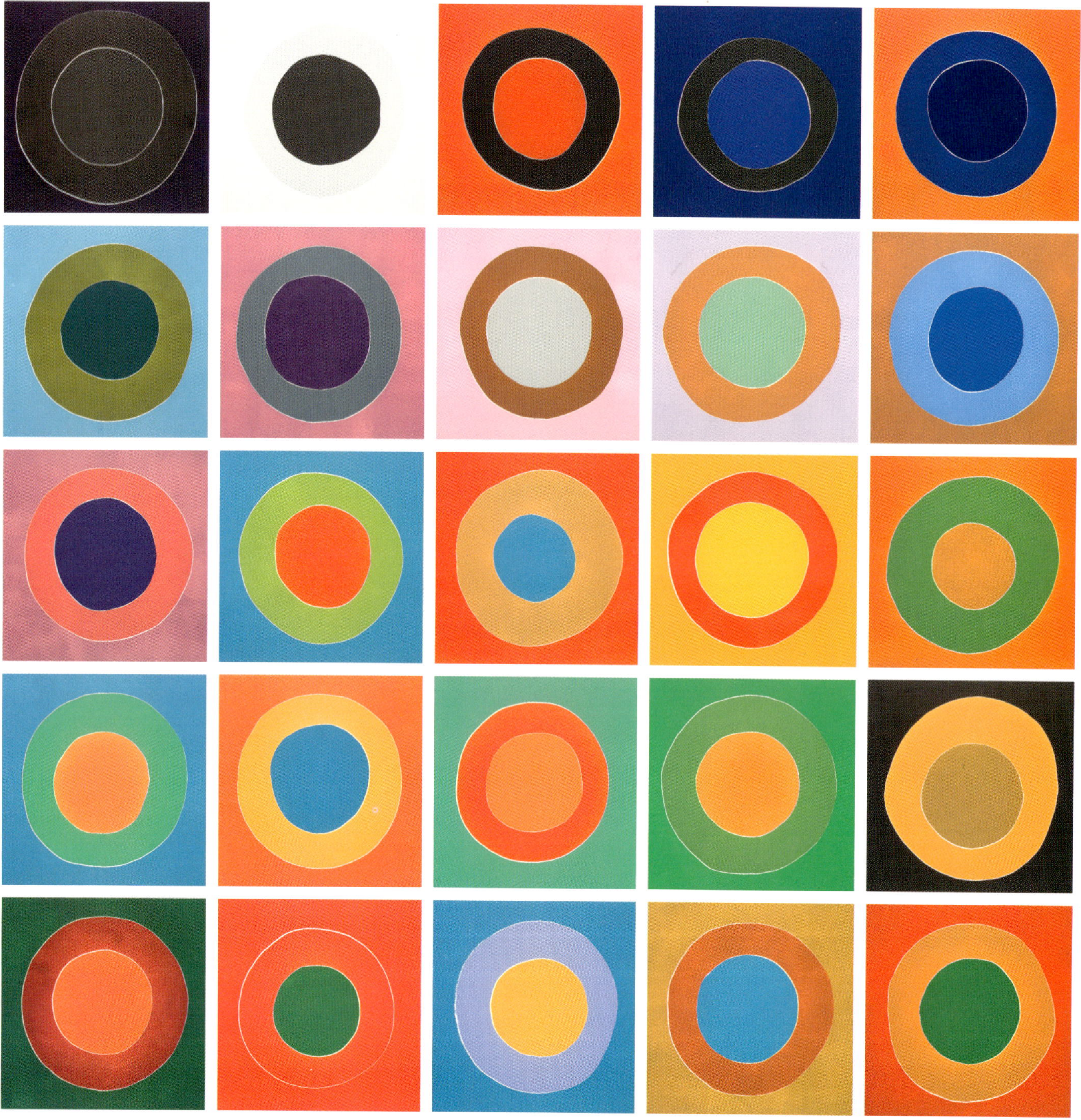

Sir Terry Frost RA (1915–2003): 'Orchard Tambourine B', printer: Hugh Stoneman (1947–2005), publisher: The Paragon Press, woodcut (B.A.T. for an edition of 35) published 2002, 37.3 x 37.3cms each (25 prints making the image). The Art Fund Hugh Stoneman Archive. Falmouth Art Gallery collection. © courtesy of the Estate of Terry Frost. FAMAG 2008.26.29

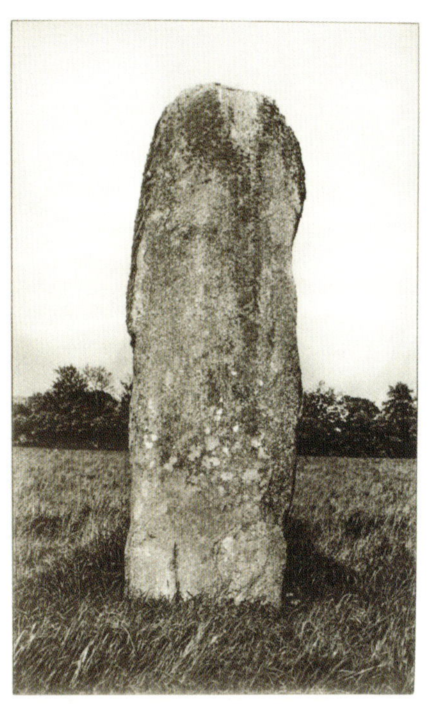

BIRD
ROCK

A ROAD WALKING JOURNEY
AT THE TIME OF SINGING BIRDS
BRITTANY
13-25 MAY 1987
SOUTH COAST TO WEST COAST TO NORTH COAST

Hamish Fulton, (born 1946): 'Bird Rock', 1988, printer: Hugh Stoneman (1947–2005), publisher: Print Centre Publications, signed, photogravure (number 44 of an edition of 50), 63 x 43cms. The Art Fund Hugh Stoneman Archive. Falmouth Art Gallery collection. FAMAG 2008.26.30

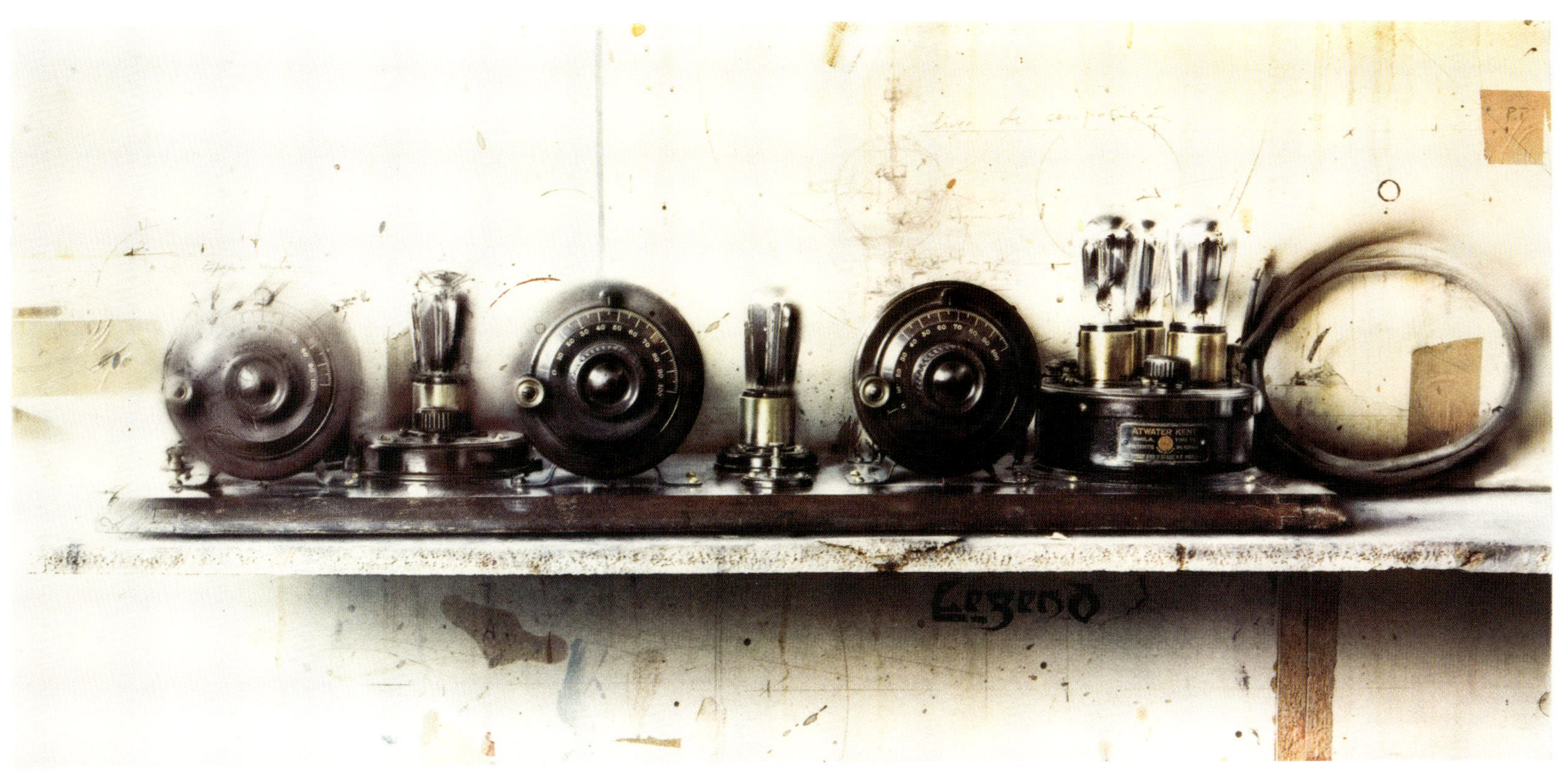

César Galicia (born 1957): 'Radio', 2003, printer: Hugh Stoneman (1947–2005), publisher: The artist, colour separation photogravure, 10.3 x 72cms. The Art Fund Hugh Stoneman Archive. Falmouth Art Gallery collection. FAMAG 2008.26.31

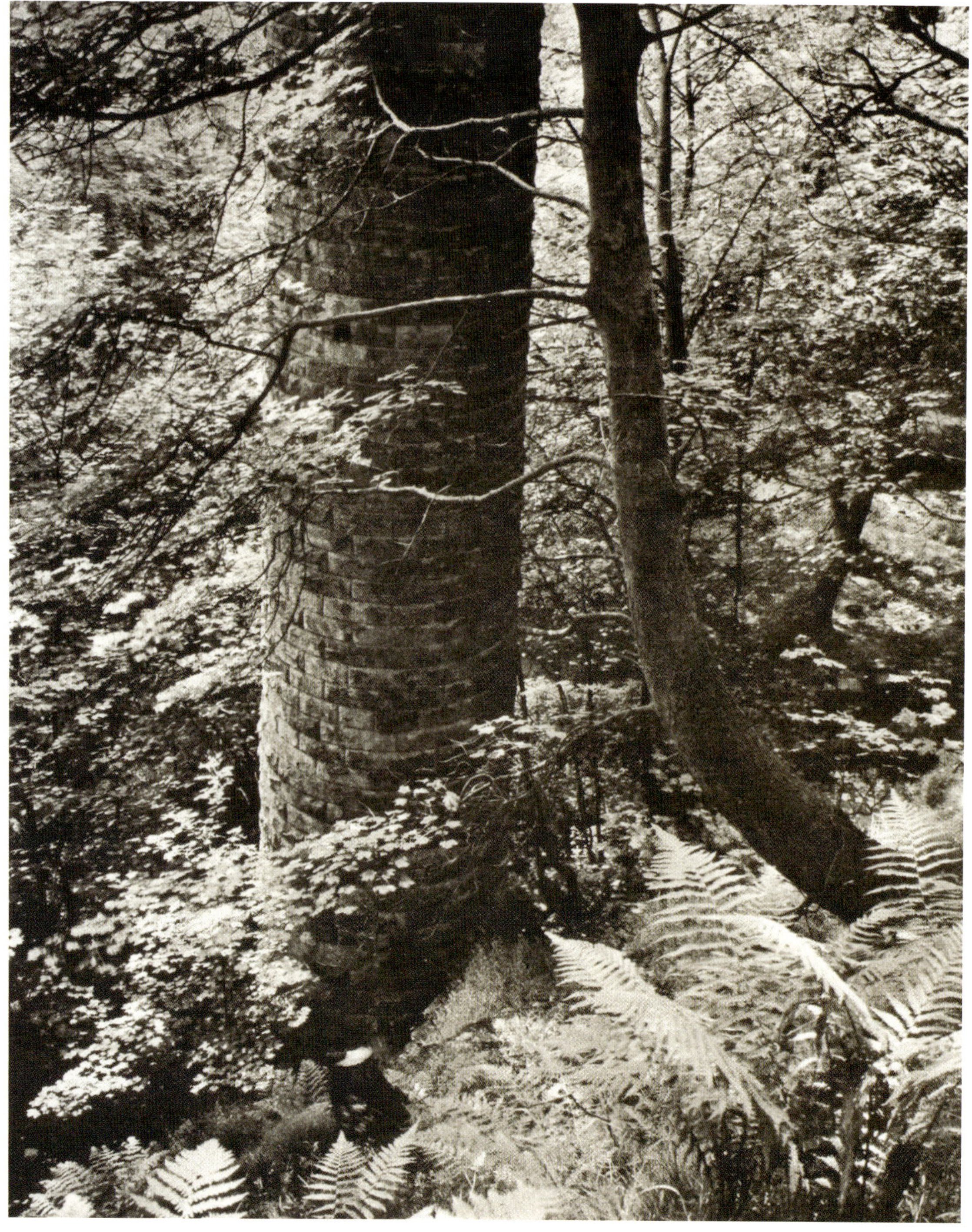

Fay Godwin (1931–2005): 'Remains of Elmet', 1979, printer: Hugh Stoneman (1947–2005), publisher: Print Centre Publications and Zwemmers 1994, signed, photogravure (number 8 of an edition of 30), 34.2 x 33.2cms. The Art Fund Hugh Stoneman Archive. Falmouth Art Gallery collection. FAMAG 2008.26.32 © The British Library Board

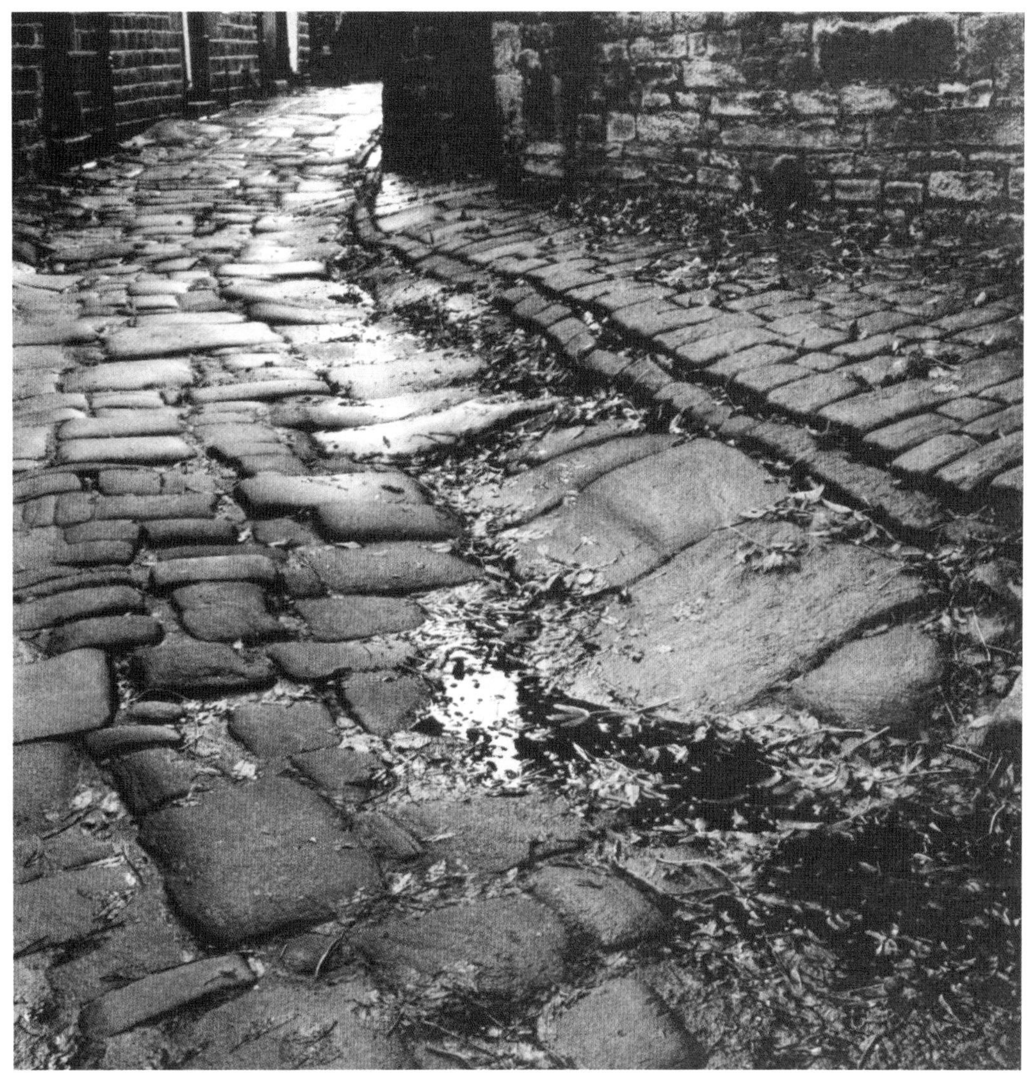

Fay Godwin (1931–2005): 'Paved Path Above Lumbutts', 1977 from the series 'The Remains of Elmet', printer: Hugh Stoneman (1947–2005), publisher: Print Centre Publications and Zwemmers 1994, signed, photogravure published by Faber (number 6 of an edition of 30), 34.2 x 33.2cms. The Art Fund Hugh Stoneman Archive. Falmouth Art Gallery collection. FAMAG2008.26.33

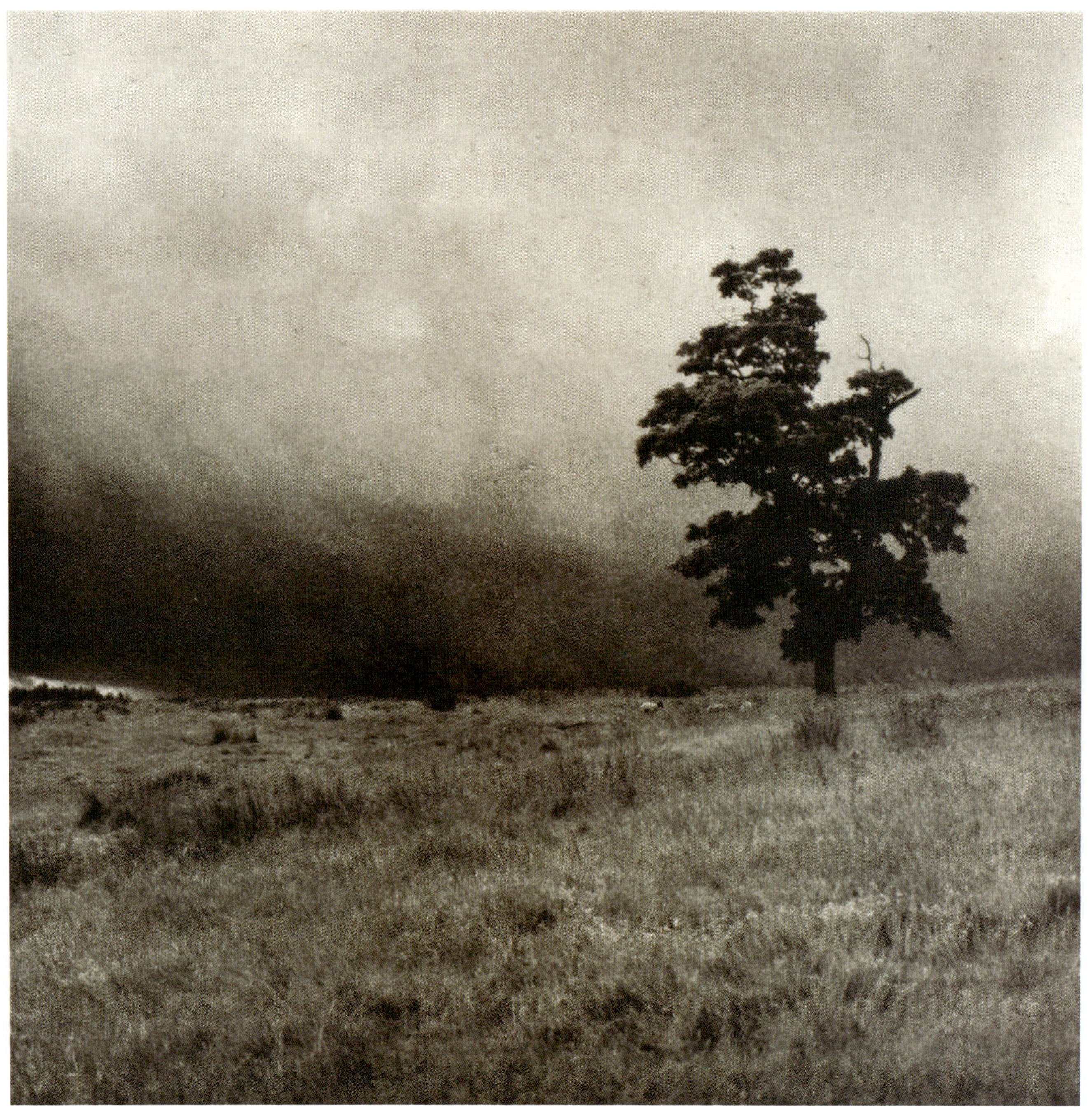

Fay Godwin (1931–2005): 'West Laithe, Heptonstall', 1977 from the series 'The Remains of Elmet', printer: Hugh Stoneman (1947–2005), publisher: Print Centre Publications and Zwemmers 1994, signed, photogravure (number 6 of an edition of 30), 34 x 33cms. The Art Fund Hugh Stoneman Archive. Falmouth Art Gallery collection. FAMAG 2008.26.34

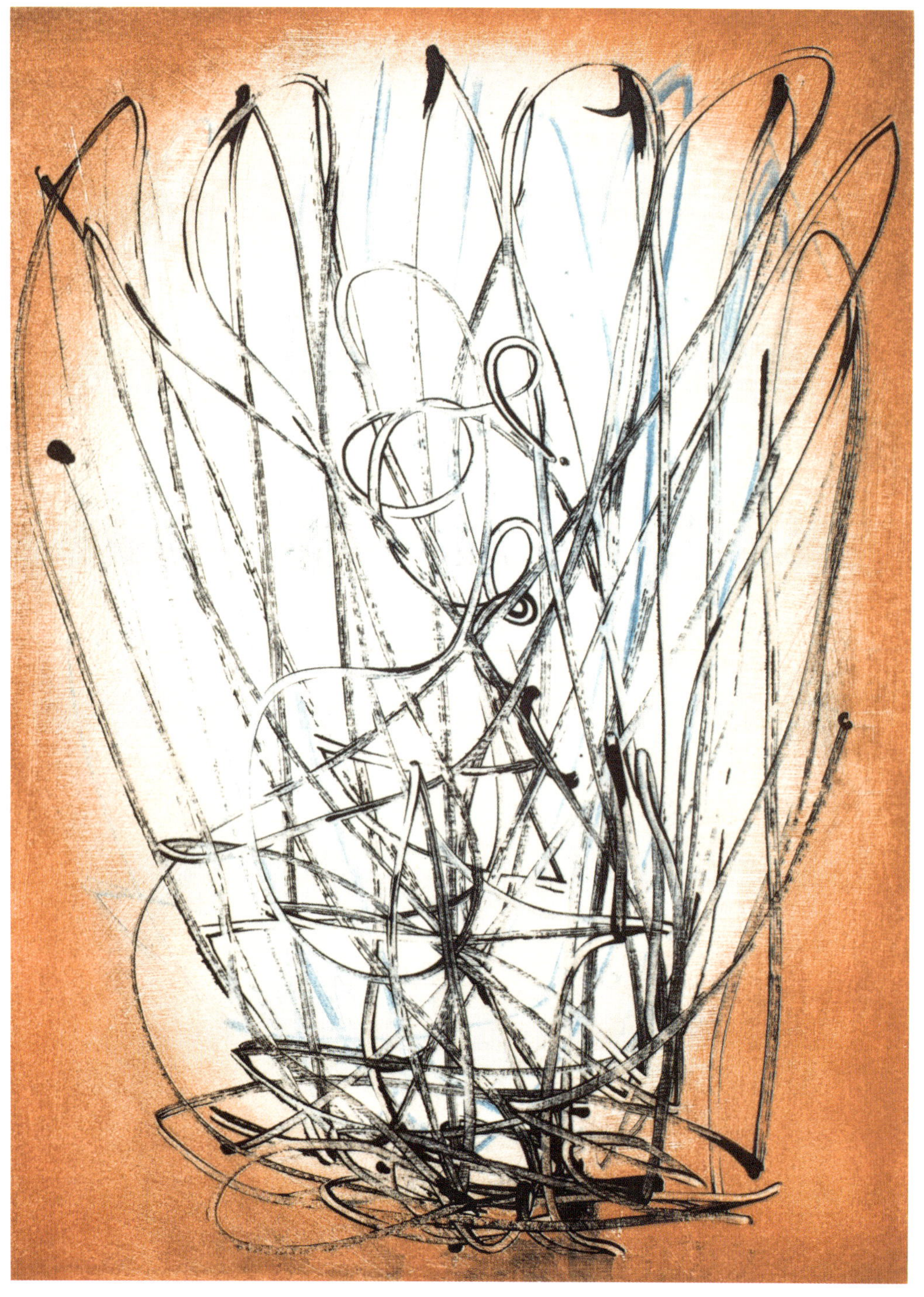

Dame Barbara Hepworth (1903–1975): 'Spring', 1957 – print produced for the Hepworth Centenary Exhibition at Tate St Ives, 2003, printer: Hugh Stoneman (1947–2005), publisher: Tate St Ives, photogravure, 58.5 x 45cms. The Art Fund Hugh Stoneman Archive. Falmouth Art Gallery collection. © Bowness, Hepworth Estate. FAMAG 2008.26.35

Patrick Heron (1920–1999): From the 'Brushworks' series of 11 etchings, 1999, printer: Hugh Stoneman (1947–2005), publisher: The Paragon Press, sugarlift etching (proof, edition of 38), 67 x 79.5cms. The Art Fund Hugh Stoneman Archive. Falmouth Art Gallery collection. © Estate of Patrick Heron. All rights reserved. DACS 2009. FAMAG 2008.26.36

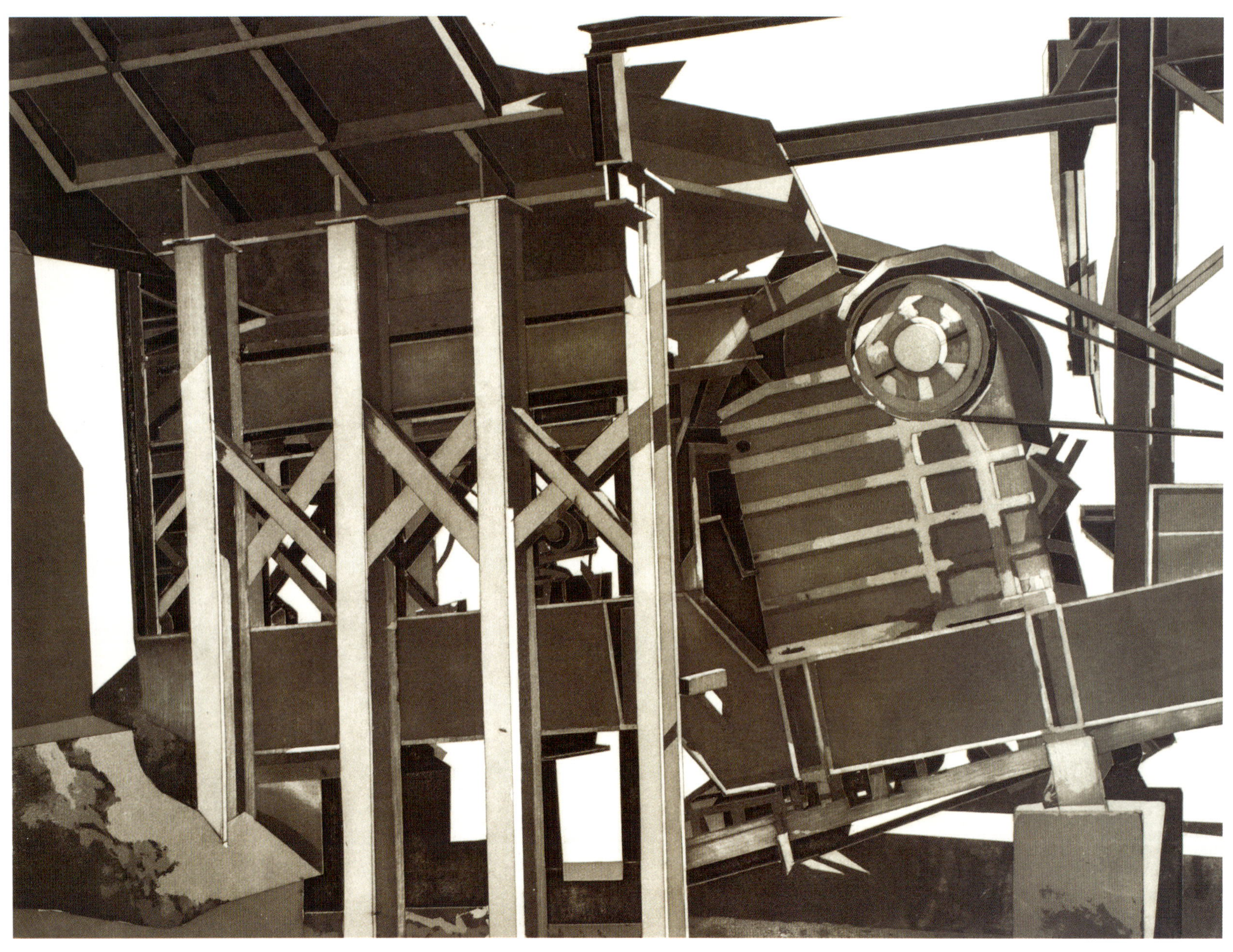

Sid Hurwitz: 'Quarry', printer: Hugh Stoneman (1947–2005), signed, aquatint (number 3 of an edition of 25), 55.8 x 75.5cms. The Art Fund Hugh Stoneman Archive. Falmouth Art Gallery collection. FAMAG 2008.26.37

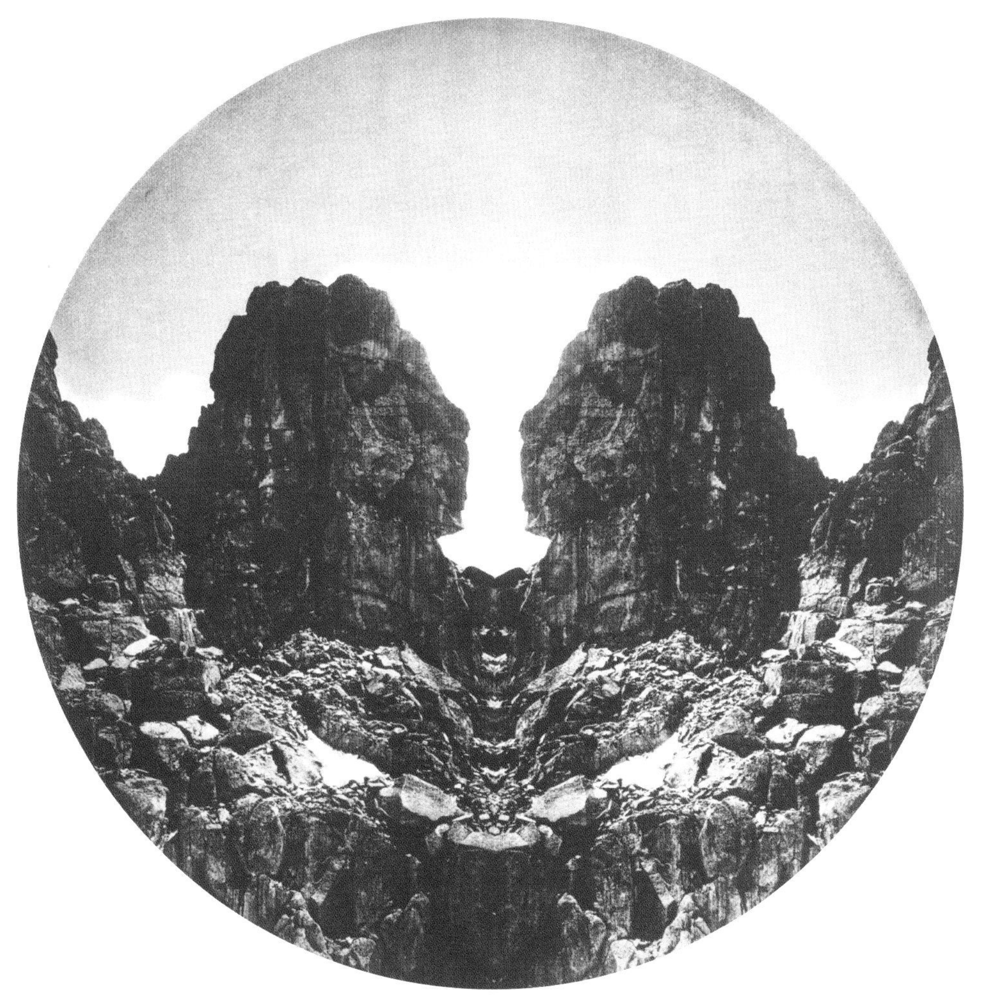

John Hilliard (born 1945): 'Plein-Air', printer: Hugh Stoneman (1947–2005), publisher: Print Centre Publications, signed and dated 1988, photogravure (number 16 of an edition of 20), 67.5 x 53cms. The Art Fund Hugh Stoneman Archive. Falmouth Art Gallery collection. FAMAG 2008.26.38

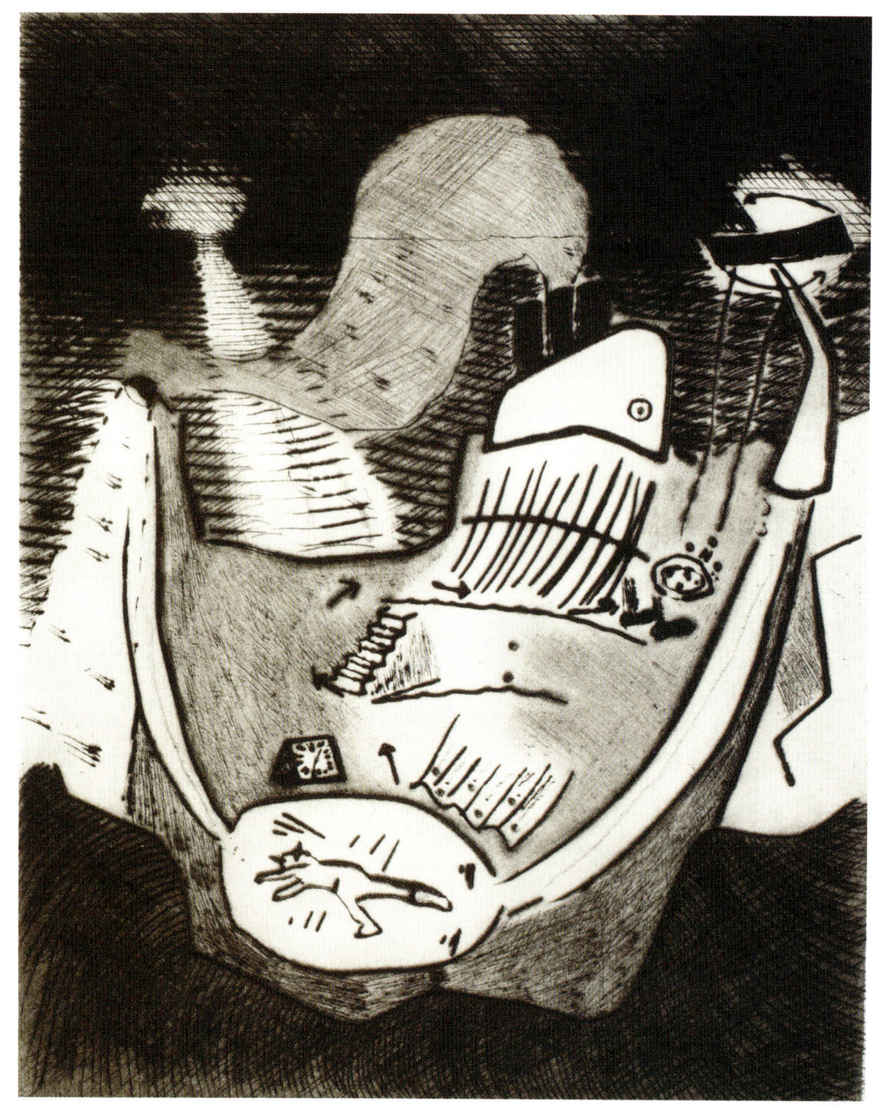

Mathew Hilton: 'Second', printer: Hugh Stoneman (1947–2005), signed and dated 1991, etching (printer's proof), 49 x 50cms. The Art Fund Hugh Stoneman Archive. Falmouth Art Gallery collection. FAMAG 2008.26.39

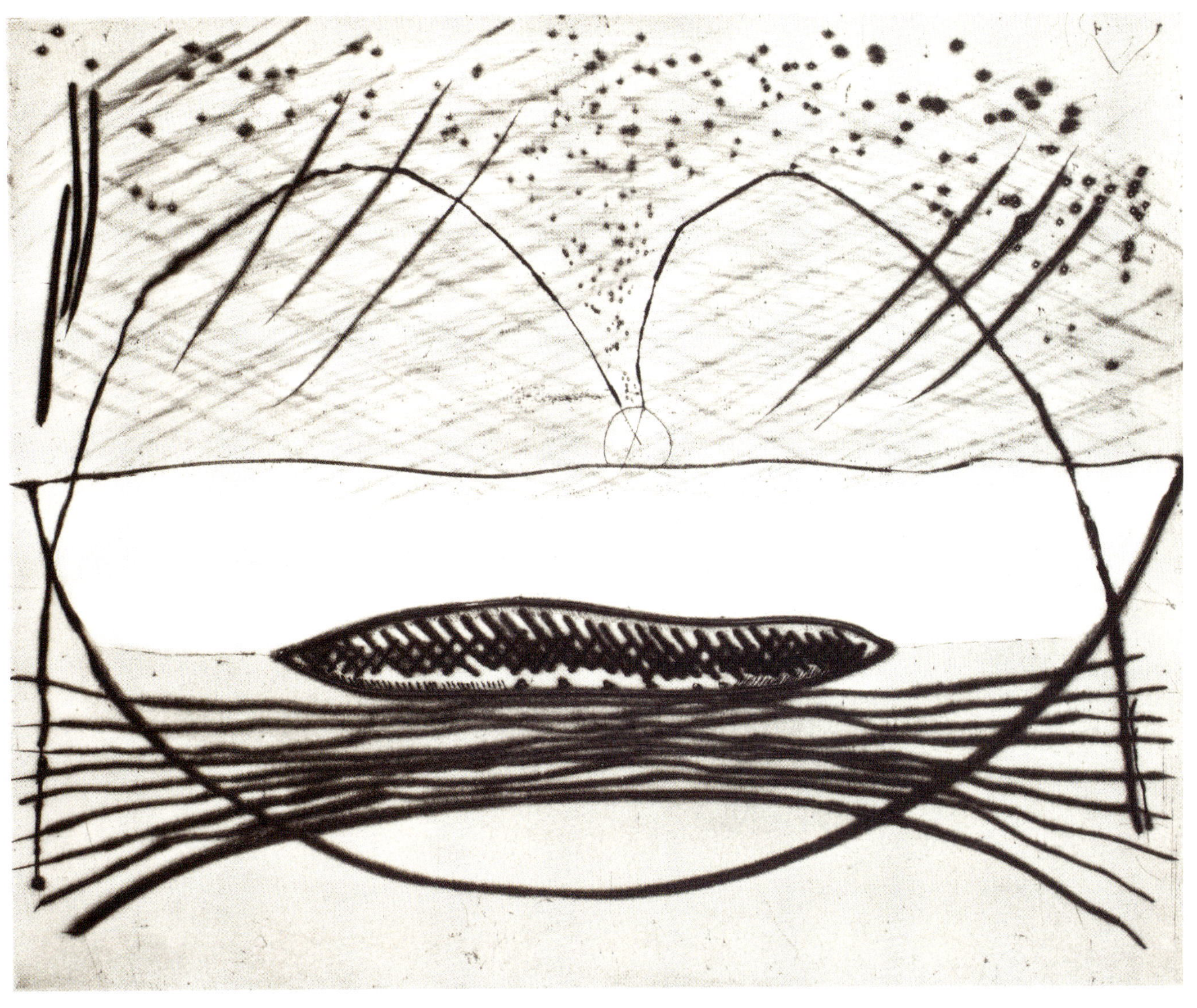

Mathew Hilton: 'Thirteenth', printer: Hugh Stoneman (1947–2005), signed and dated 1991, etching (printer's proof), 49 x 50cms. The Art Fund Hugh Stoneman Archive. Falmouth Art Gallery collection. FAMAG 2008.26.40

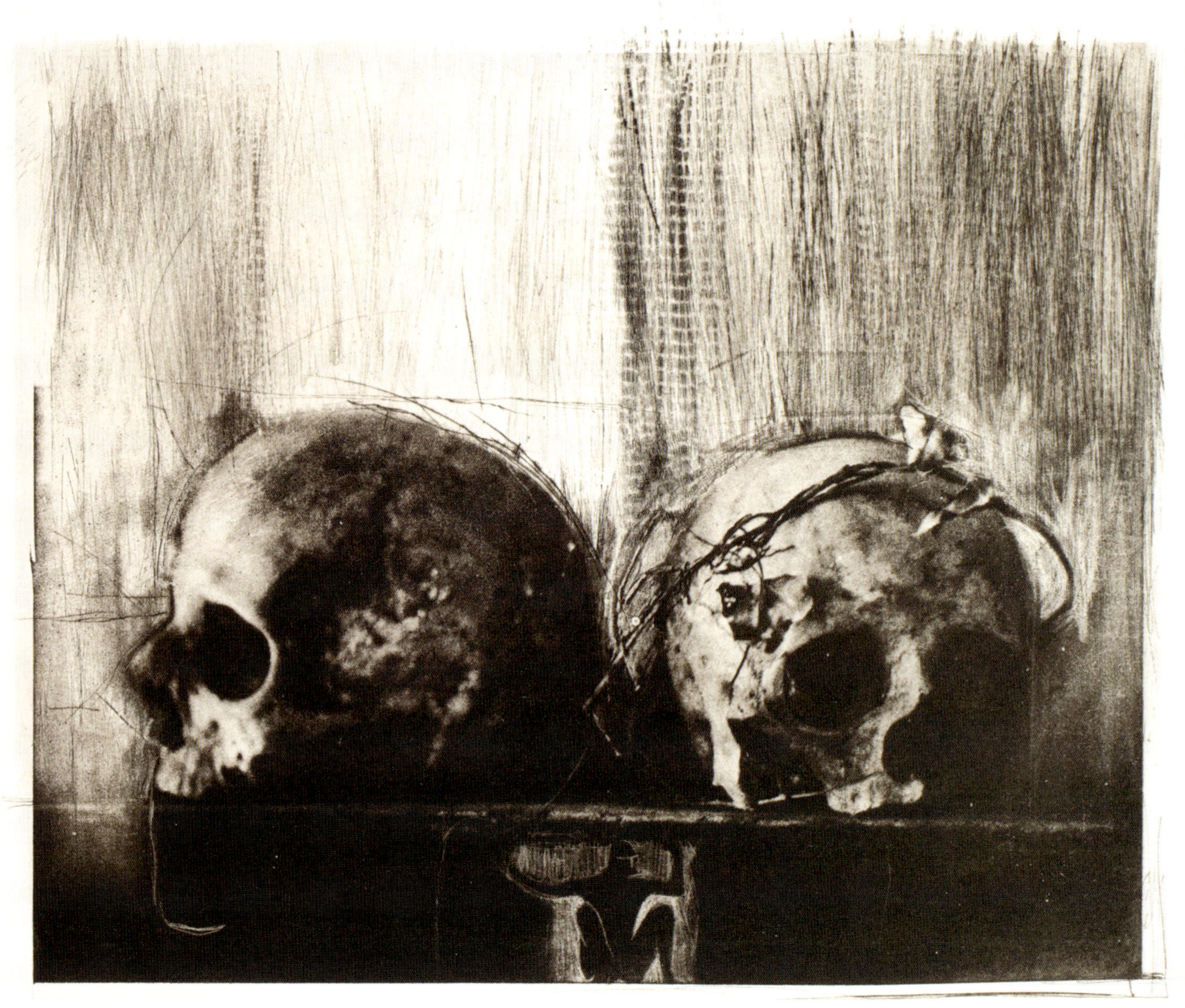

David Hiscock (born 1956): No. 7 from the series 'Seven Ages', printer: Hugh Stoneman (1947–2005), publisher: Print Centre Publications, signed and dated 1990, photogravure etching (number 29 of an edition of 50), 43 x 53cms. The Art Fund Hugh Stoneman Archive. Falmouth Art Gallery collection. FAMAG 2008.26.41

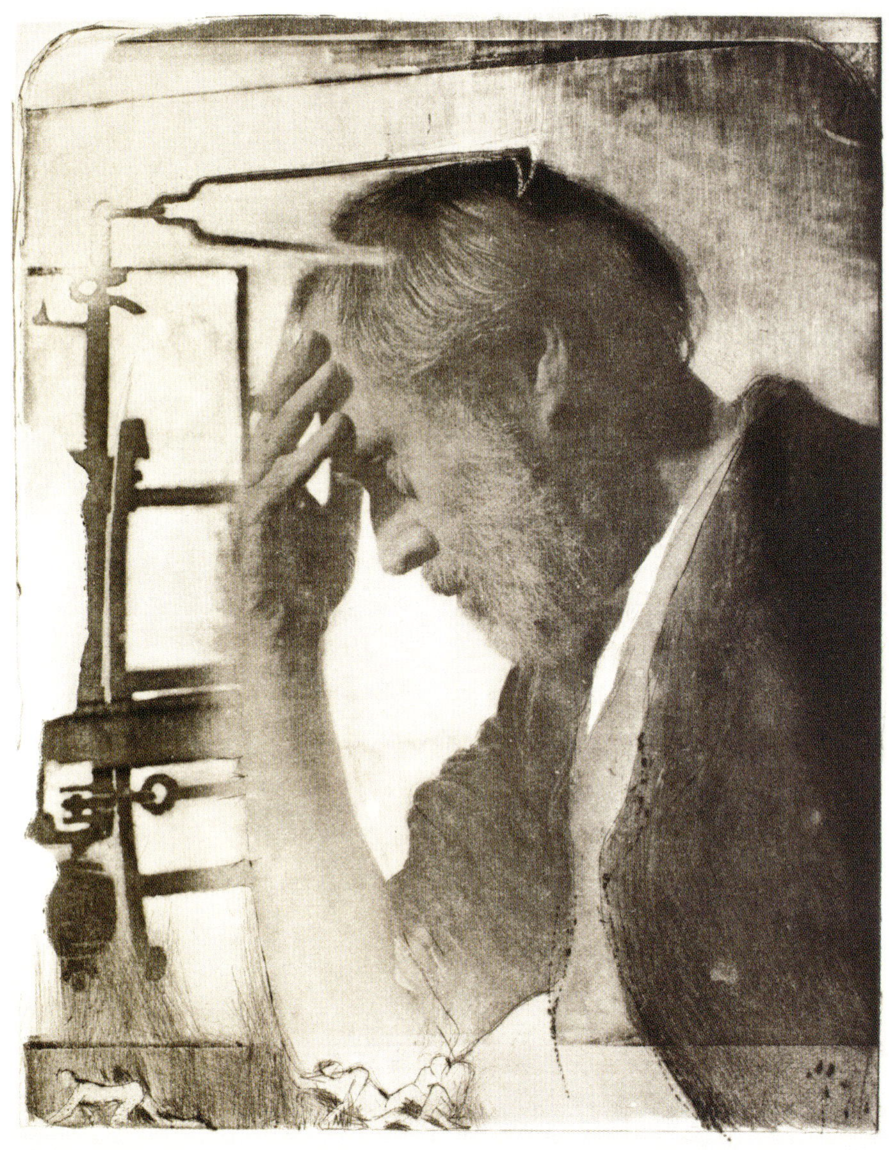

David Hiscock (born 1956): 'Old Man' – No. 6 from the series 'Seven Ages', printer: Hugh Stoneman (1947–2005), publisher: Print Centre Publications, signed and dated 1990, photogravure etching (number 29 of an edition of 50), 53 x 43cms. The Art Fund Hugh Stoneman Archive. Falmouth Art Gallery collection. FAMAG 2008.26.42

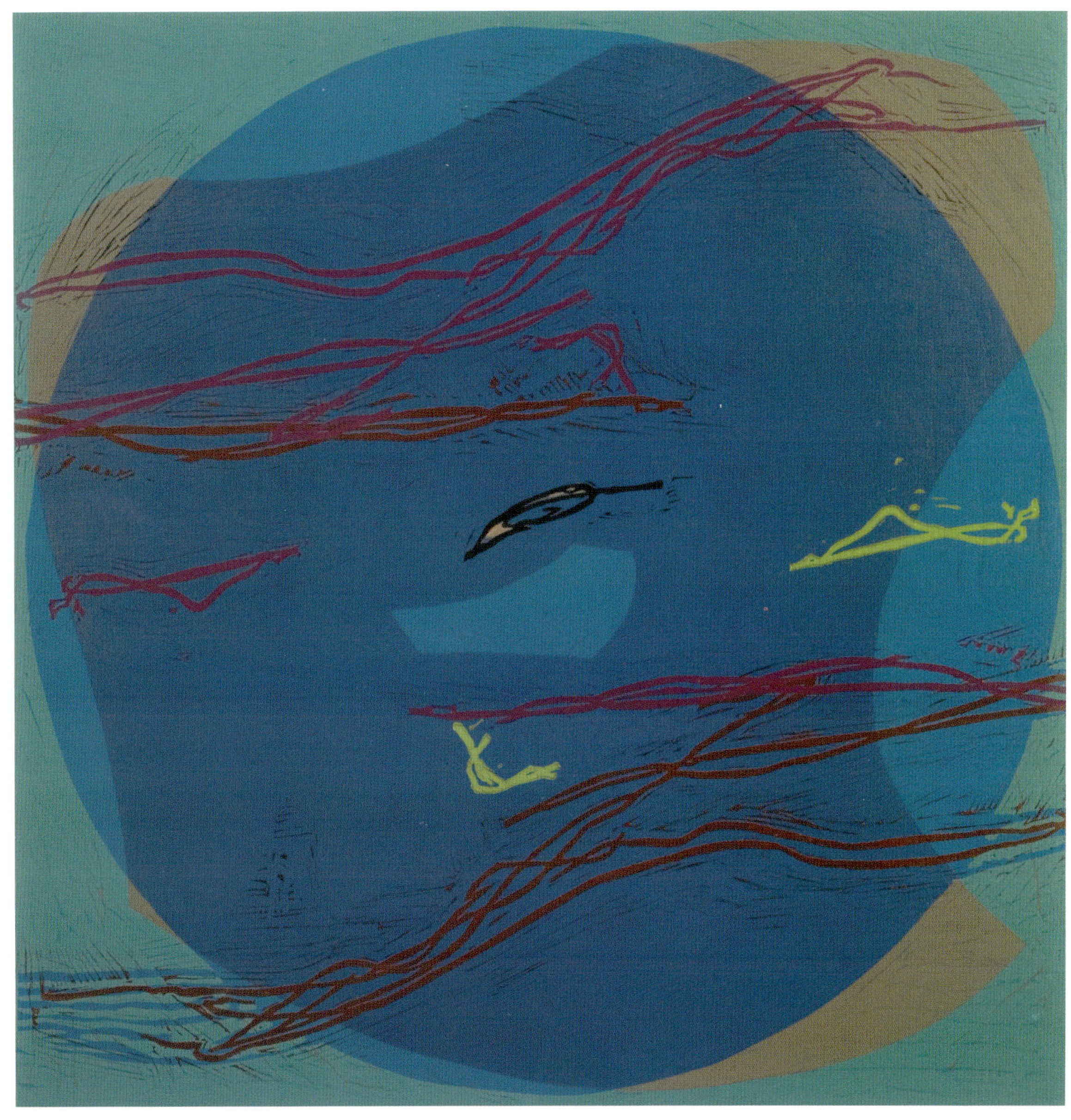

Gordon House (1932–2004): 'Deep Circle', printer: Hugh Stoneman (1947–2005), signed and dated 1991, linocut (H.C. 1), 72 x 60.5cms. The Art Fund Hugh Stoneman Archive. Falmouth Art Gallery collection. FAMAG 2008.26.43

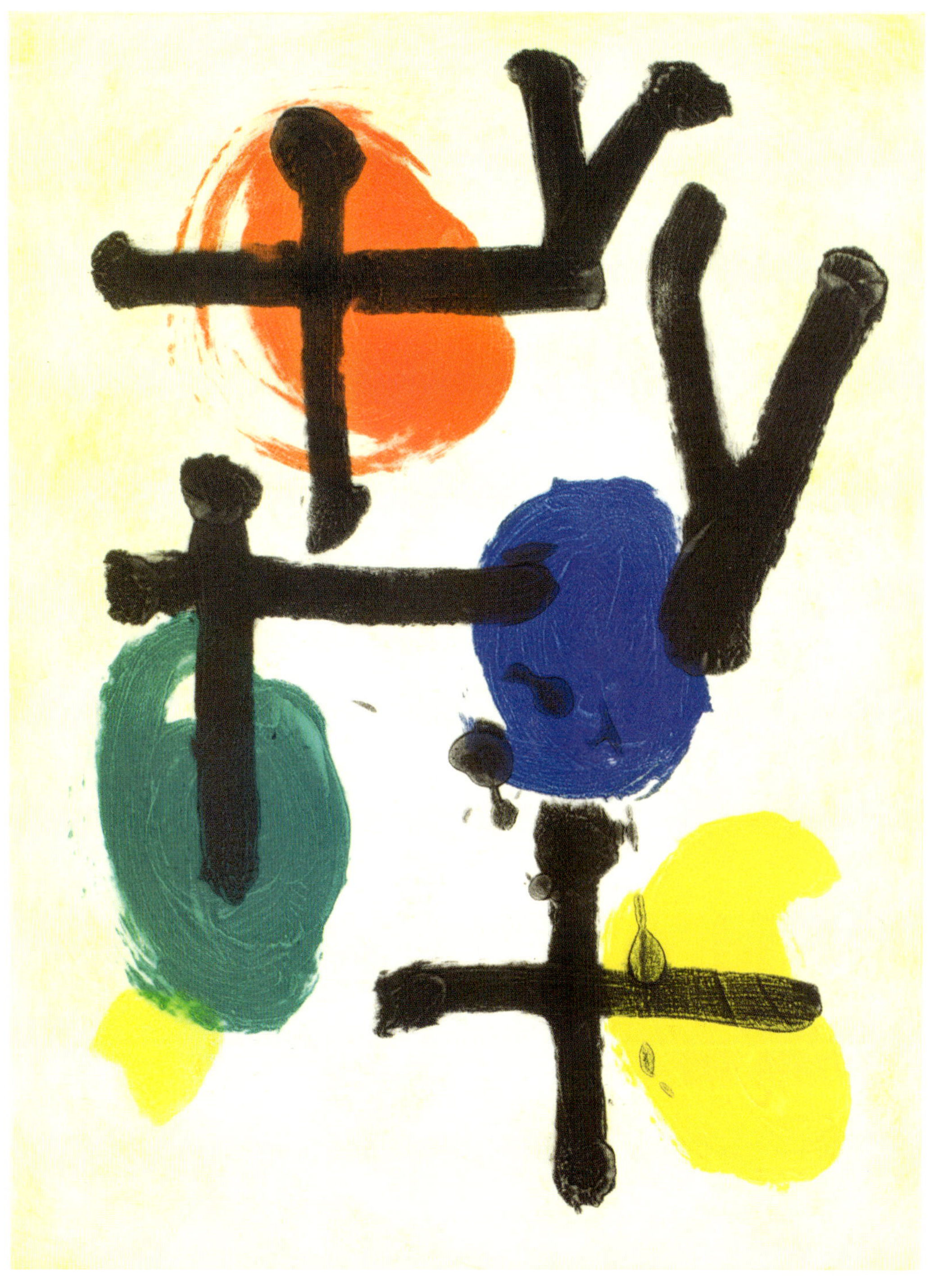

John Hoyland RA (born 1934): 'Endless Poem', 2006, printer: Hugh Stoneman (1947–2005), publisher: Stoneman Graphics, signed and dated 2006, photogravure and carborundum (printer's proof 1), 75.5 x 57cms. The Art Fund Hugh Stoneman Archive. Falmouth Art Gallery collection. FAMAG 2008.26.44

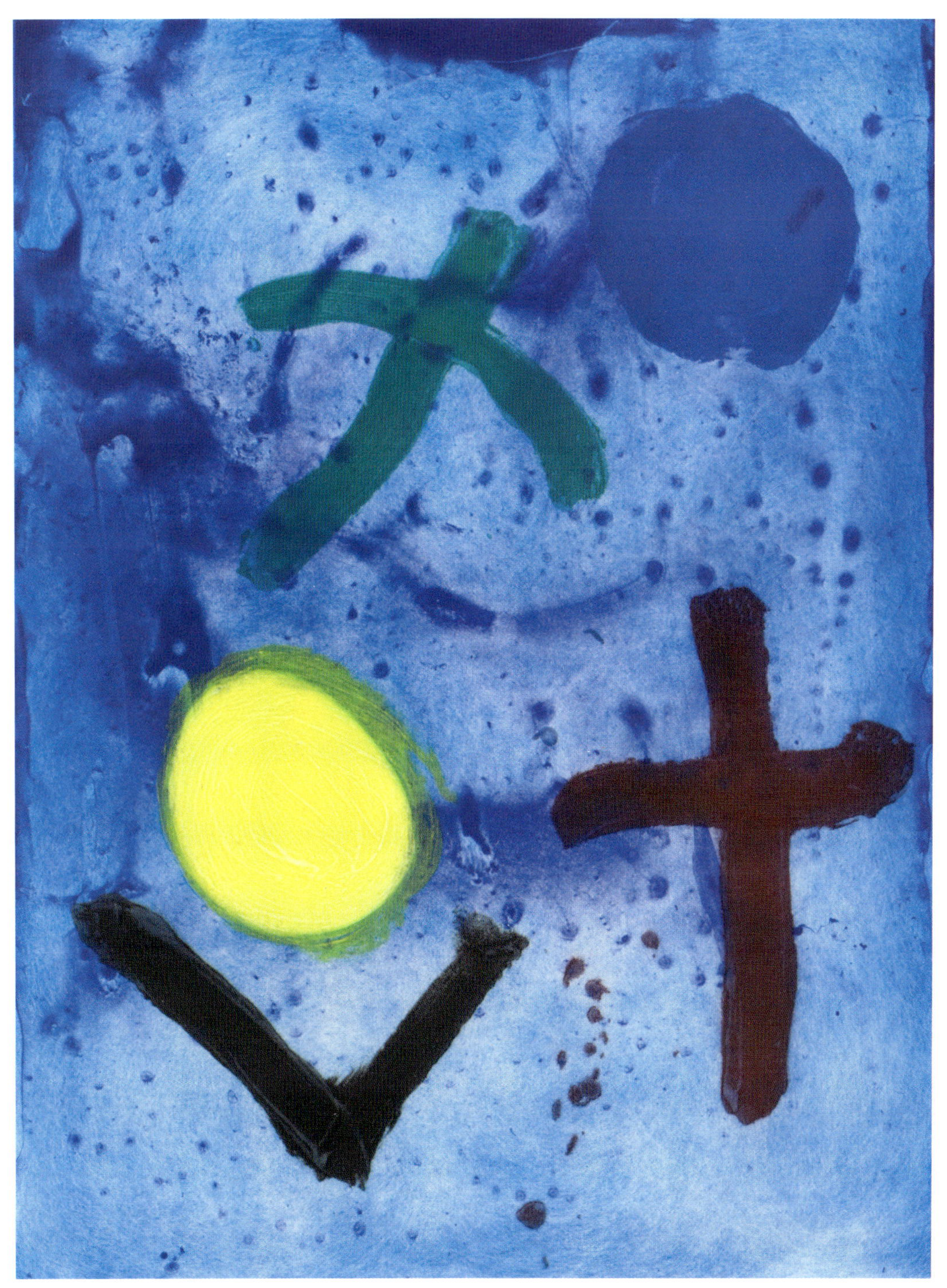

John Hoyland RA (born 1934): 'Flying Wild', 2006, printer: Hugh Stoneman (1947–2005), publisher: Stoneman Graphics, signed and dated 2006, photogravure and carborundum (artist's proof), 75.5 x 57cms. The Art Fund Hugh Stoneman Archive. Falmouth Art Gallery collection. FAMAG 2008.26.45

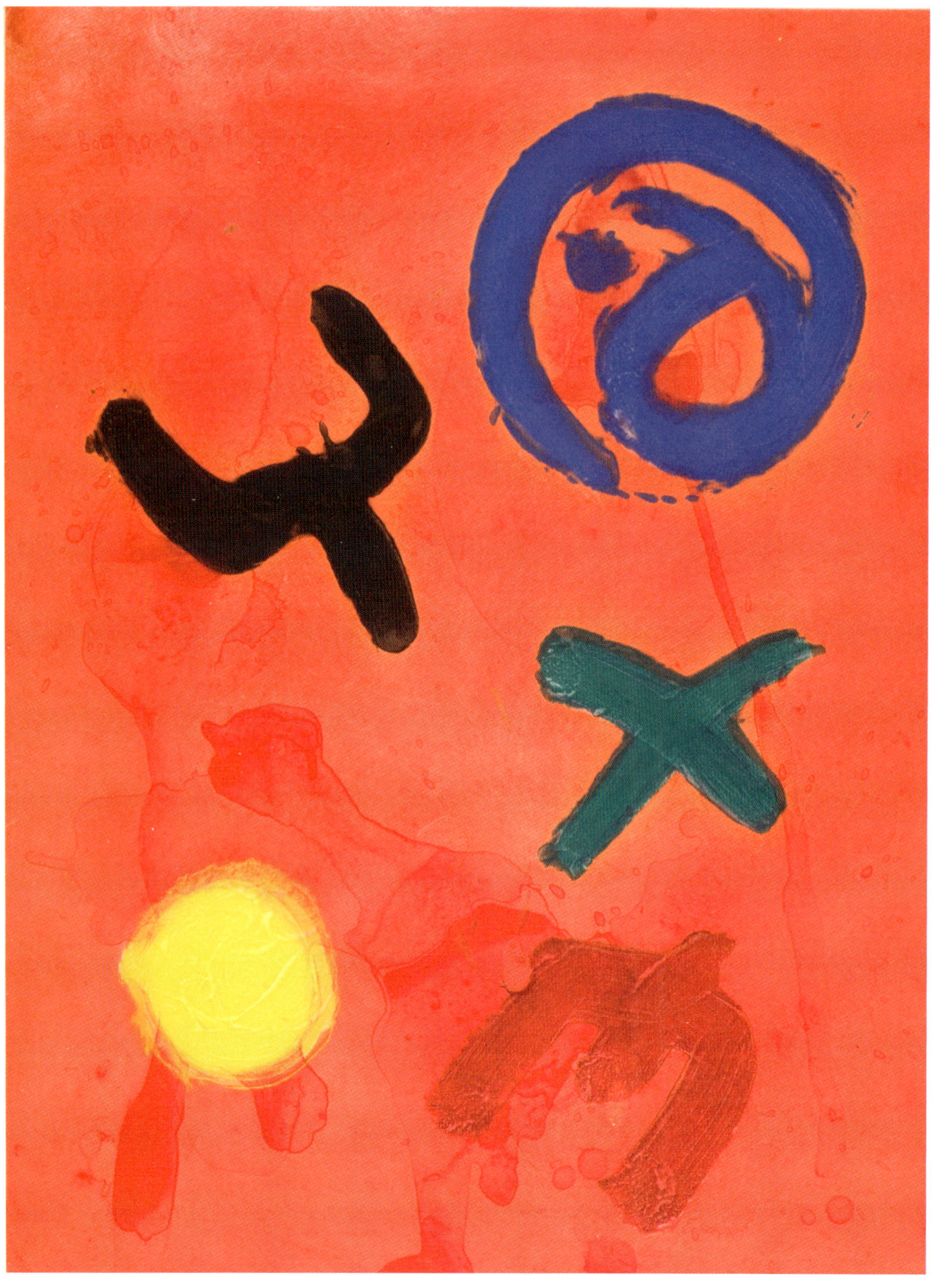

John Hoyland RA (born 1934): 'Secret Summer', 2006, printer: Hugh Stoneman (1947–2005), publisher: Stoneman Graphics, signed and dated 2006, photogravure and carborundum (printer's proof 1), 75.5 x 57cms. The Art Fund Hugh Stoneman Archive. Falmouth Art Gallery collection. FAMAG 2008.26.46

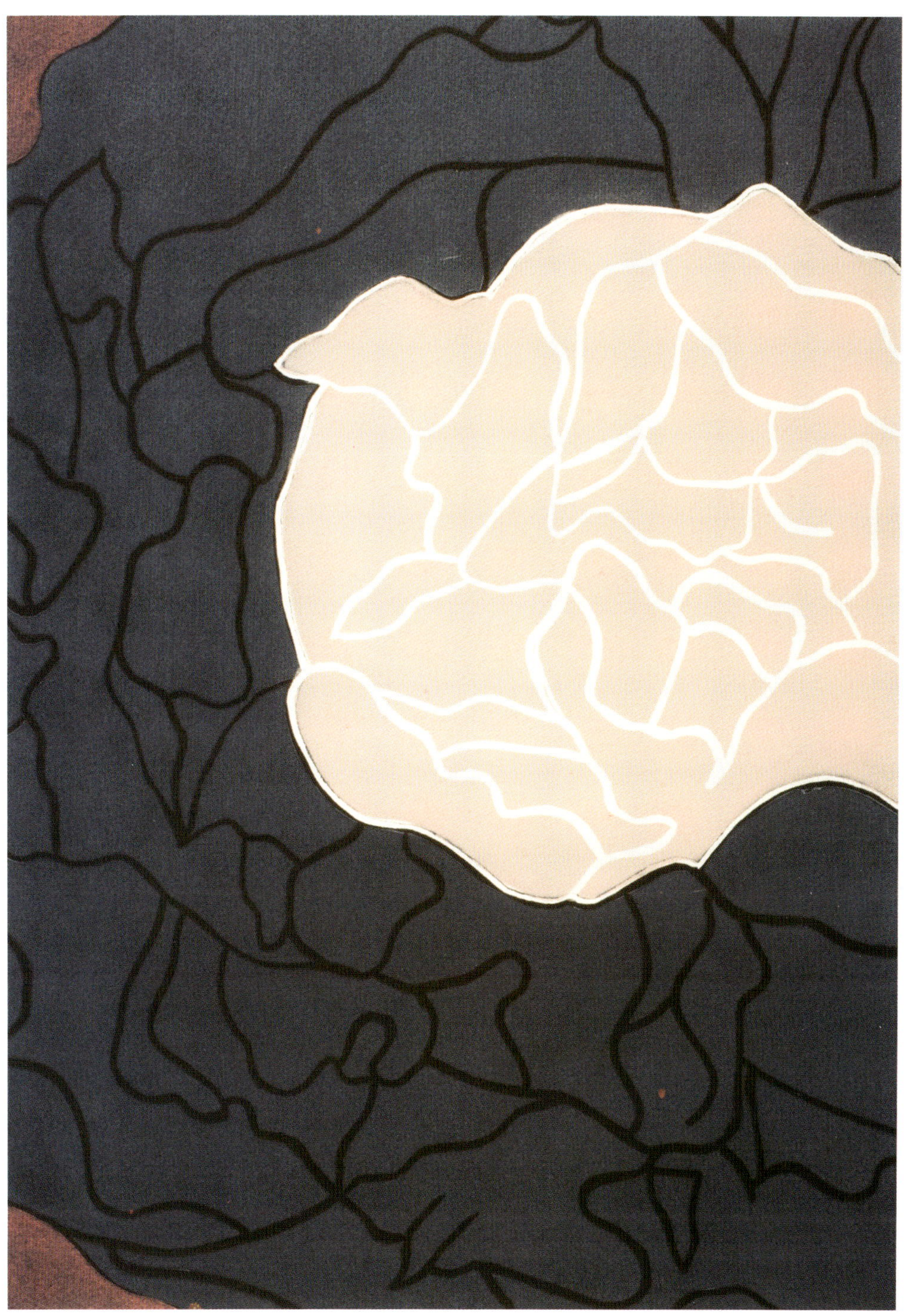

Gary Hume RA (born 1962): 'Here's Flowers 7', printer: Hugh Stoneman (1947–2005), publisher: Paragon Press, signed and dated 2006, linocut with hand colouring (printer's proof) (number 2 of an edition of 2), 77.5 x 58.5cms. The Art Fund Hugh Stoneman Archive. Falmouth Art Gallery collection. FAMAG 2008.26.47

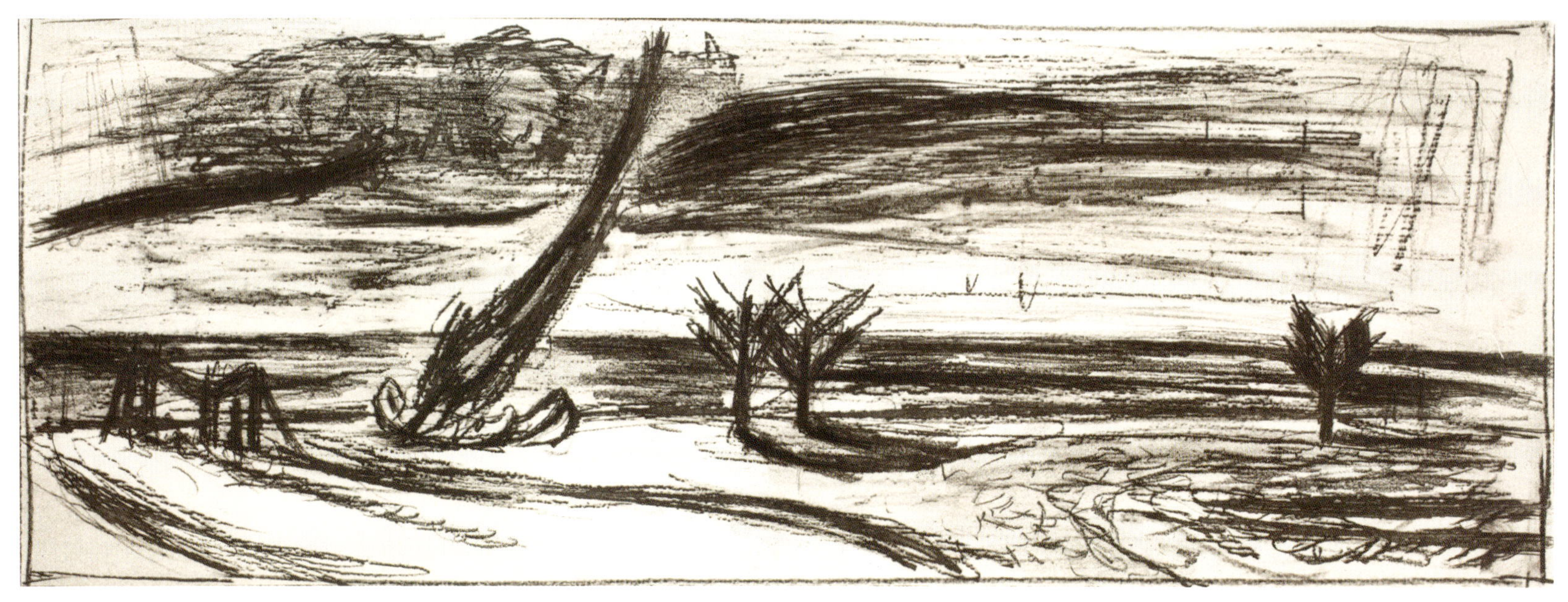

Andrzej Jackowski (born 1947): 'Dawn Ghosts', printer: Hugh Stoneman (1947–2005), publisher: Print Centre Publications, signed and dated 1988, etching (B.A.T.), 46.5 x 67cms. The Art Fund Hugh Stoneman Archive. Falmouth Art Gallery collection. FAMAG 2008.26.48

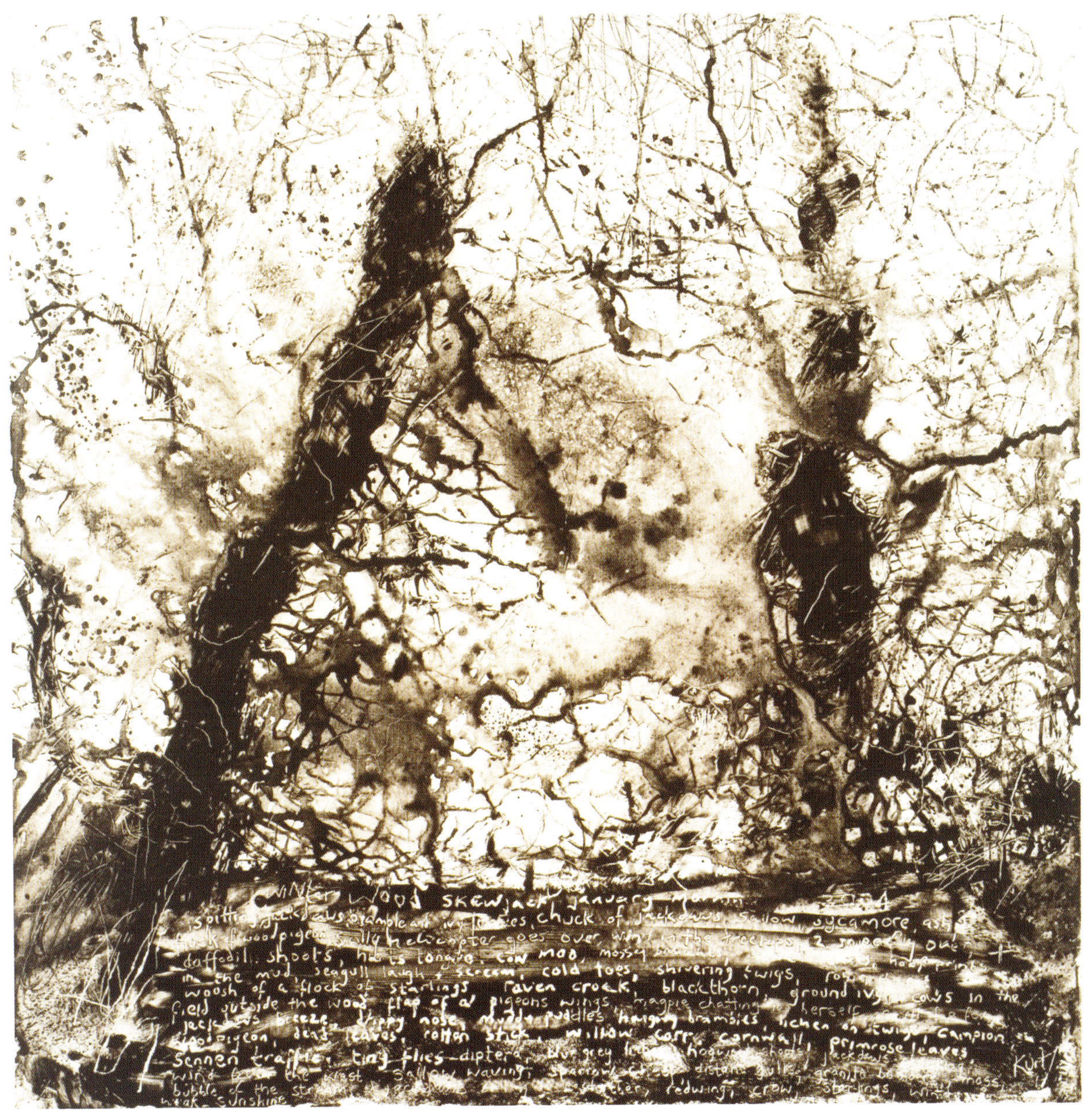

Kurt Jackson (b.1961): 'Winter wood (brown)', printer: Hugh Stoneman (1947–2005), publisher: The artist, signed and dated 2004, etching (B.A.T.), 70.5 x 70.5cms. The Art Fund Hugh Stoneman Archive. Falmouth Art Gallery collection. FAMAG 2008.26.49

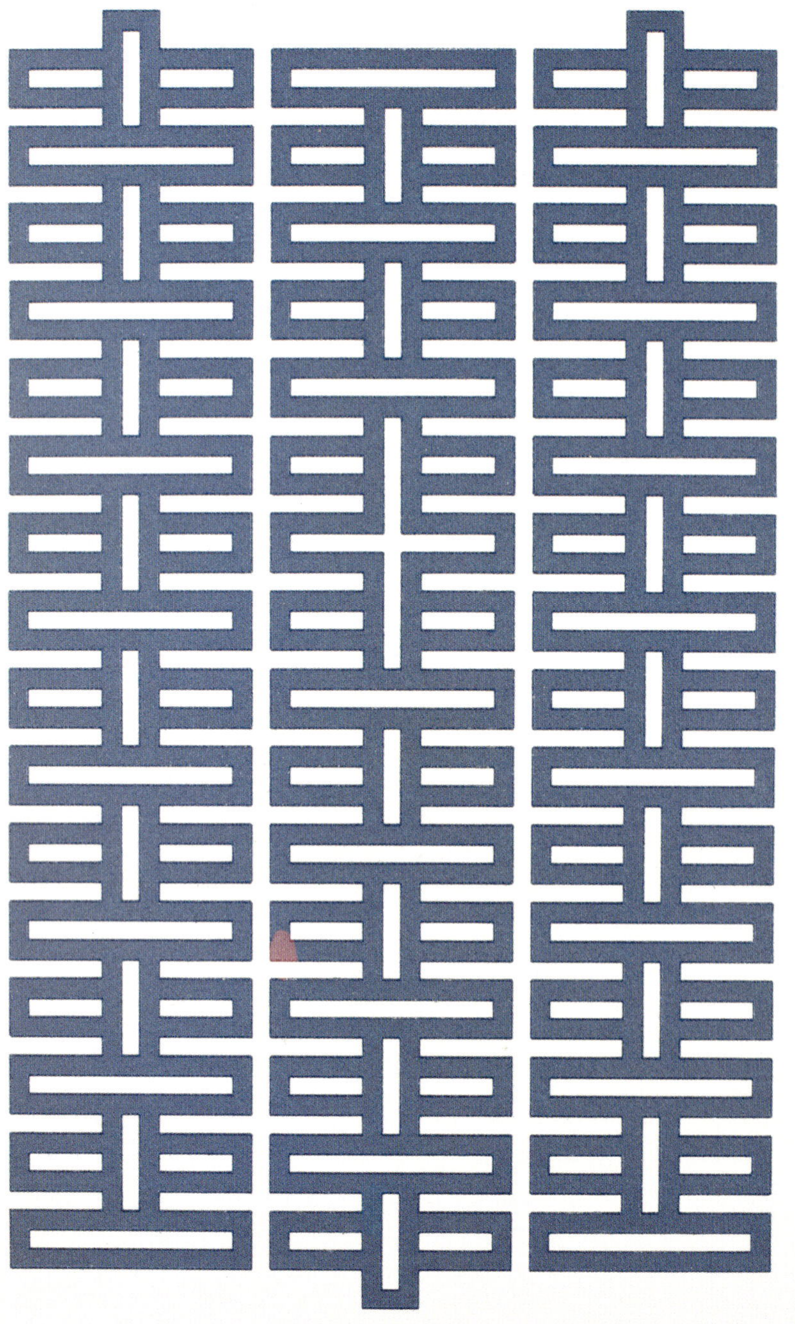

Tess Jaray (born 1937): 'The Serpent and the Cross' from the 'Wakefield' etchings, printer: Hugh Stoneman (1947–2005), signed and dated 1993, etching (number 14 of an edition of 20), 57 x 43cms. The Art Fund Hugh Stoneman Archive. Falmouth Art Gallery collection. FAMAG 2008.26.50

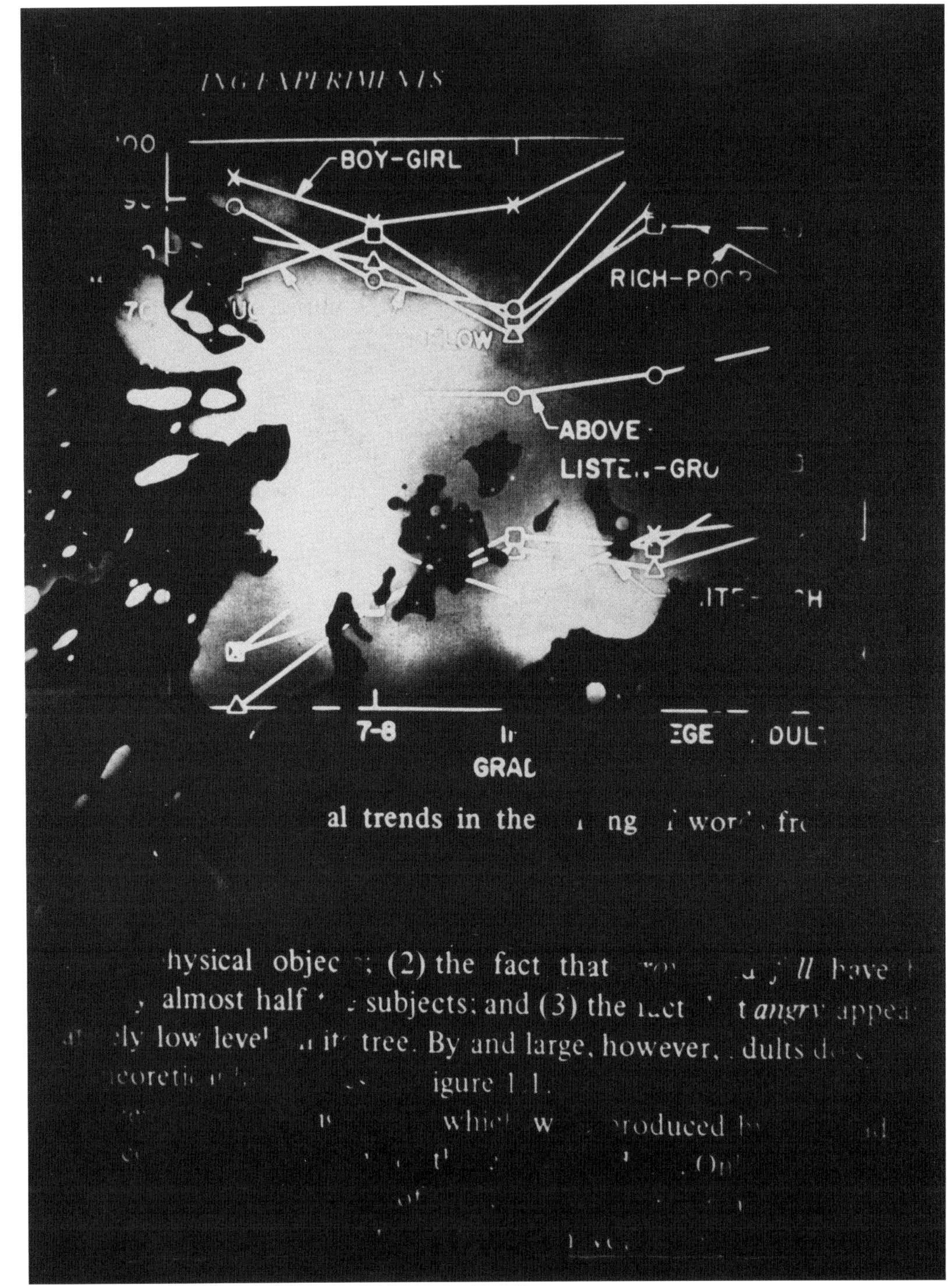

John Latham (1921–2006): From five photo etchings, 2004, printer: Hugh Stoneman (1947–2005), publisher: artHester, embossed with John Latham's studio stamp, etching, 97.5 x 76.5cms. The Art Fund Hugh Stoneman Archive. Falmouth Art Gallery collection. FAMAG 2008.26.51

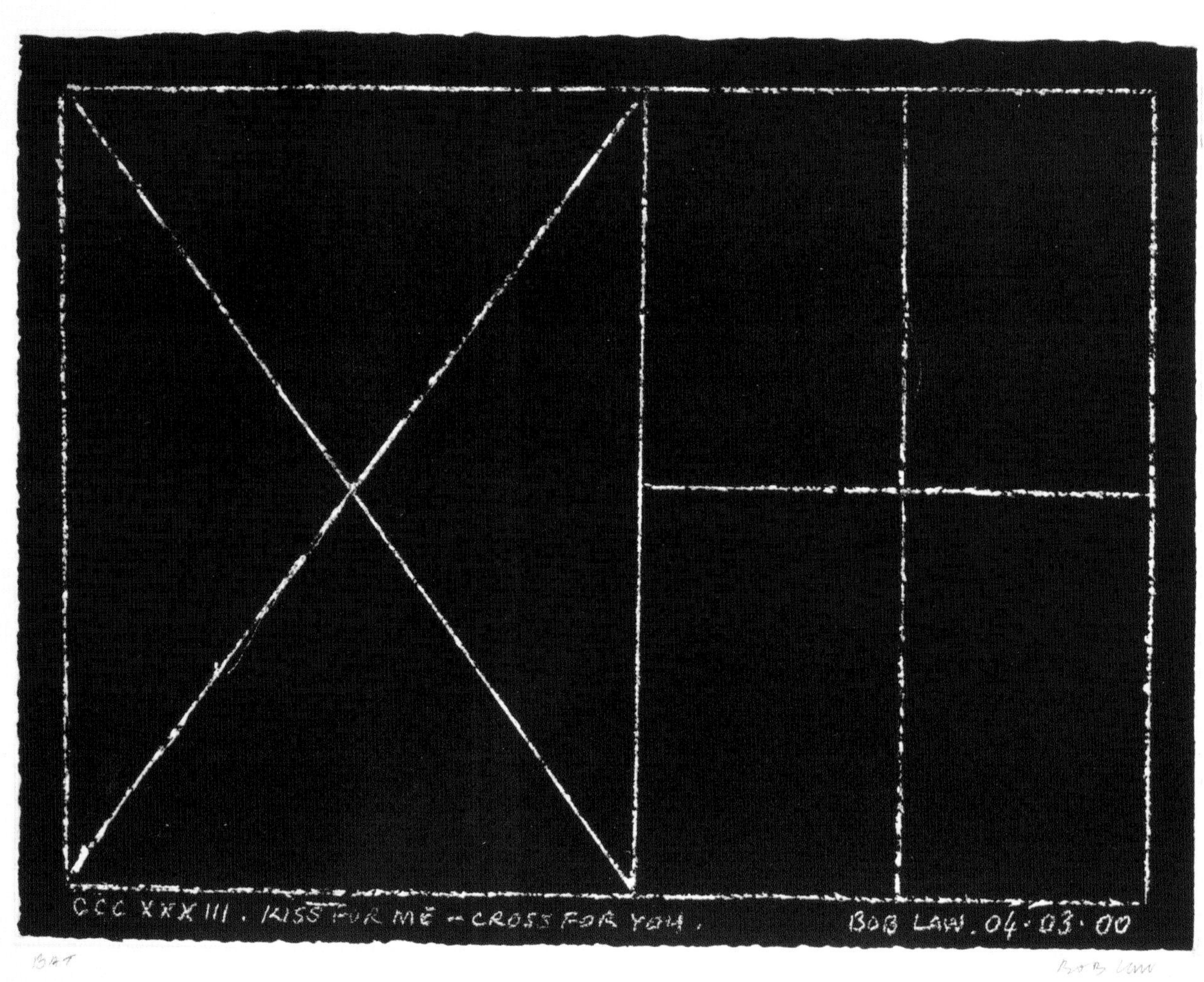

Bob Law (1934–2004): 'Kiss For Me – Cross For You', from the series 'Kisses and Crosses', printer: Hugh Stoneman (1947–2005), publisher: artHester, signed and dated 04.03. 2000, photogravure (B.A.T.), 47 x 54cms. The Art Fund Hugh Stoneman Archive. Falmouth Art Gallery collection. FAMAG 2008.26.52

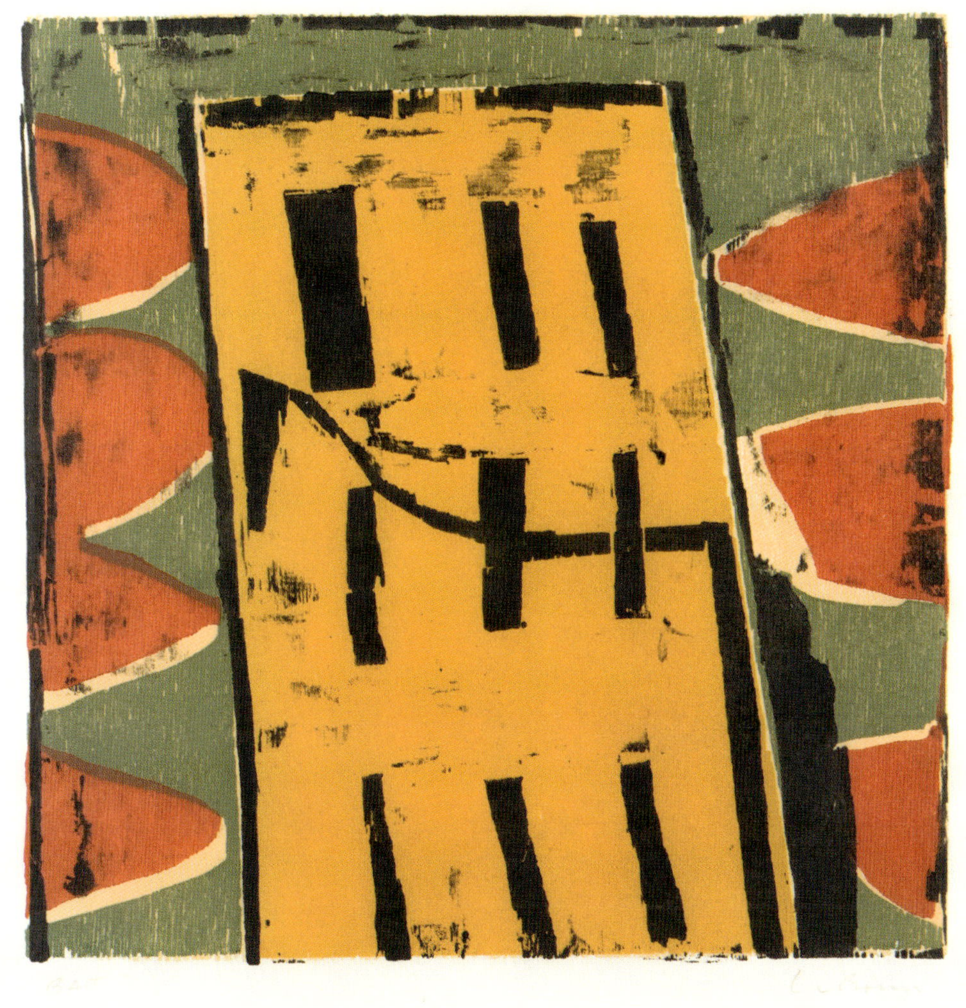

Christopher Le Brun RA (born 1951): 'Yellow Tower', 1998, printer: Hugh Stoneman (1947–2005), publisher: The Paragon Press and Marlborough Graphics, signed, woodcut (B.A.T.), 65 x 89cms. The Art Fund Hugh Stoneman Archive. Falmouth Art Gallery collection. FAMAG 2008.26.53

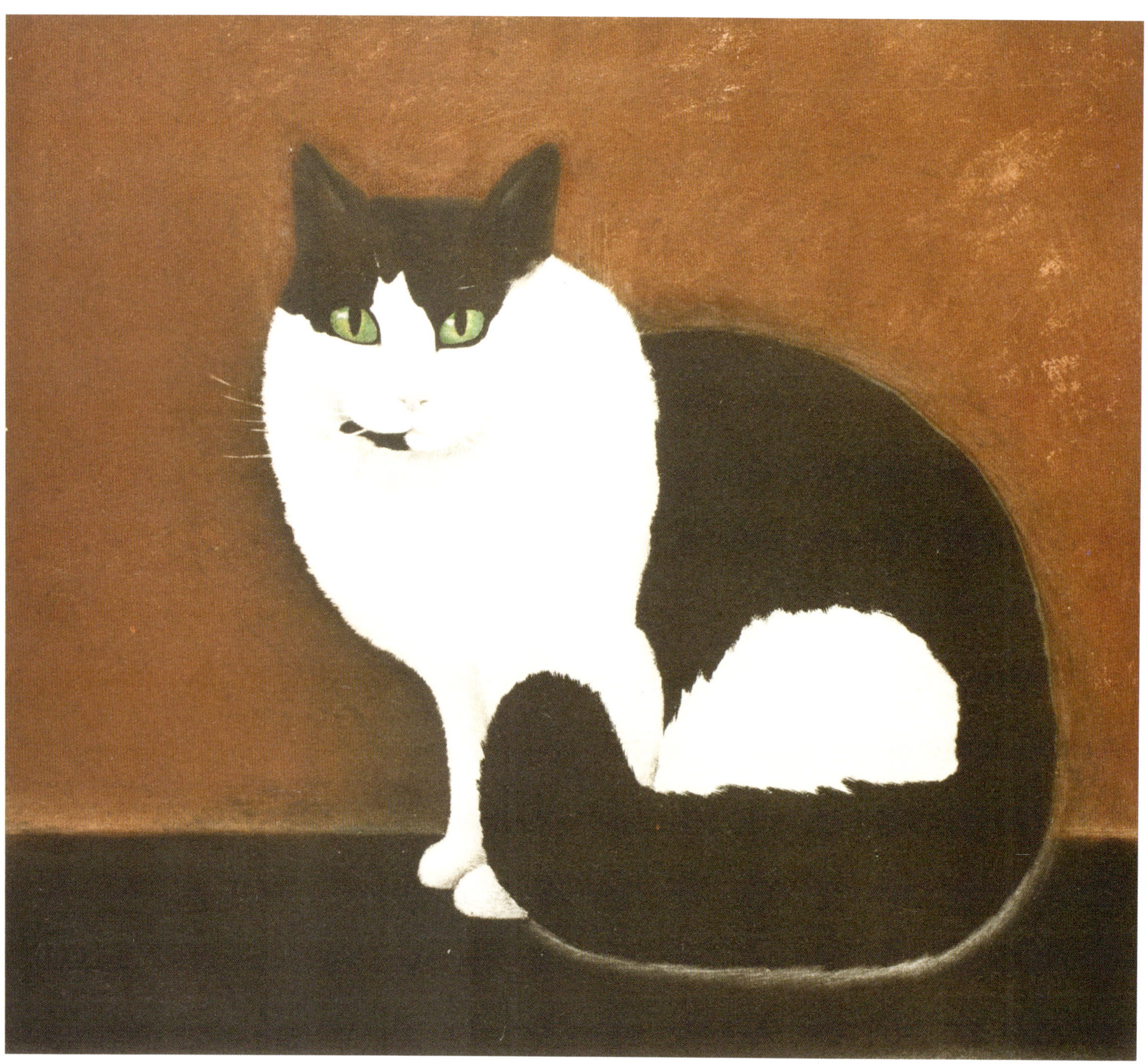

Martin Leman (born 1934): 'Panda', printer: Hugh Stoneman (1947–2005), signed and dated 1989, etching (B.A.T.), 38.5 x 44.7cms. The Art Fund Hugh Stoneman Archive. Falmouth Art Gallery collection. FAMAG 2008.26.54

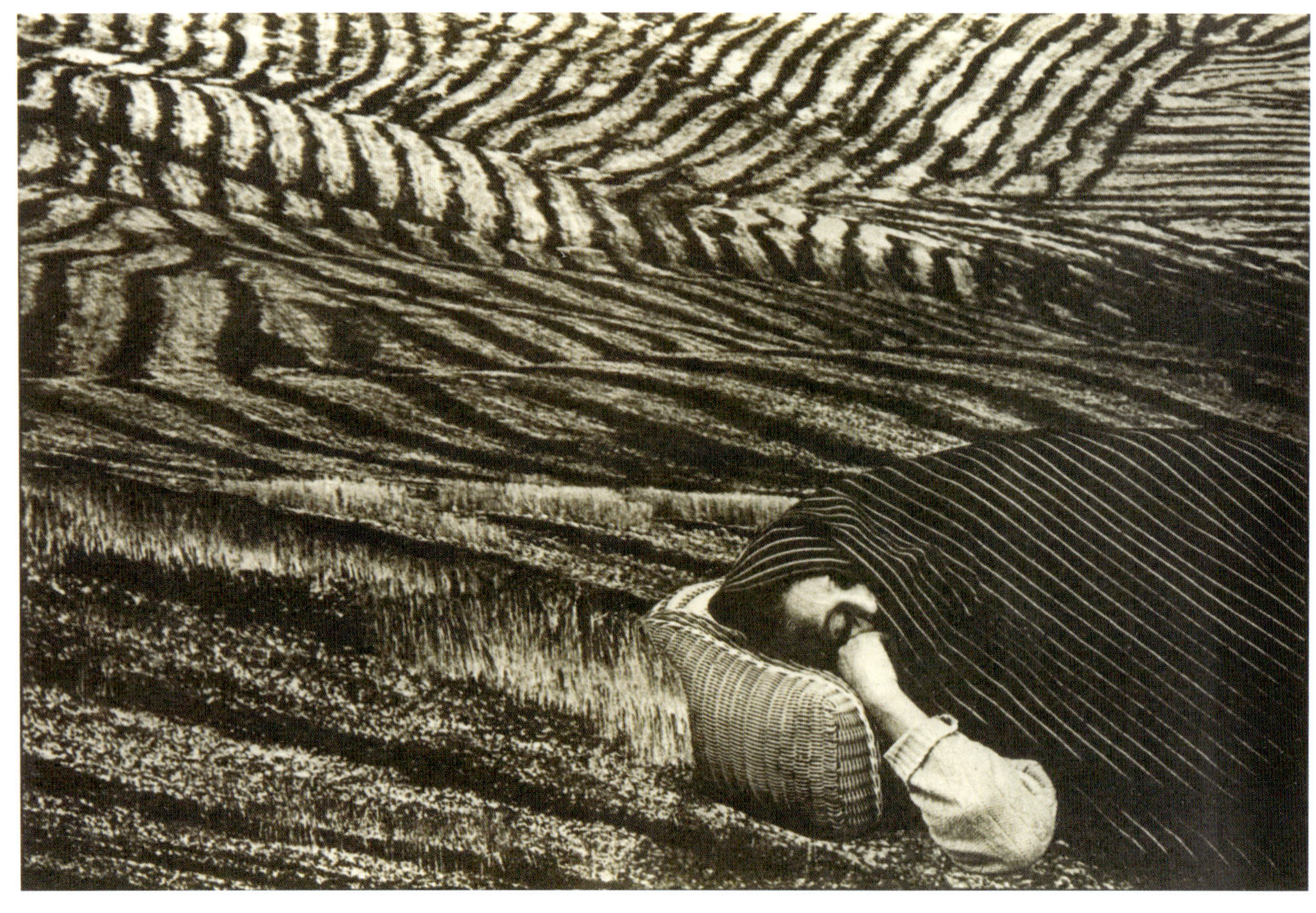

Mick Lindberg: No. 1 from the series 'Misplaced People', printer: Hugh Stoneman (1947–2005), photogravure, 18.5 x 13.5cms.
The Art Fund Hugh Stoneman Archive. Falmouth Art Gallery collection. FAMAG 2008.26.55

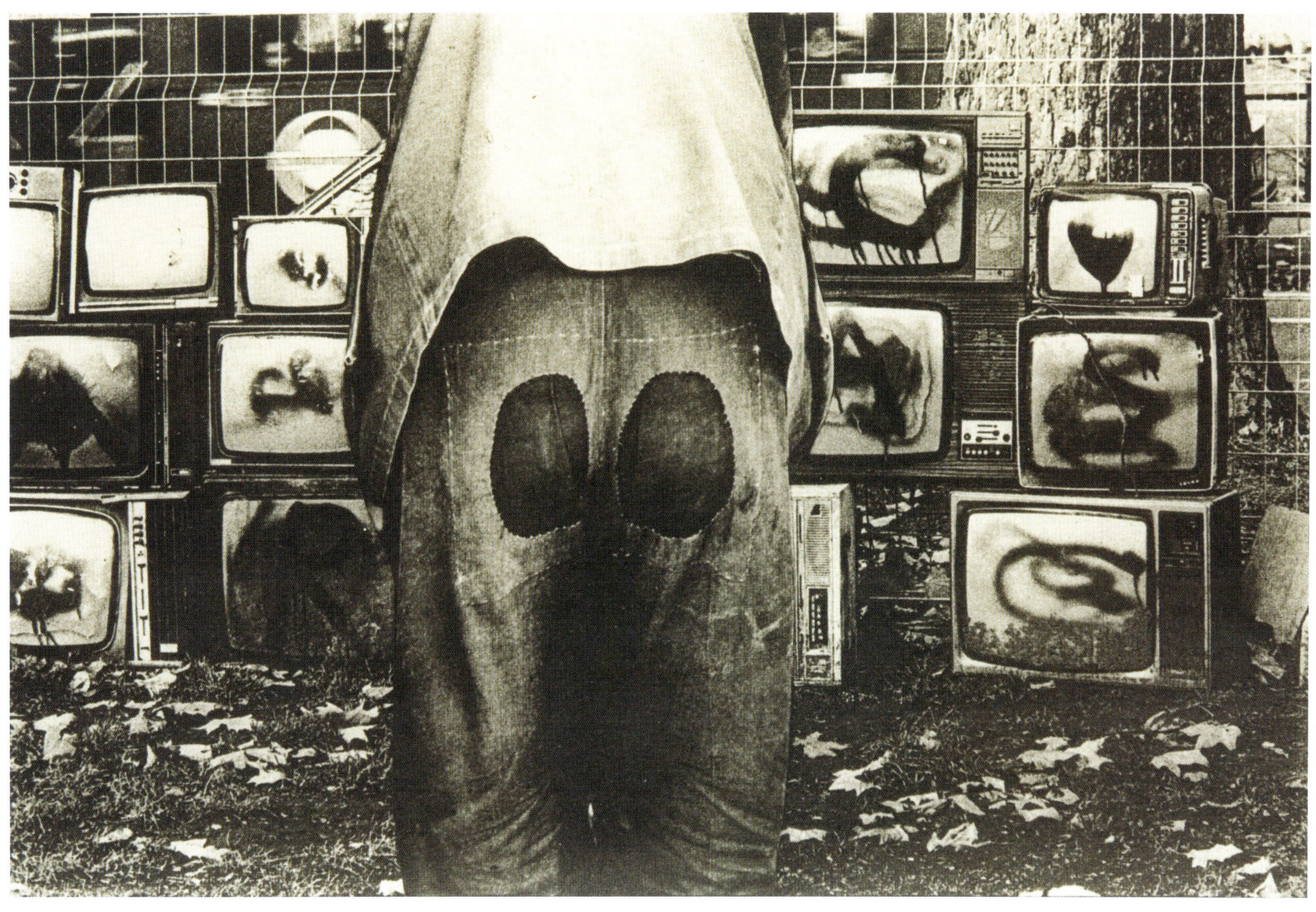

Mick Lindberg: No. 2 from the series 'Misplaced People', printer: Hugh Stoneman (1947–2005), photogravure, 18.5 x 13.5cms. The Art Fund Hugh Stoneman Archive. Falmouth Art Gallery collection. FAMAG 2008.26.56

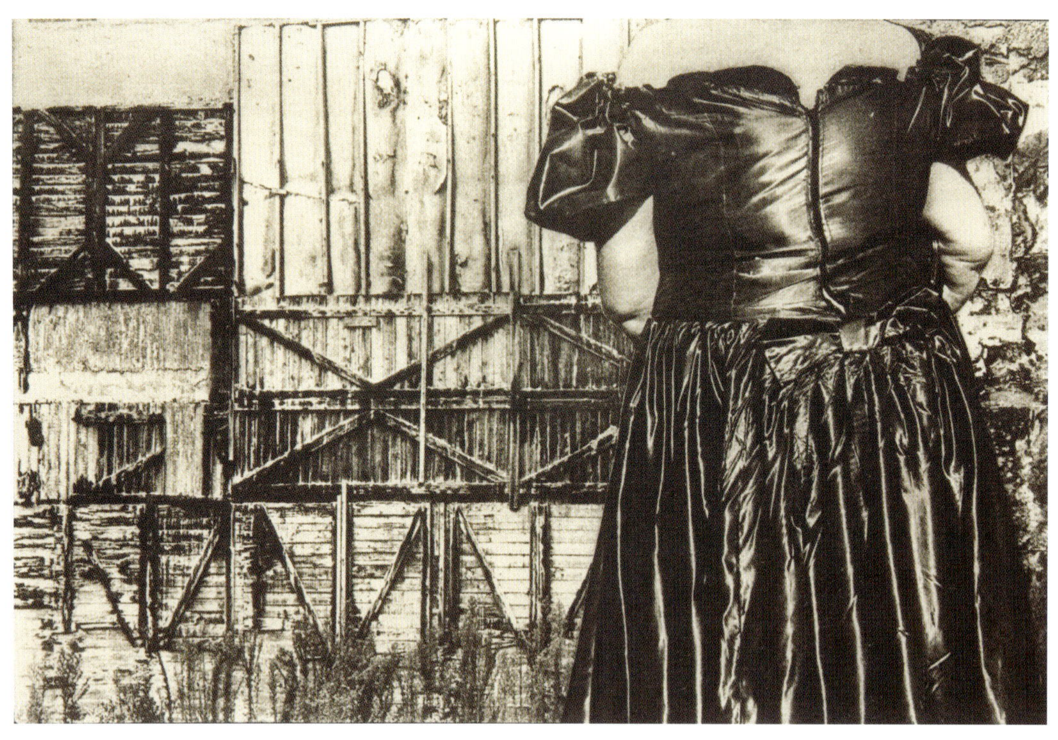

Mick Lindberg: No. 3 from the series 'Misplaced People', printer: Hugh Stoneman (1947–2005), photogravure, 18.5 x 13.5cms. Art Fund Hugh Stoneman Archive. Falmouth Art Gallery collection. FAMAG 2008.26.57

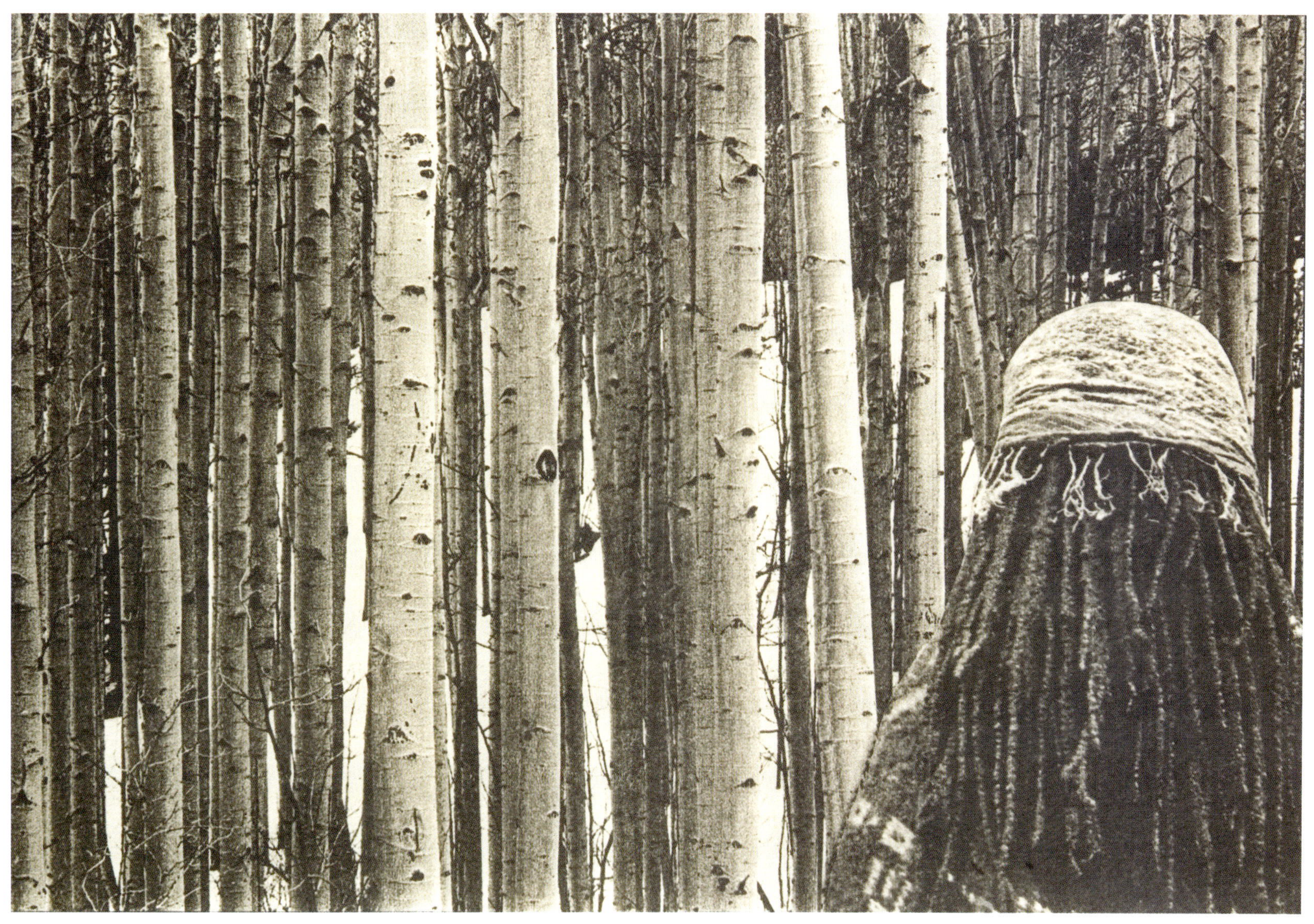

Mick Lindberg: No. 4 from the series 'Misplaced People', printer: Hugh Stoneman (1947–2005), photogravure, 18.5 x 13.5cms. The Art Fund Hugh Stoneman Archive. Falmouth Art Gallery collection. FAMAG 2008.26.58

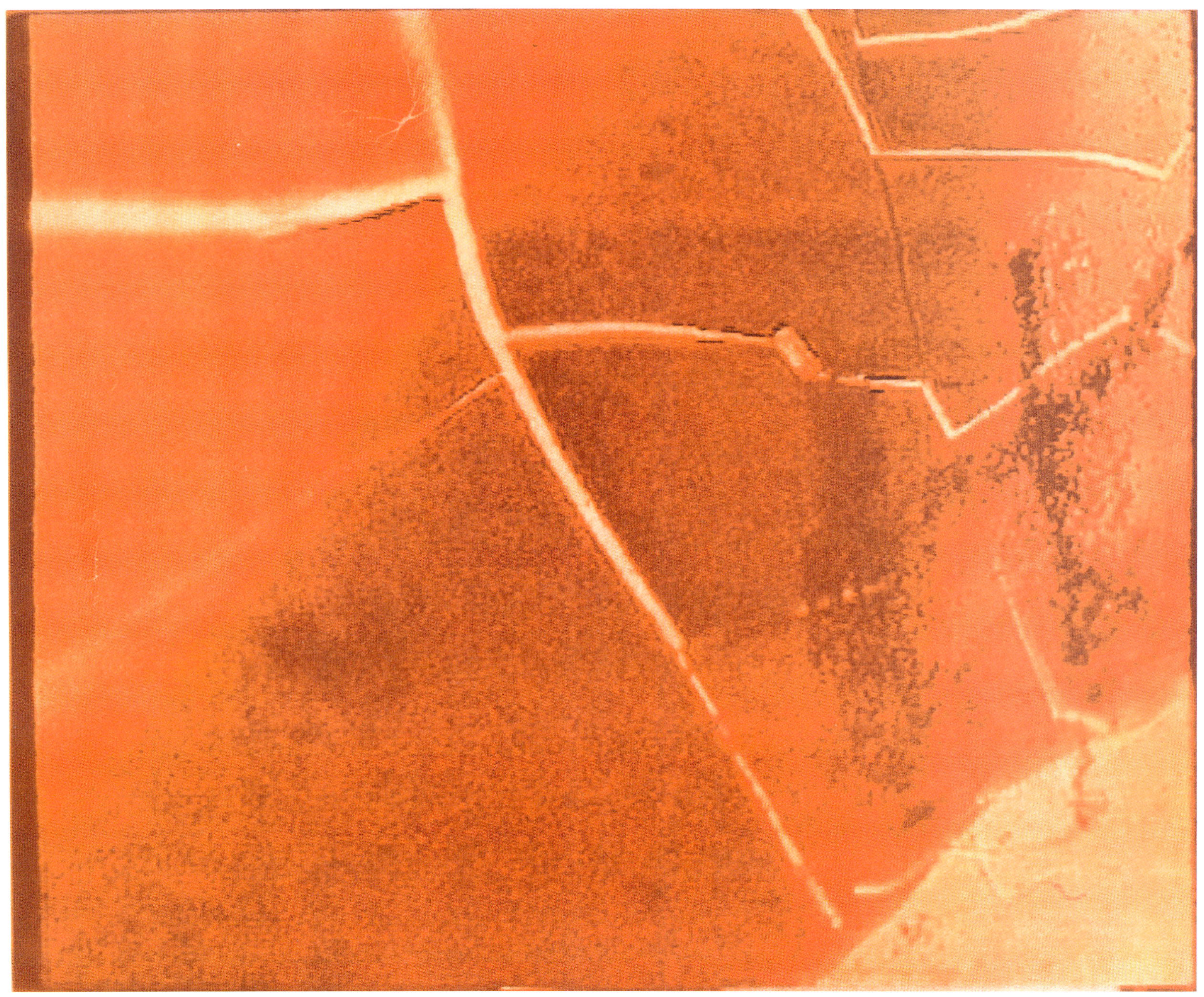

Adam Lowe (born 1959): 'Emulsion 3', printer: Hugh Stoneman (1947–2005), publisher: The Paragon Press, signed photogravure etching published 2000 (B.A.T.), 49.7 x 65cms. The Art Fund Hugh Stoneman Archive. Falmouth Art Gallery collection. FAMAG 2008.26.59

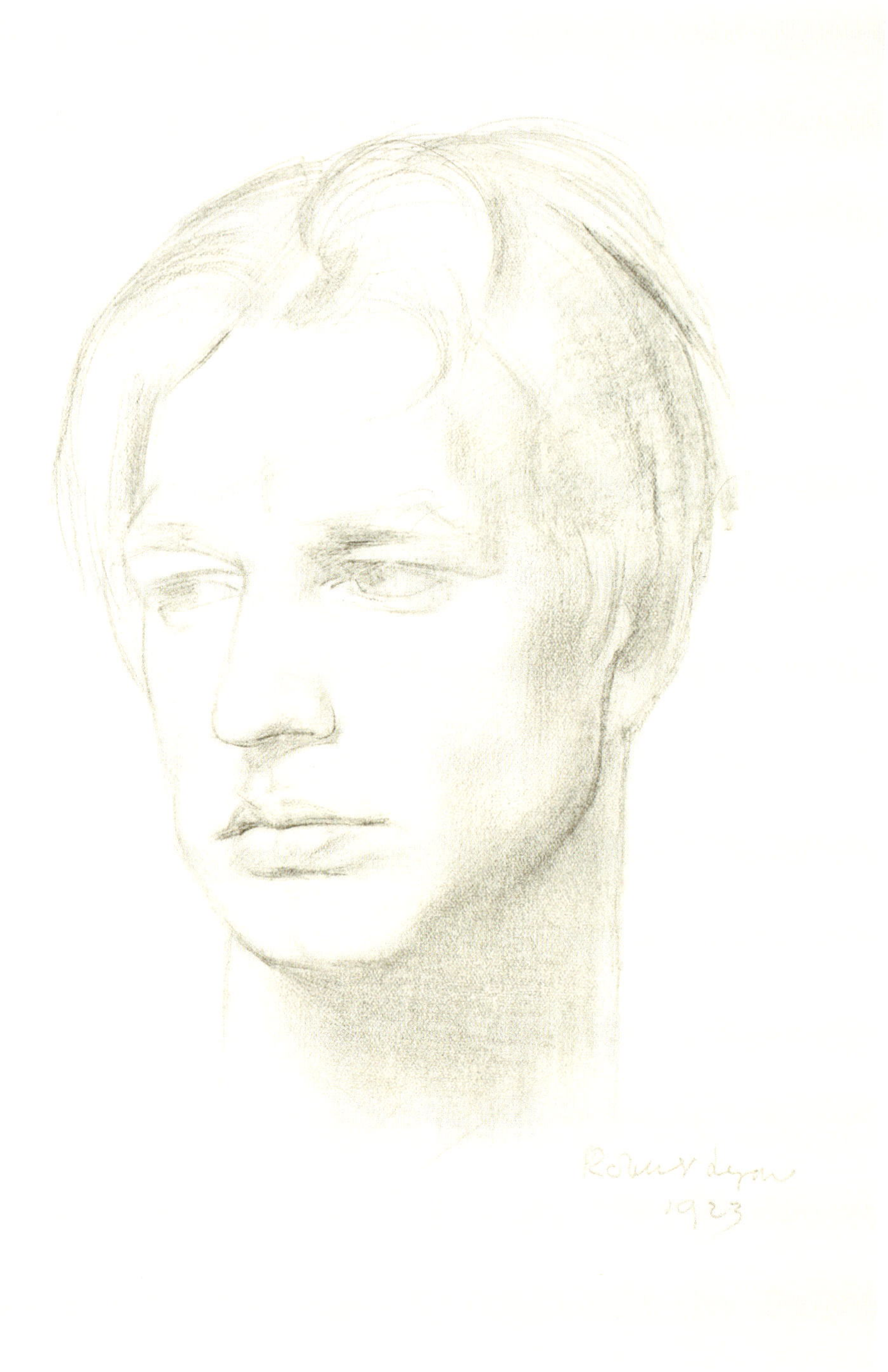

Robert Lyon (1894–1978): 'Head of Henry Moore', printer: Hugh Stoneman (1947–2005), photogravure, 34.8 x 25cms. The Art Fund Hugh Stoneman Archive. Falmouth Art Gallery collection. FAMAG 2008.26.60

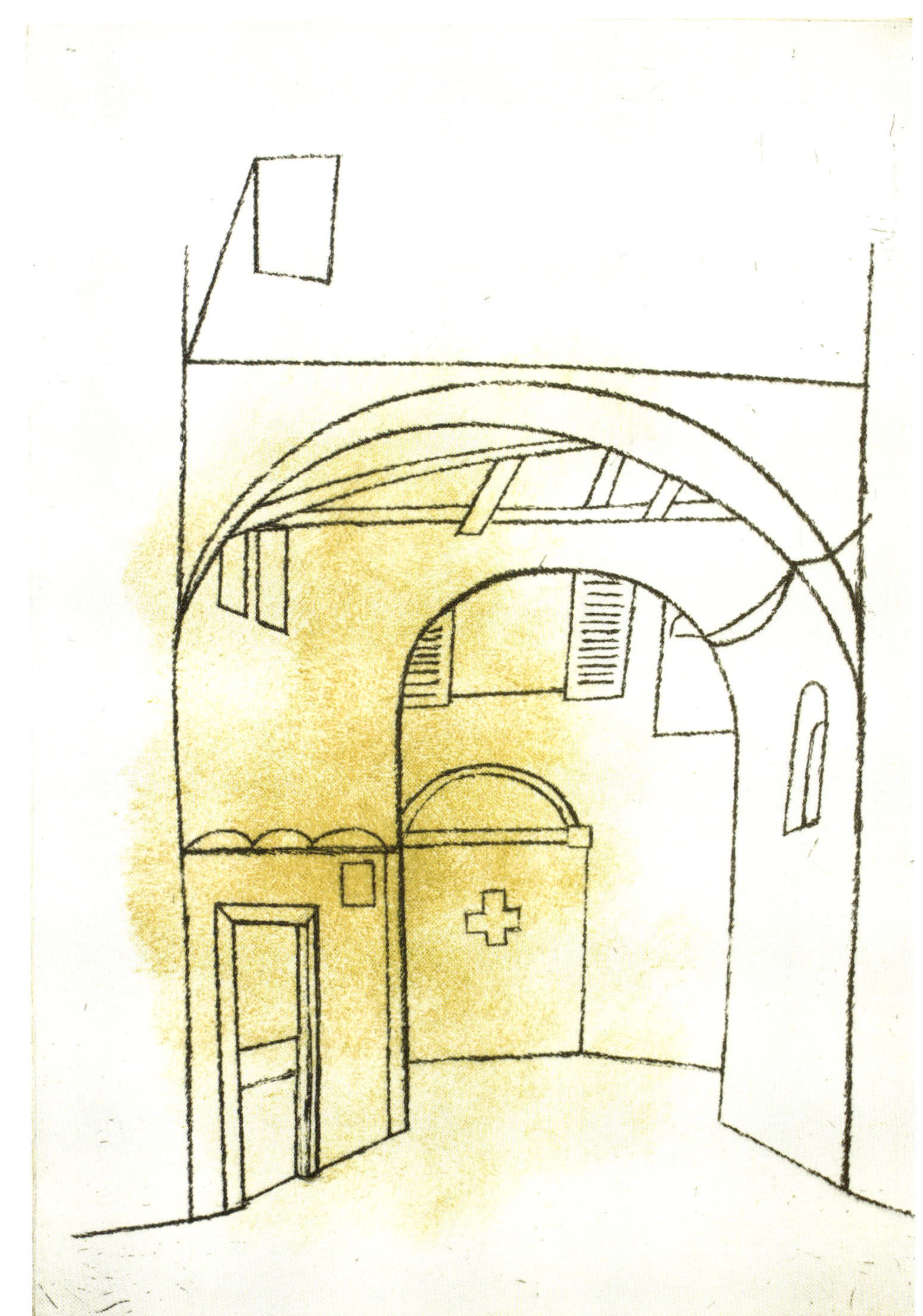

Alexander MacKenzie (1923–2002): 'Lucca', printer: Hugh Stoneman (1947–2005), publisher: Austin Desmond, signed and dated 2002, etching and aquatint (printer's proof 1), 41.3 x 38.4cms. The Art Fund Hugh Stoneman Archive. Falmouth Art Gallery collection. FAMAG 2008.26.61

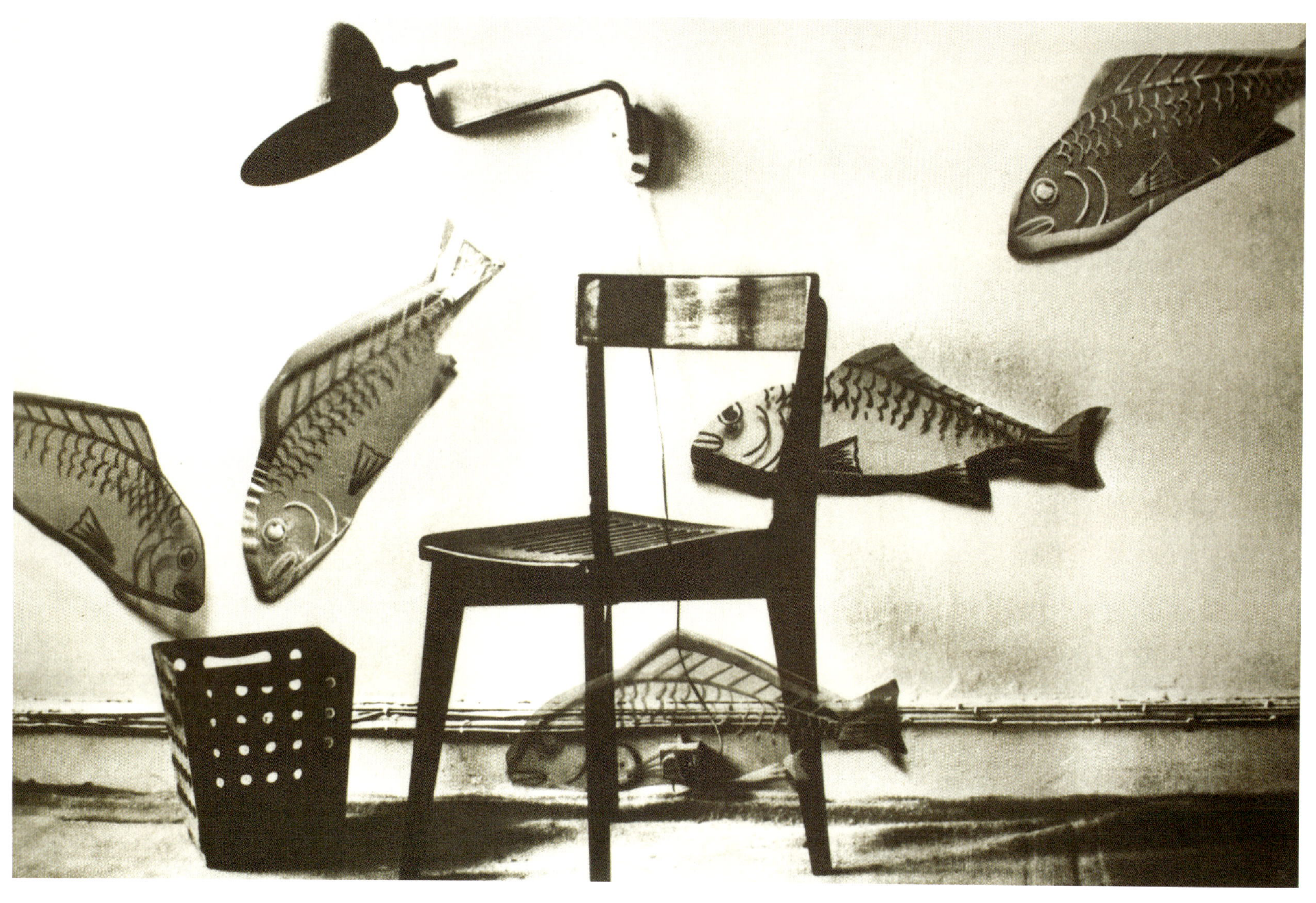

Mari Mahr (born 1941): 'Friday Alternative', printer: Hugh Stoneman (1947–2005), publisher: Print Centre Publications, signed and dated 1983, photogravure (number 16 of an edition of 50), 39 x 52cms. The Art Fund Hugh Stoneman Archive. Falmouth Art Gallery collection. FAMAG 2008.26.62

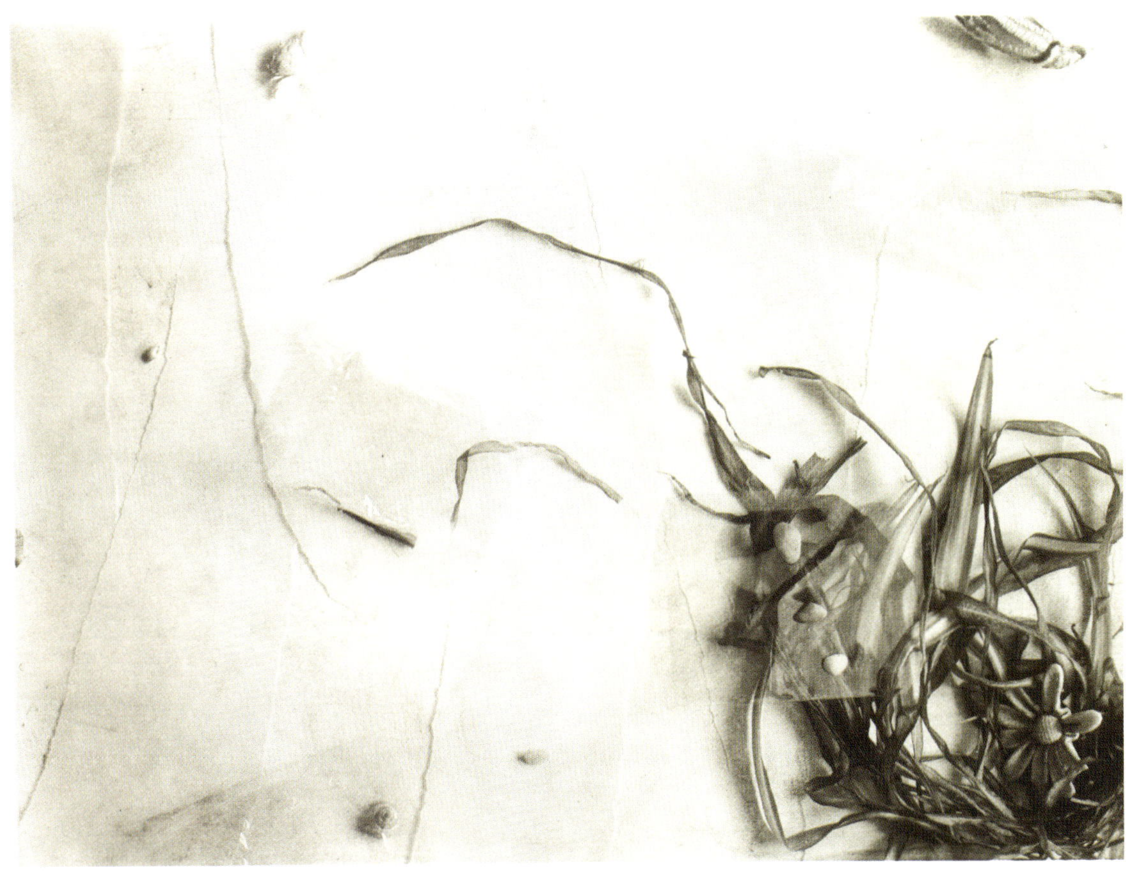

Pradip Malde (born 1957): 'Head of a Drowned Woman – After Shunei', printer: Hugh Stoneman (1947–2005), publisher: Print Centre Publications, signed and dated 1987, photogravure (number 23 of an edition of 50), 36.5 x 41cms. The Art Fund Hugh Stoneman Archive. Falmouth Art Gallery collection. FAMAG 2008.26.63

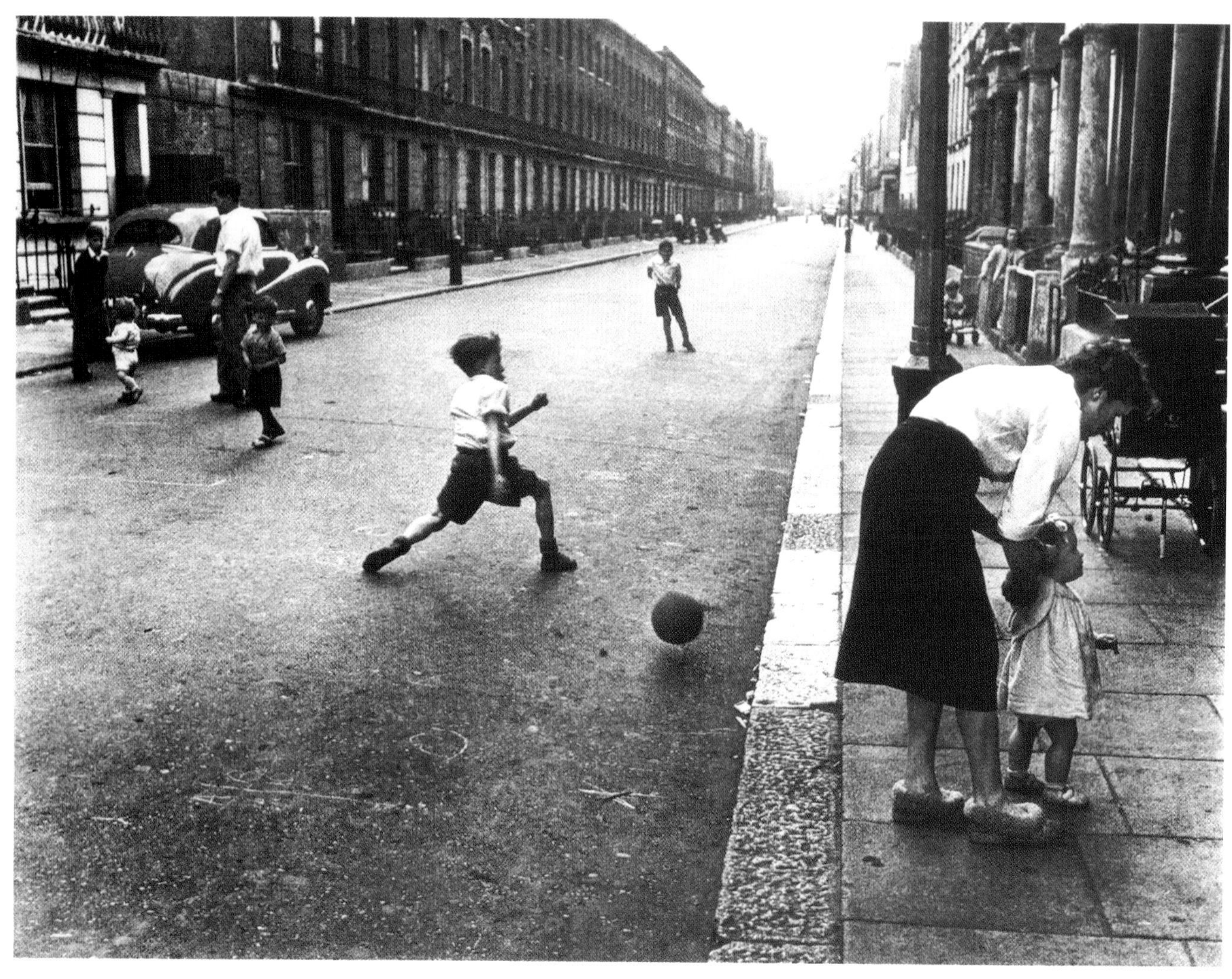

Roger Mayne (born 1929): 'Footballers, Southam Street', 1956, printer: Hugh Stoneman (1947–2005), publisher: The Notting Hill Improvements Group, signed 2004, photogravure (printer's proof 1) published 2005, 57 x 70.5cms. The Art Fund Hugh Stoneman Archive. Falmouth Art Gallery collection. FAMAG 2008.26.64

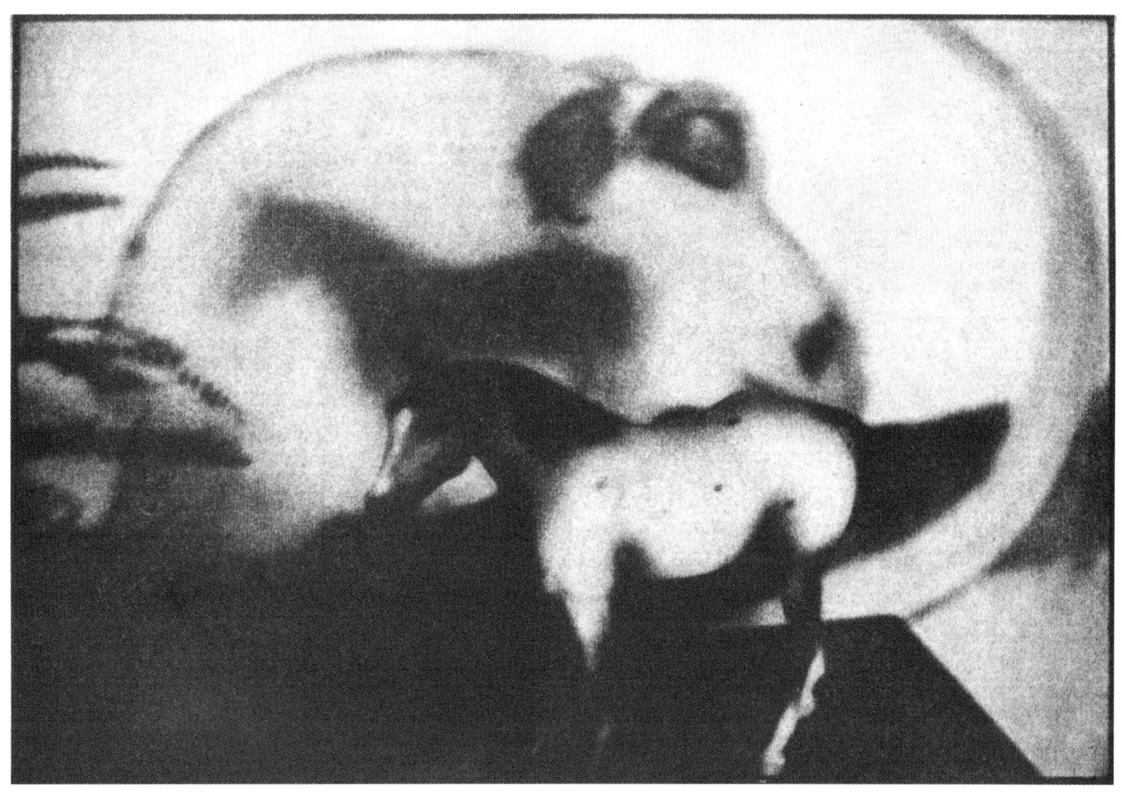

Linda McCartney (1941–1998): 'Horse', printer: Hugh Stoneman (1947–2005), photogravure, 48 x 60.5cms. © 1996 Paul McCartney. Photographer: Linda McCartney. The Art Fund Hugh Stoneman Archive. Falmouth Art Gallery collection. FAMAG 2008.26.65

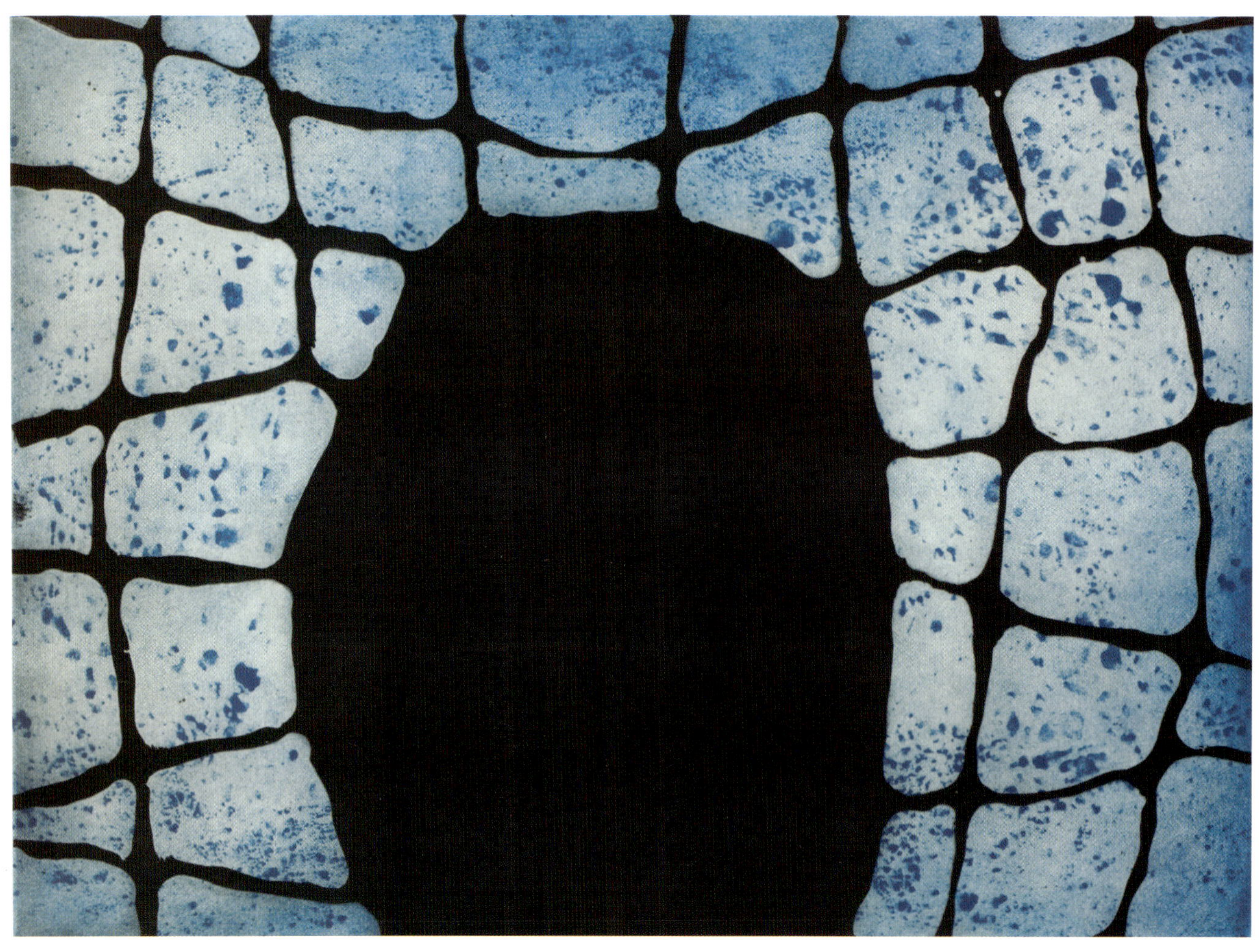

Ian McKeever RA (born 1946): 'Between Space and Time No. 4', printer: Hugh Stoneman (1947–2005), publisher: Paragon Press, signed and dated 1996, aquatint etching (printer's proof 1), 50 x 66cms. The Art Fund Hugh Stoneman Archive. Falmouth Art Gallery collection. FAMAG 2008.26.66

Ian McKeever RA (born 1946): 'Coloured Etching 5', printer: Hugh Stoneman (1947–2005), signed and dated 1996, etching (printer's proof), 69 x 52.7cms. The Art Fund Hugh Stoneman Archive. Falmouth Art Gallery collection. FAMAG 2008.26.67

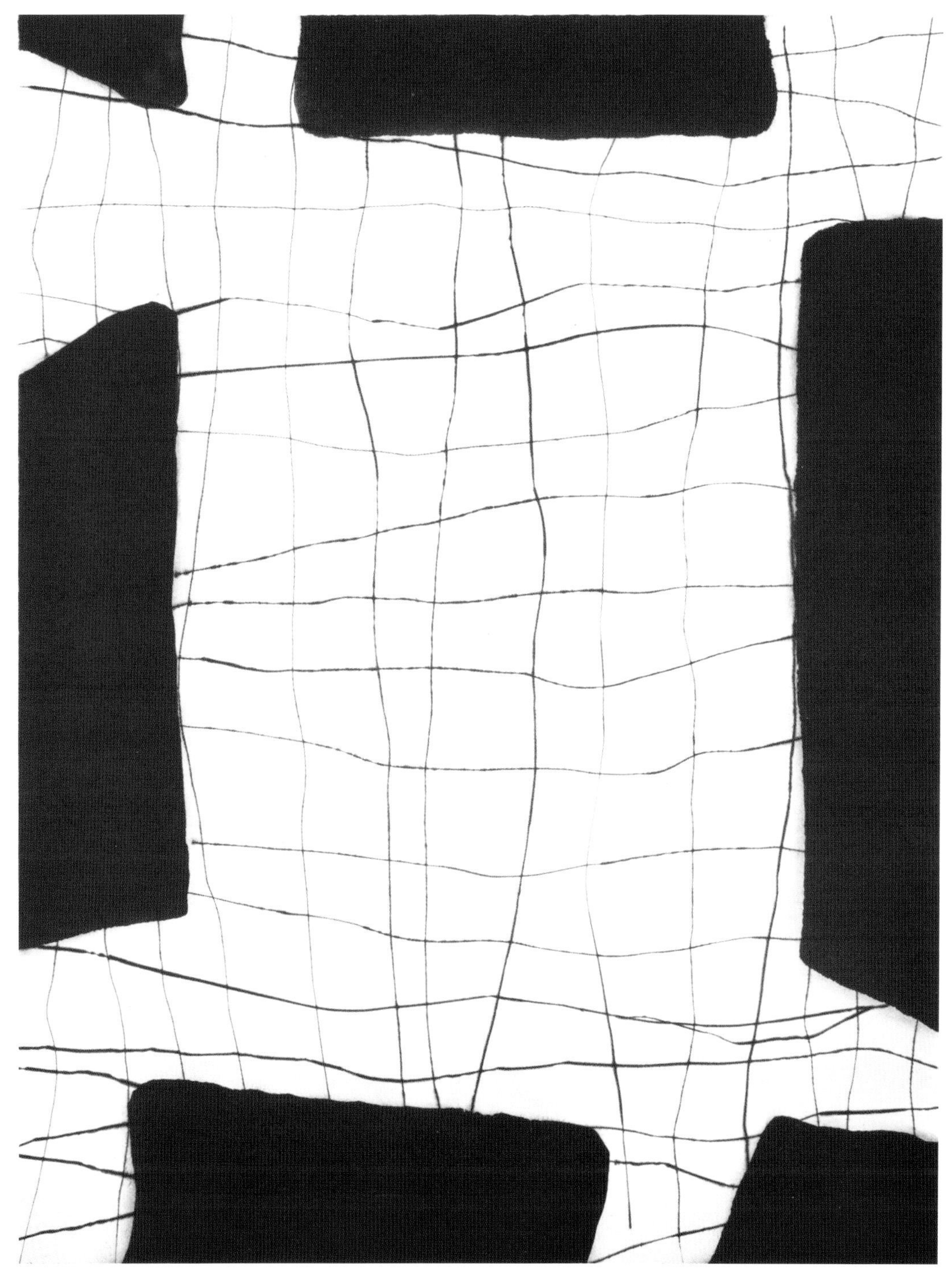

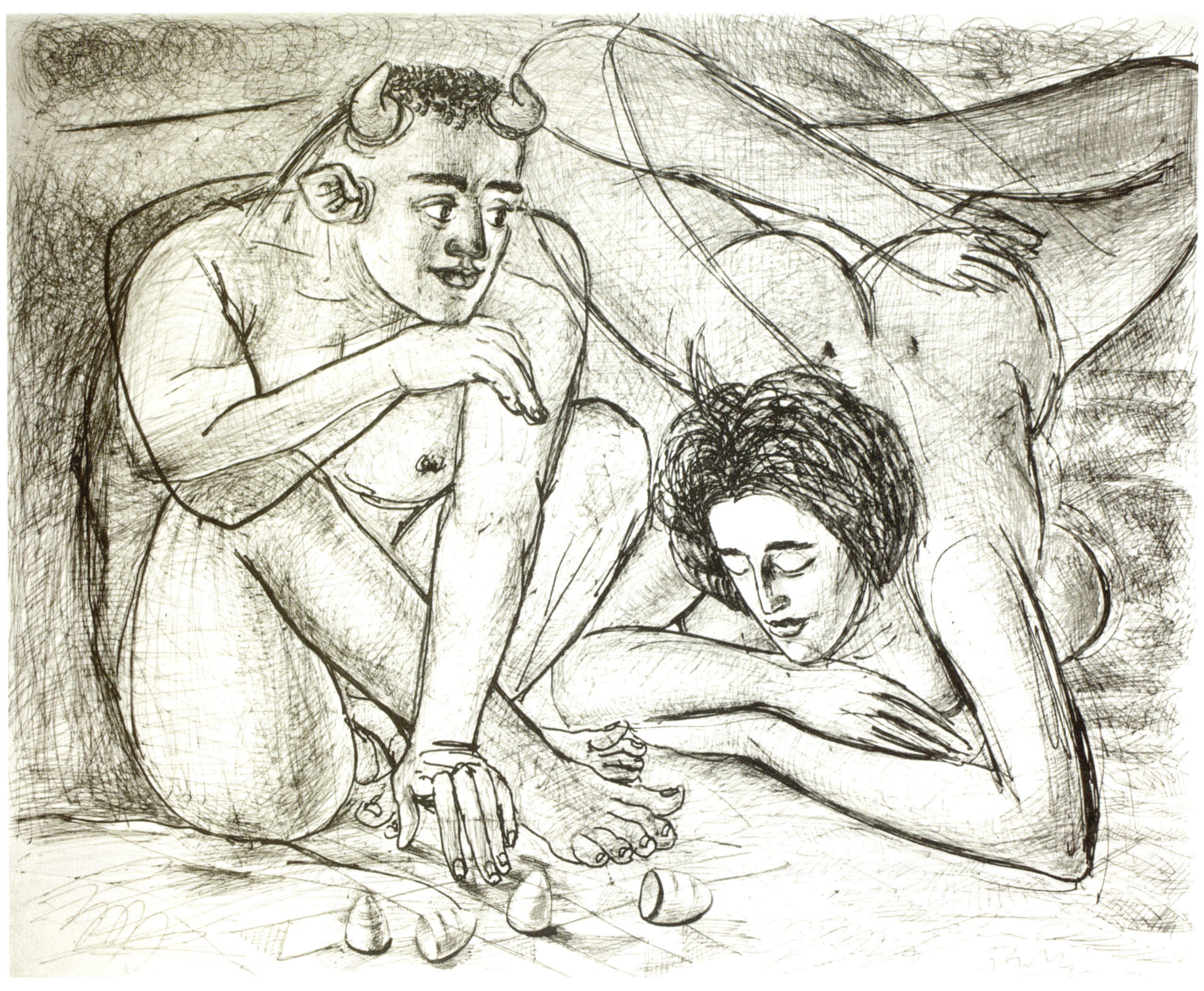

Dhruva Mistry RA (born 1957): 'The Couple', printer: Hugh Stoneman (1947–2005), publisher: Print Centre Publications, signed, etching (number 19 of an edition of 50), 49 x 58.5cms. The Art Fund Hugh Stoneman Archive. Falmouth Art Gallery collection. FAMAG 2008.26.68

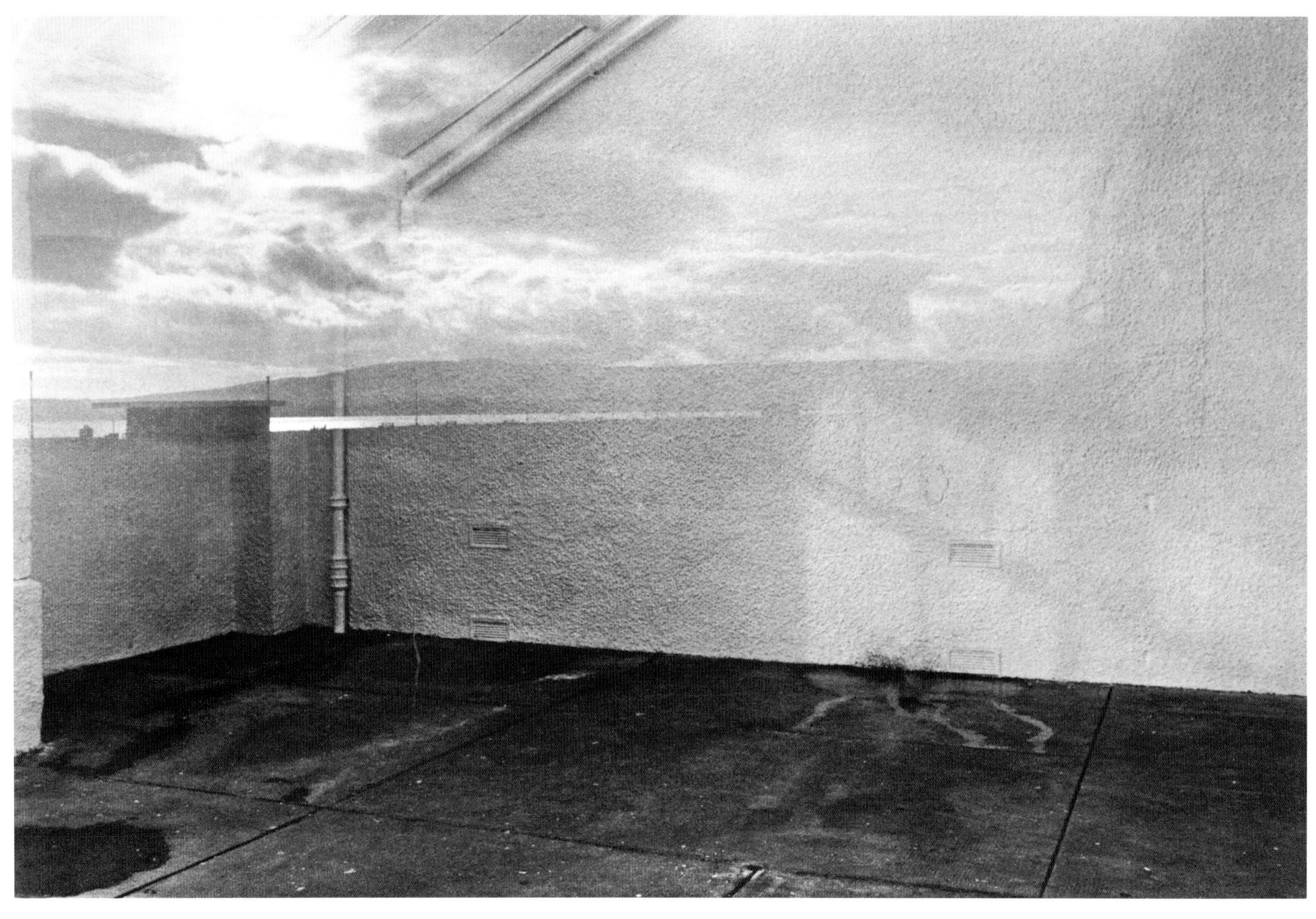

Raymond Moore (1920–1987): 'Ayr', 1979, printer: Hugh Stoneman (1947–2005), photogravure, 45.7 x 51.5cms. The Art Fund Hugh Stoneman Archive. Falmouth Art Gallery collection. FAMAG 2008.26.69

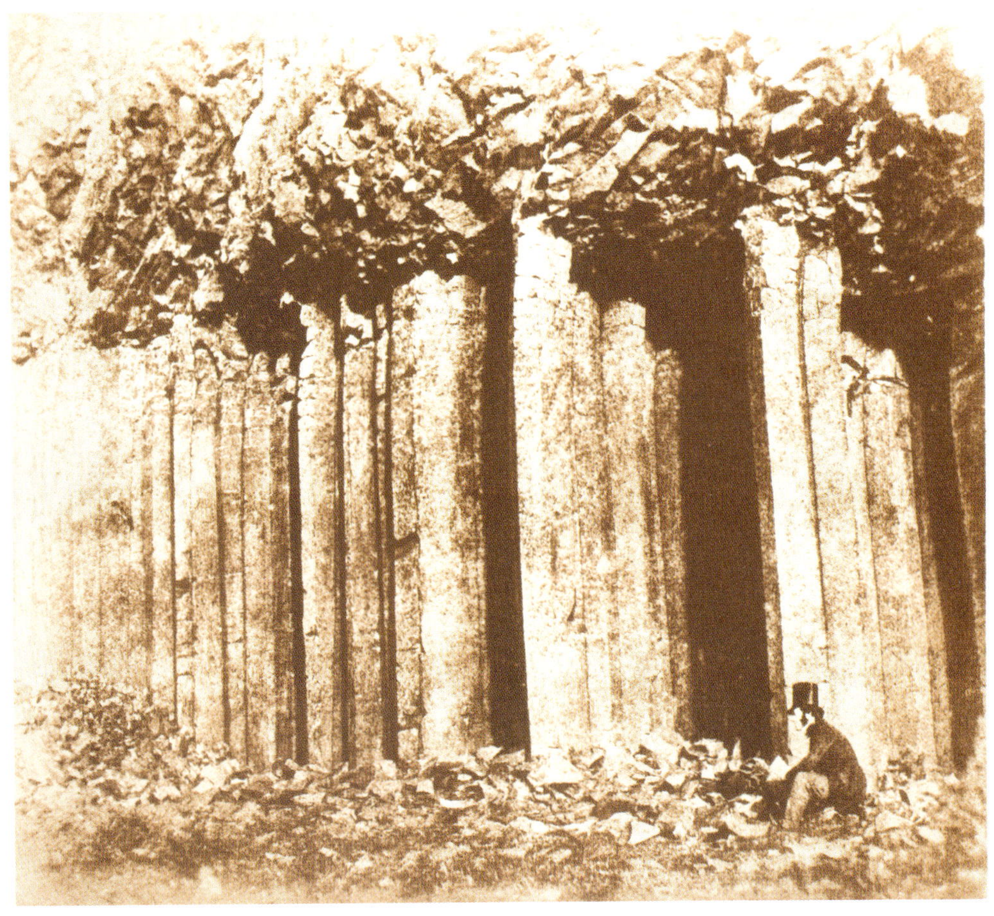

John Muir Wood (1805–1892): 'Recollections, Self Portrait at Staffa', printer: Hugh Stoneman (1947–2005), photogravure, 40 x 46.5cms. The Art Fund Hugh Stoneman Archive. Falmouth Art Gallery collection. FAMAG 2008.26.70

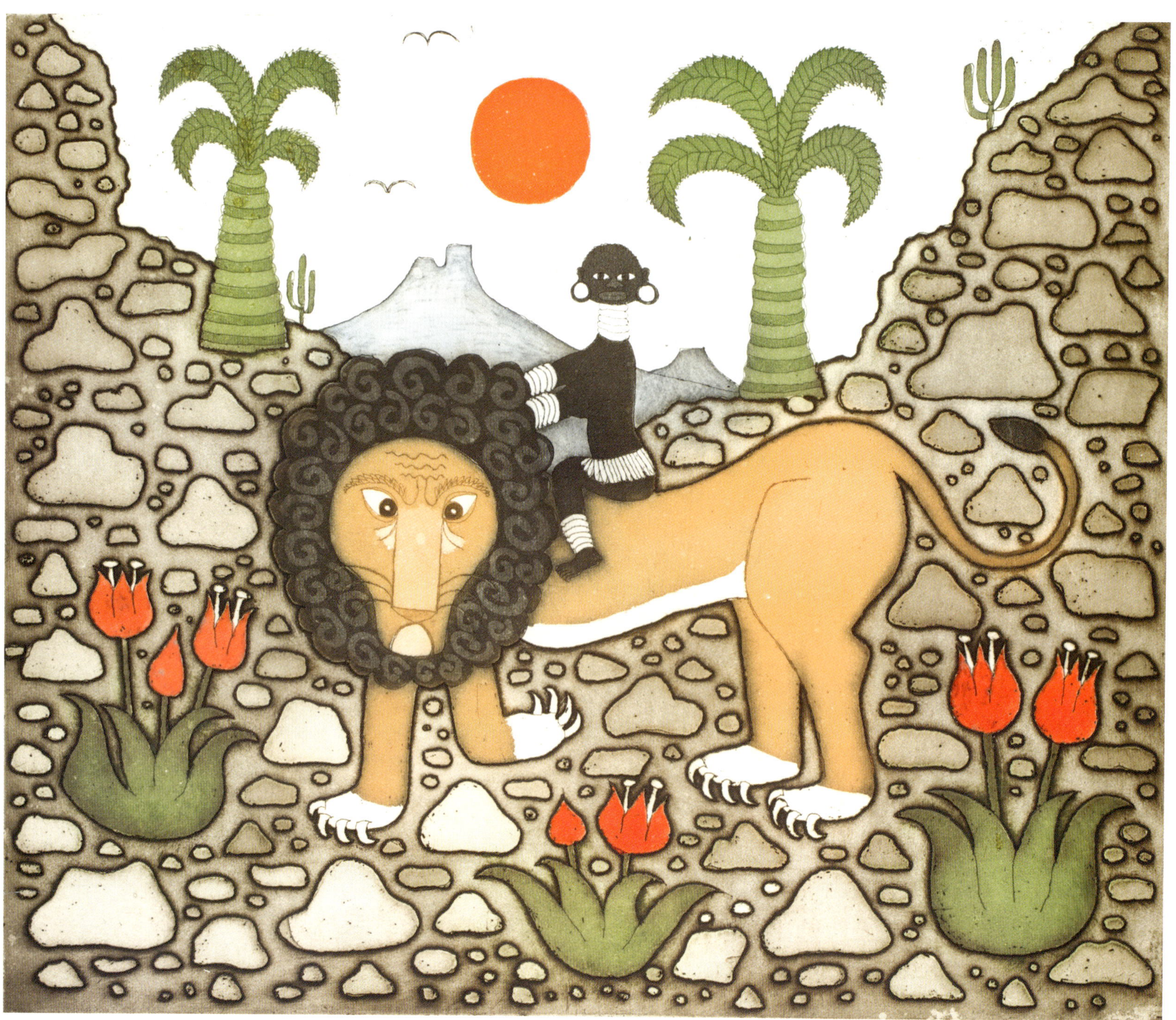

Andrew Murray (1917–1998): 'Little Girl on a Lion', printer: Hugh Stoneman (1947–2005), signed, aquatint, 49.8 x 55cms. The Art Fund Hugh Stoneman Archive. Falmouth Art Gallery collection. FAMAG 2008.26.71

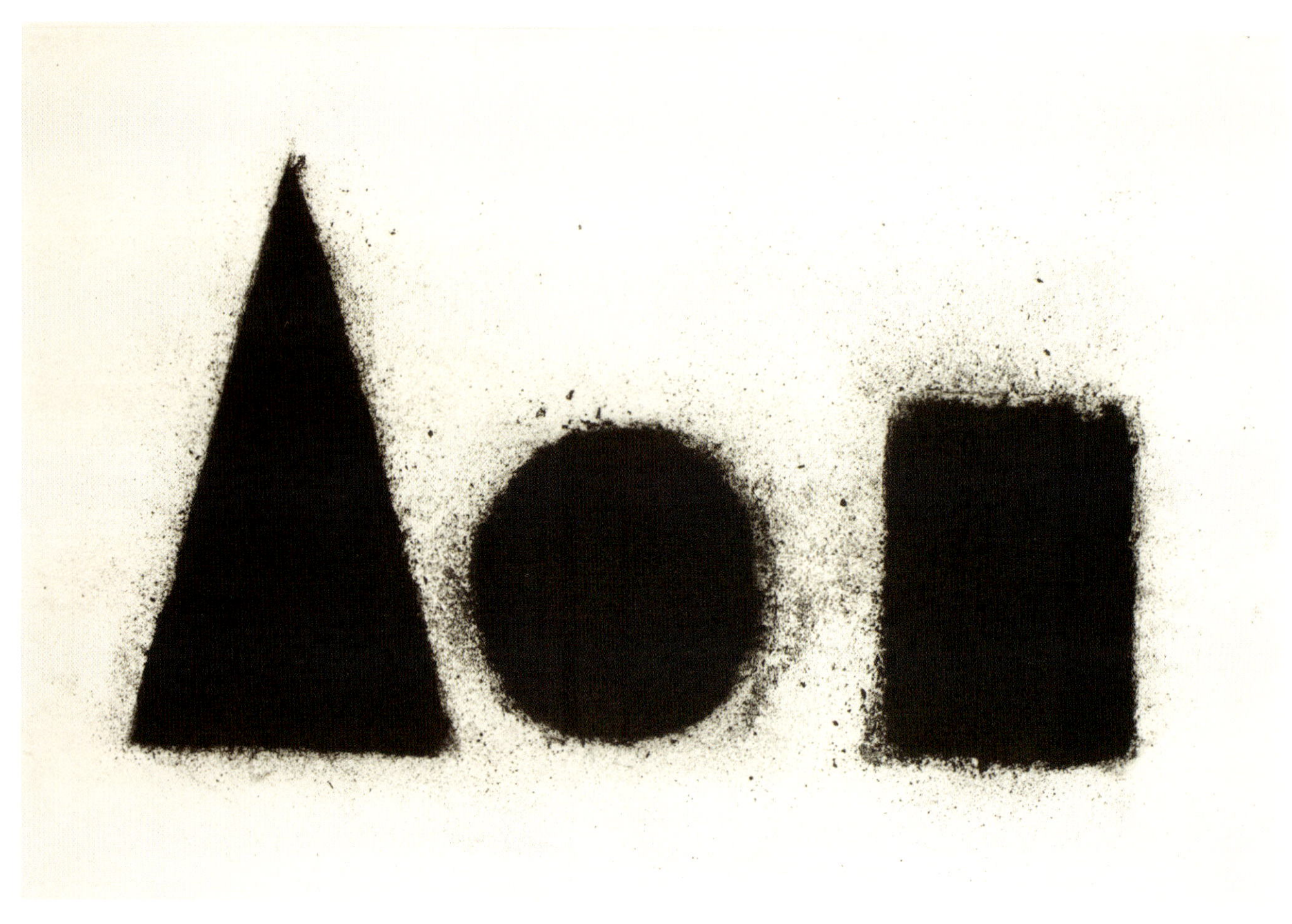

David Nash RA (born 1945): 'Pyramid, Sphere, Cube', 2004, printer: Hugh Stoneman (1947–2005), publisher: Tate St Ives, signed and dated 2004, aquatint etching (B.A.T.), 44.5 x 58.7cms. The Art Fund Hugh Stoneman Archive. Falmouth Art Gallery collection. FAMAG 2008.26.72

Paul Neagu (1938–2004): 'Untitled,' printer: Hugh Stoneman (1947–2005), signed and dated 1972, etching (number 13 of an edition of 30), 65.7 x 40.5cms. The Art Fund Hugh Stoneman Archive. Falmouth Art Gallery collection. FAMAG 2008.26.73

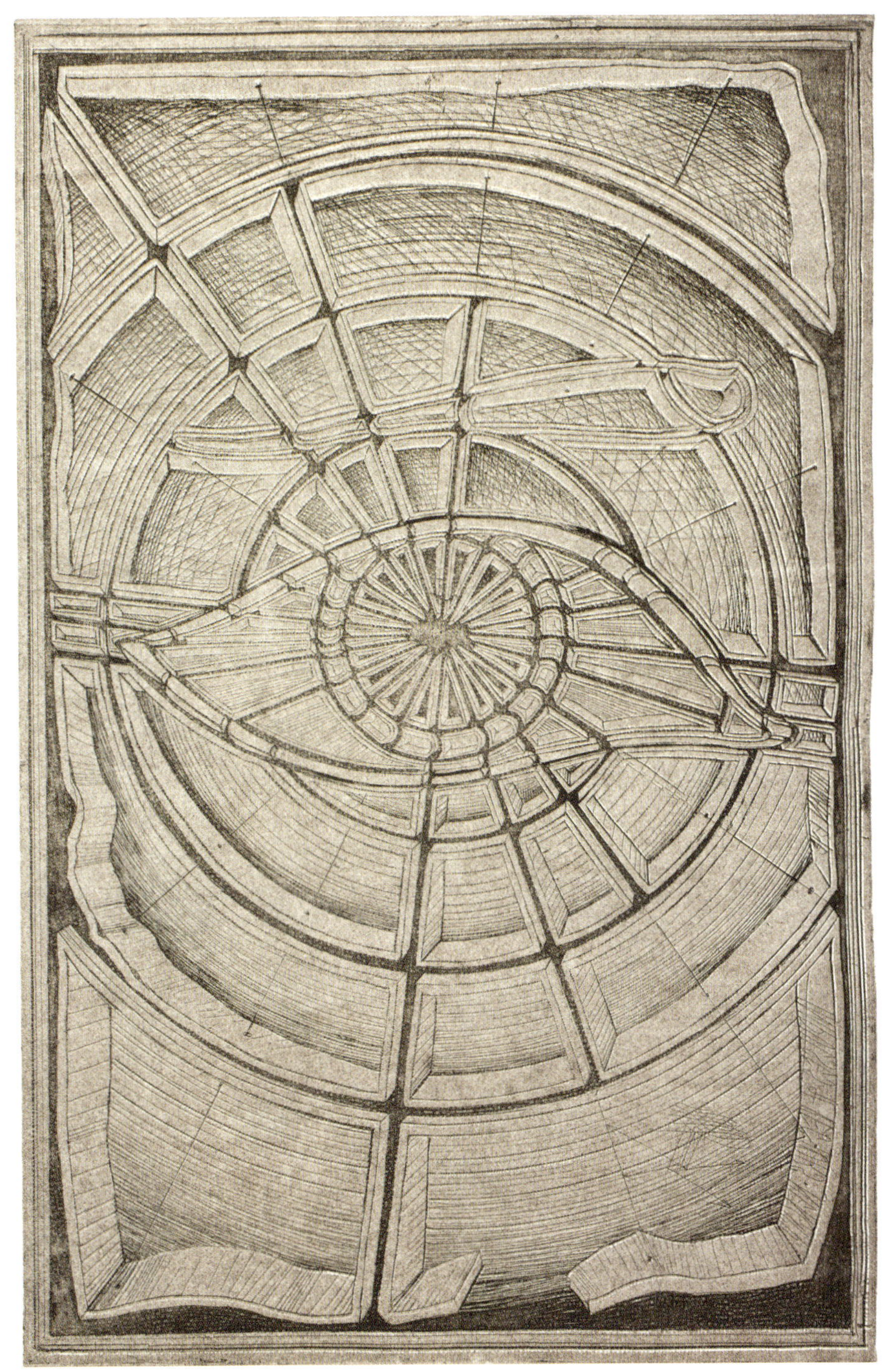

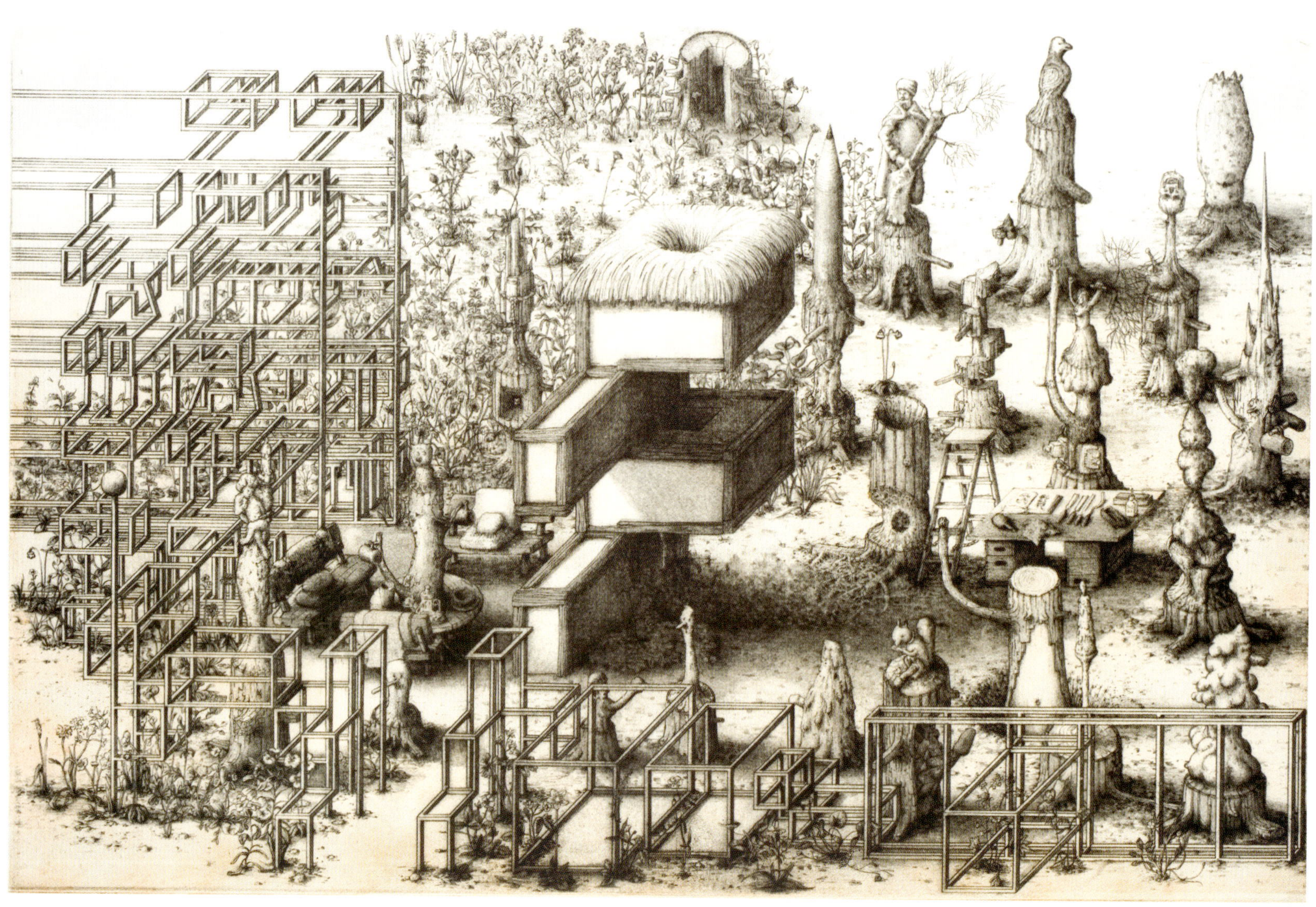

Paul Noble (born 1963): 'Paul's Place', printer: Hugh Stoneman (1947–2005), signed and dated 2002, etching (B.A.T.), 65.5 x 86cms. The Art Fund Hugh Stoneman Archive. Falmouth Art Gallery collection. FAMAG 2008.26.74

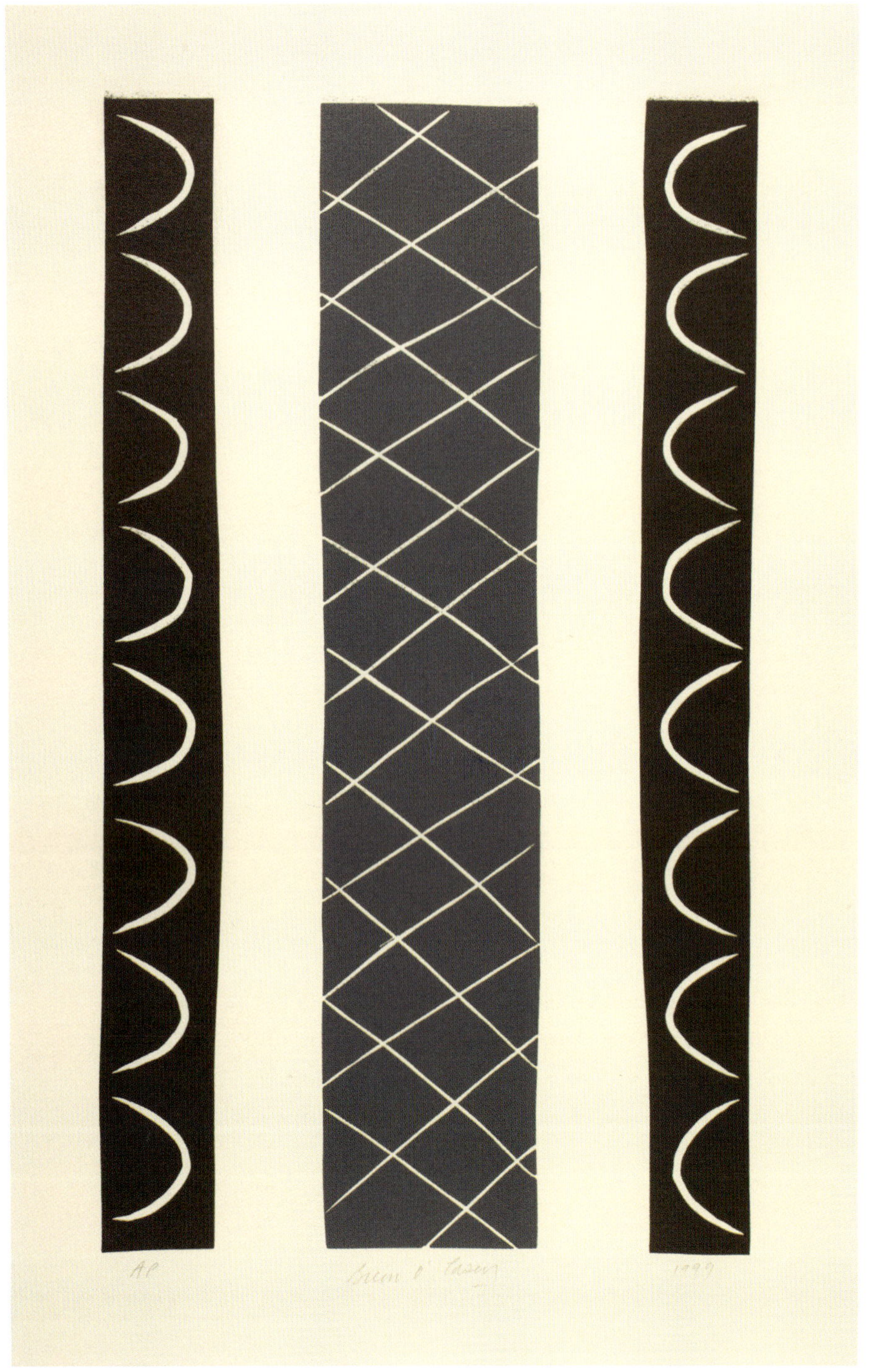

Breon O'Casey (b.1928): 'Grey Centre', 1999, printer: Hugh Stoneman (1947–2005), publisher: special editions, signed and dated 1999, linocut (artist's proof), 49 x 28.5cms. The Art Fund Hugh Stoneman Archive. Falmouth Art Gallery collection. FAMAG 2008.26.75

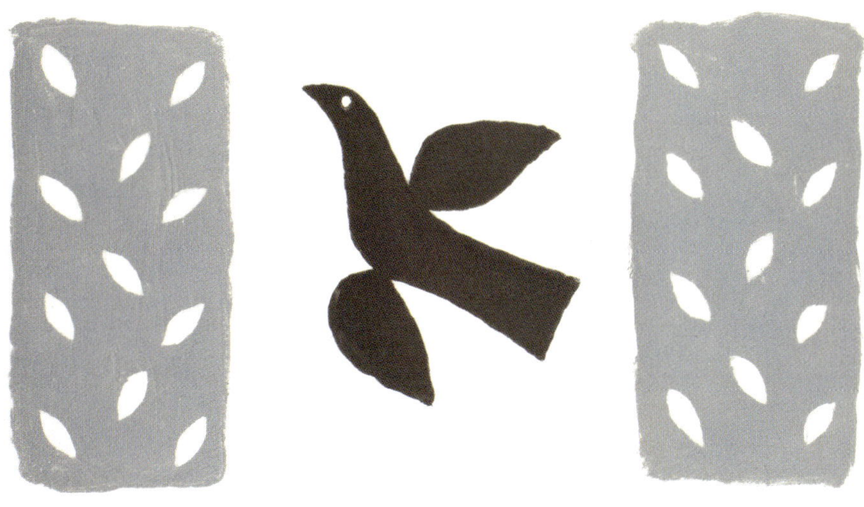

Breon O'Casey (b.1928): 'Black Bird in Grey', printer: Hugh Stoneman (1947–2005), publisher: special editions, signed and dated 2005, carborundum (number 14 of an edition of 25), 57.5 x 75.5cms. The Art Fund Hugh Stoneman Archive. Falmouth Art Gallery collection. FAMAG 2008.26.76

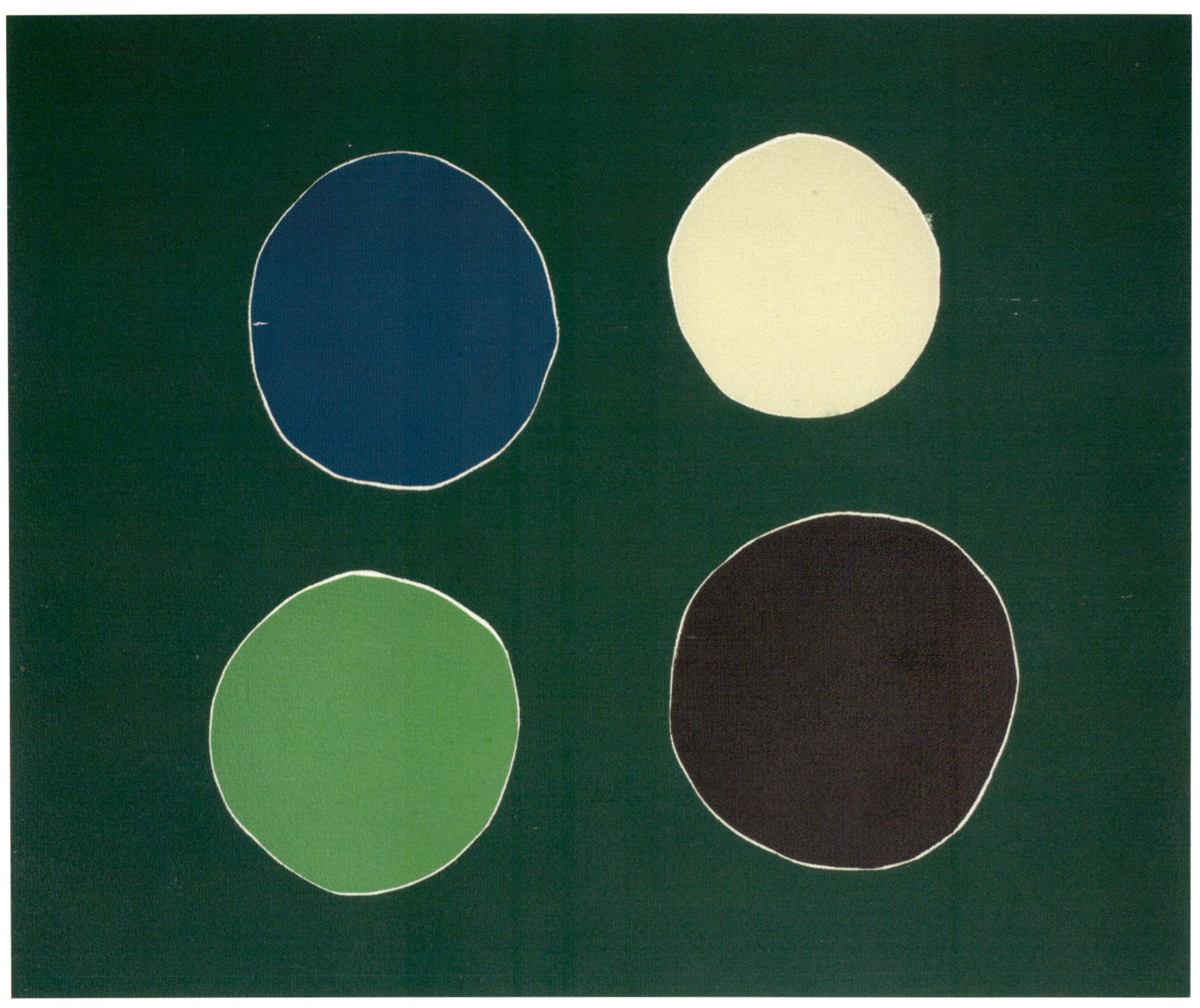

Breon O'Casey (b.1928): 'Four Circles', printer: Hugh Stoneman (1947–2005), publisher: special editions, signed and dated MM III (2003), woodcut (number 15 of an edition of 15), 41 x 70.7cms. The Art Fund Hugh Stoneman Archive. Falmouth Art Gallery collection. FAMAG 2008.26.77

John O'Connor (1913–2004): 'John Taverner', printer: Hugh Stoneman (1947–2005), signed and dated 1974, etching (number 1 of an edition of 100), 53.5 x 38cms. The Art Fund Hugh Stoneman Archive. Falmouth Art Gallery collection. FAMAG 2008.26.78

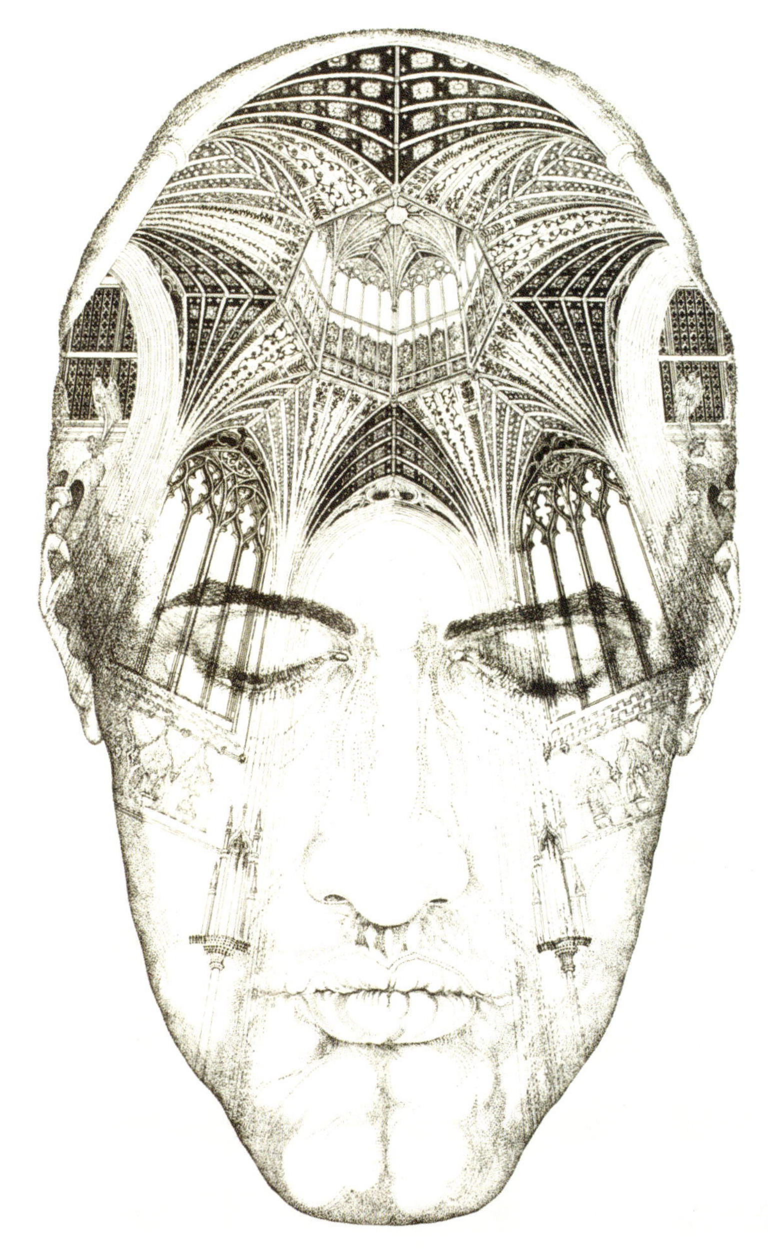

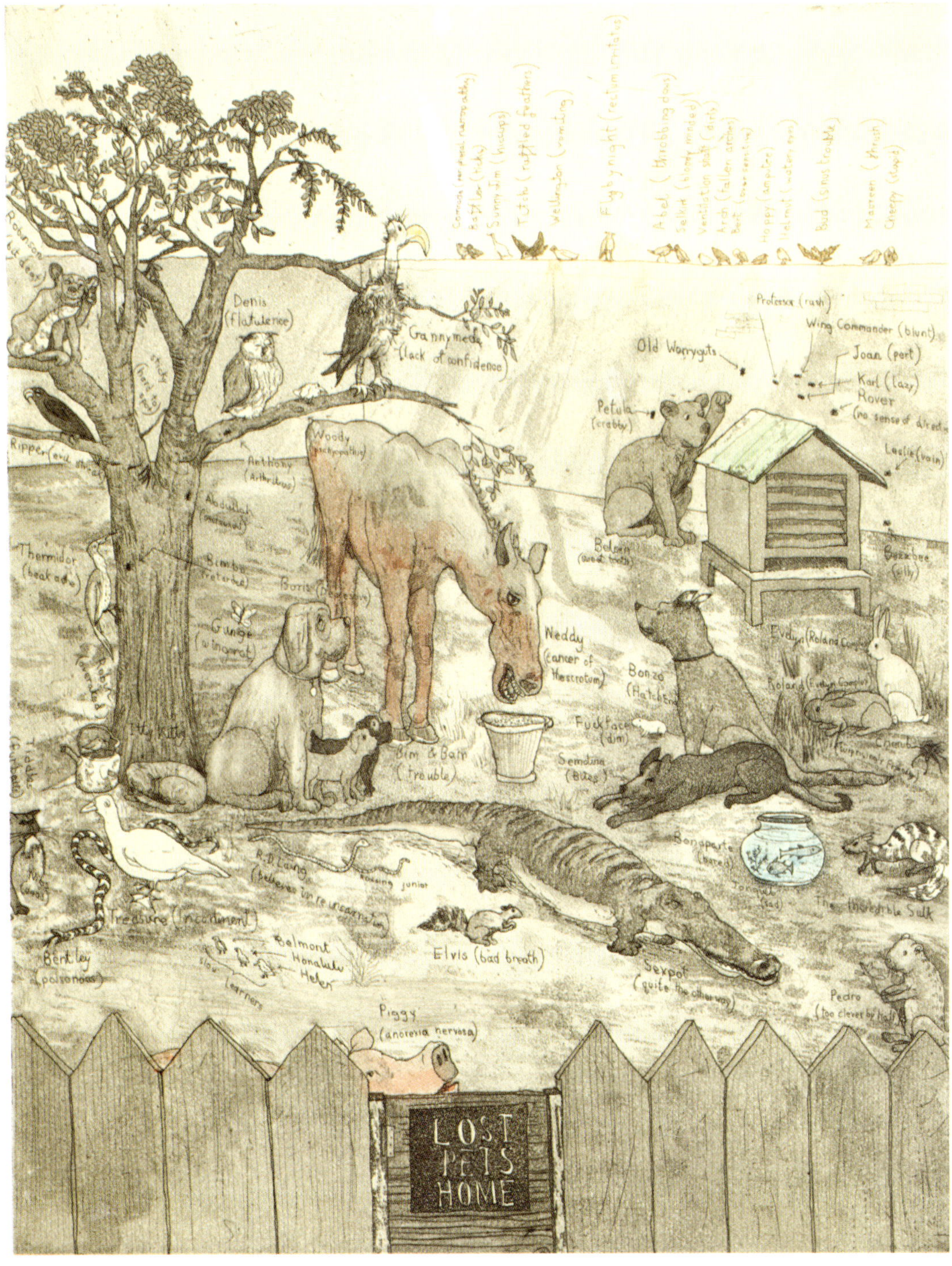

Chris Orr RA (born 1943): 'Sixty Six Lost Pets & their Problems', printer: Hugh Stoneman (1947–2005), signed and dated 1980, etching (number 32 of an edition of 50), 66.5 x 48cms. The Art Fund Hugh Stoneman Archive. Falmouth Art Gallery collection. FAMAG 2008.26.79

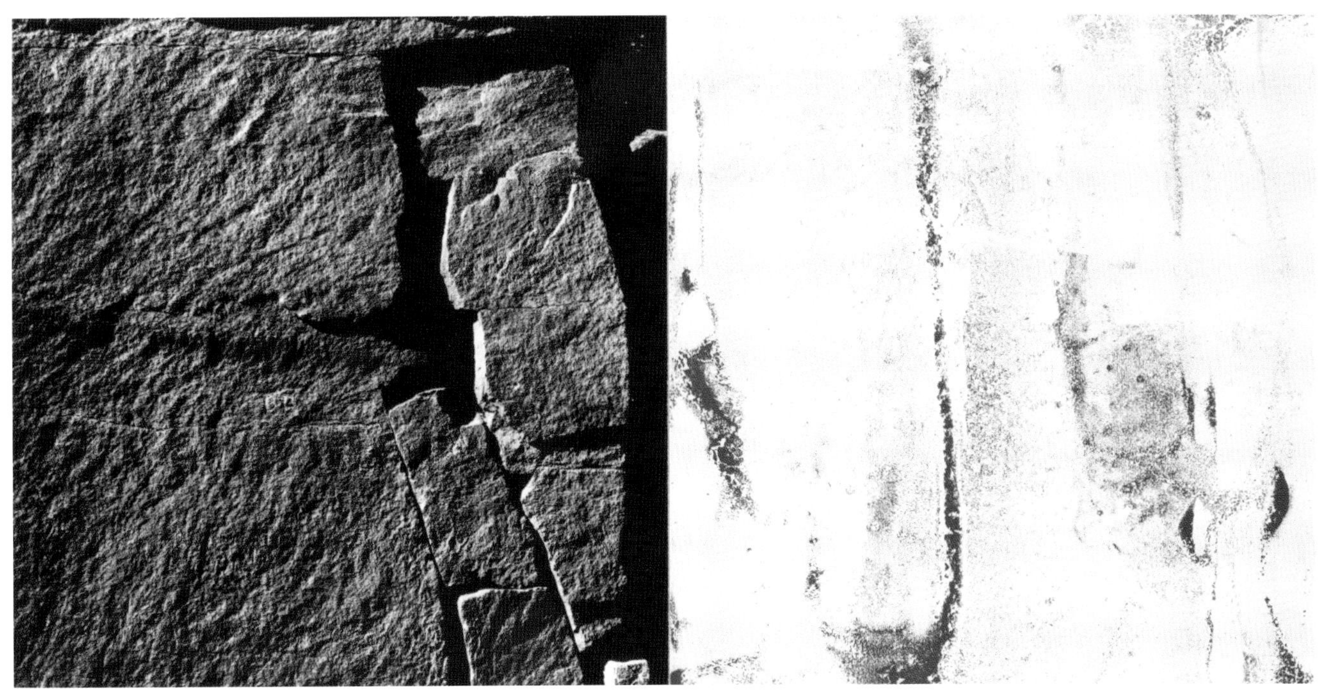

Michael Porter (born 1948): 'Shining Cliff VI', printer: Hugh Stoneman (1947–2005), signed and dated 1999, photograph and etching (number 6 of an edition of 10), 49.5 x 33cms. The Art Fund Hugh Stoneman Archive. Falmouth Art Gallery collection. FAMAG 2008.26.80

Matthew Radford (born 1953): No.3 from the series 'Newsreel', printer: Hugh Stoneman (1947–2005), publisher: Alan Cristea Gallery, signed and dated 2002, etching (B.A.T.), 38 x 33.5cms. The Art Fund Hugh Stoneman Archive. Falmouth Art Gallery collection. FAMAG 2008.26.81

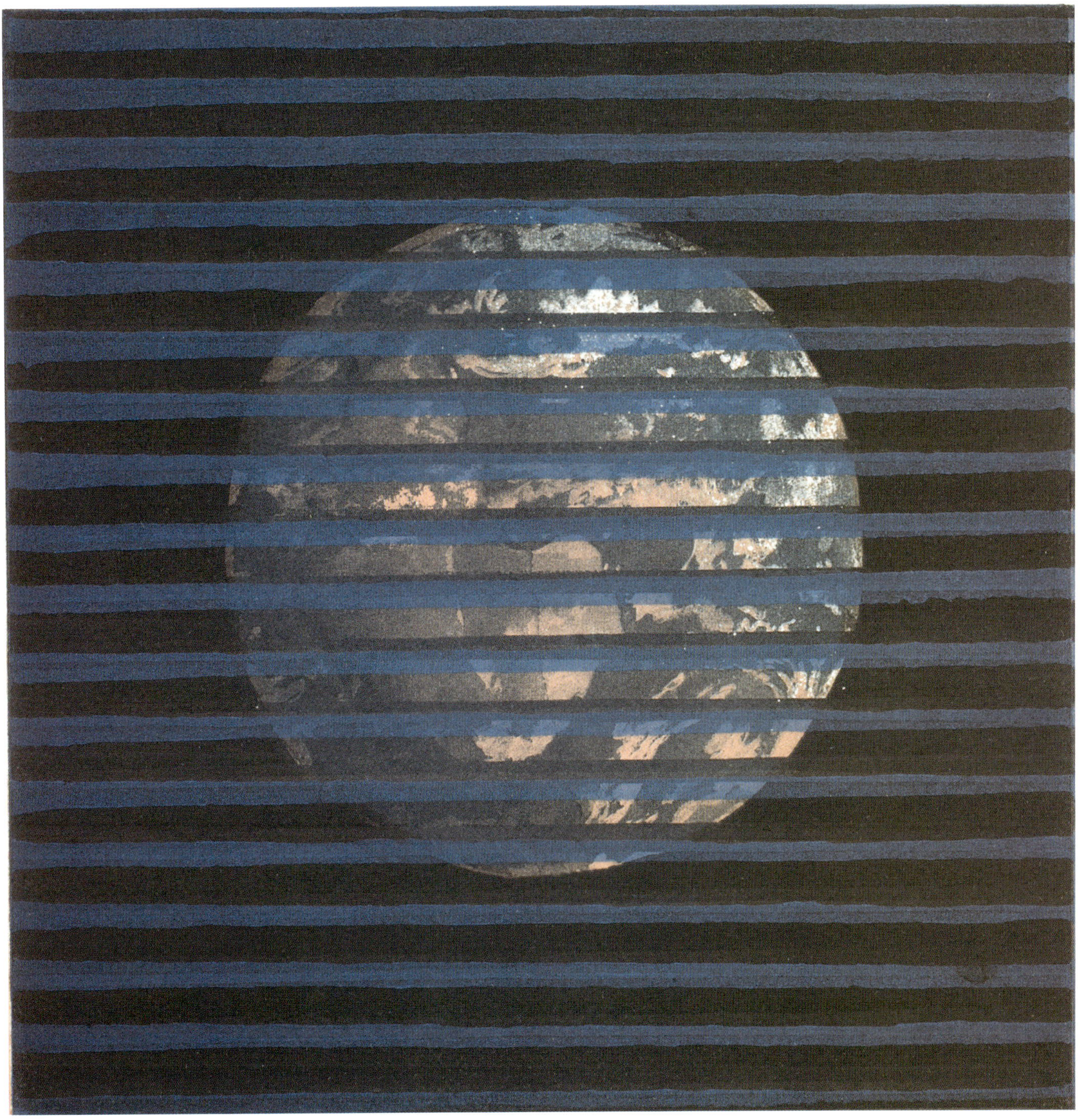

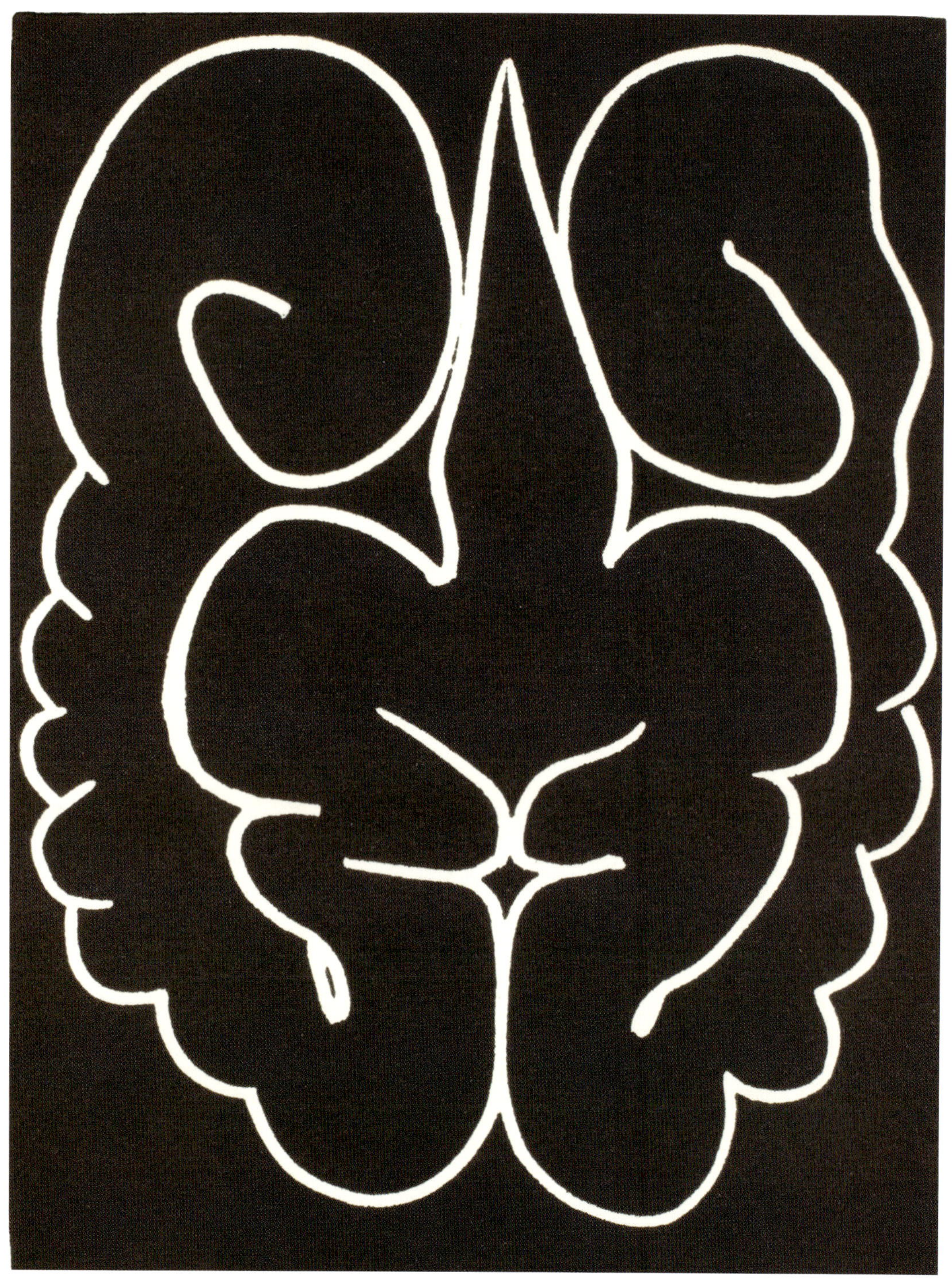

Peter Randall-Page (born 1954): 'Walnut V', printer: Hugh Stoneman (1947–2005), signed and dated 2000, linocut (B.A.T.), 33.3 x 26cms. The Art Fund Hugh Stoneman Archive. Falmouth Art Gallery collection. FAMAG 2008.26.82

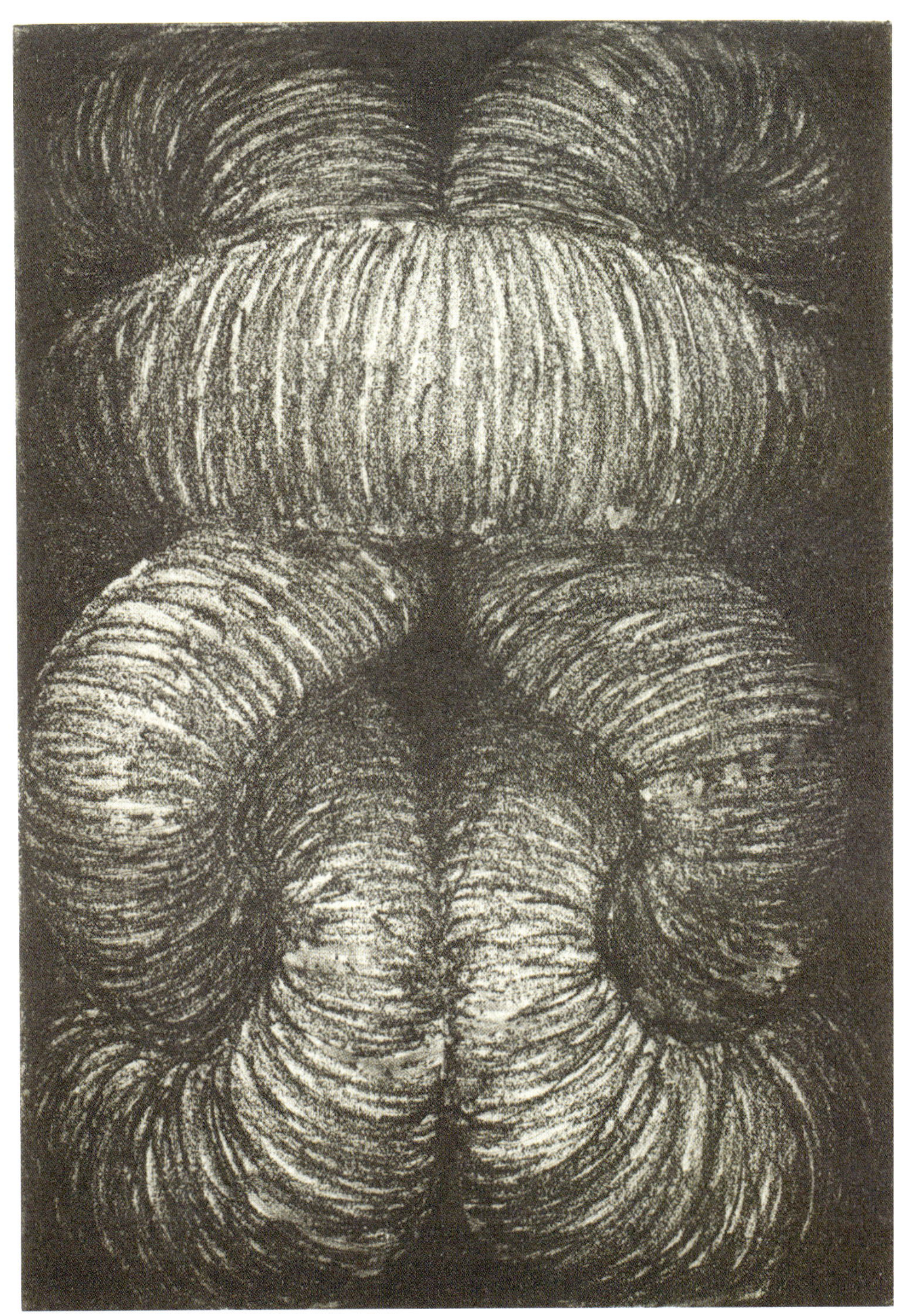

Peter Randall Page (born 1954): 'Untitled' – etching five, 1992, printer: Hugh Stoneman (1947–2005), signed, etching (B.A.T.), 34 x 26.4cms. The Art Fund Hugh Stoneman Archive. Falmouth Art Gallery collection. FAMAG 2008.26.83

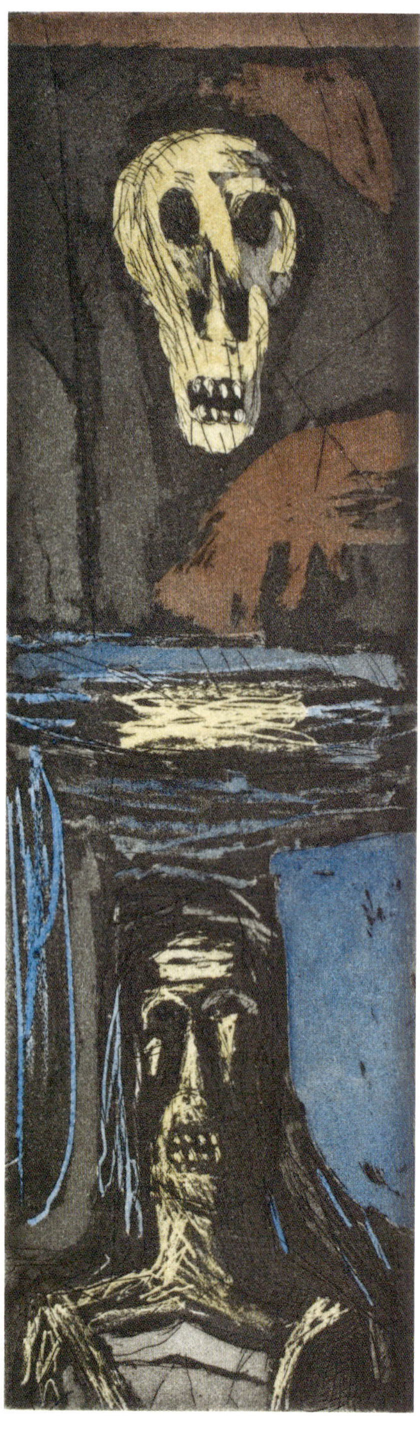

Michael Rees (born 1962): 'Bone Dreams', printer: Hugh Stoneman (1947–2005), signed and dated 1997, etching (printer's proof), 44.5 x 37cms. The Art Fund Hugh Stoneman Archive. Falmouth Art Gallery collection. FAMAG 2008.26.84

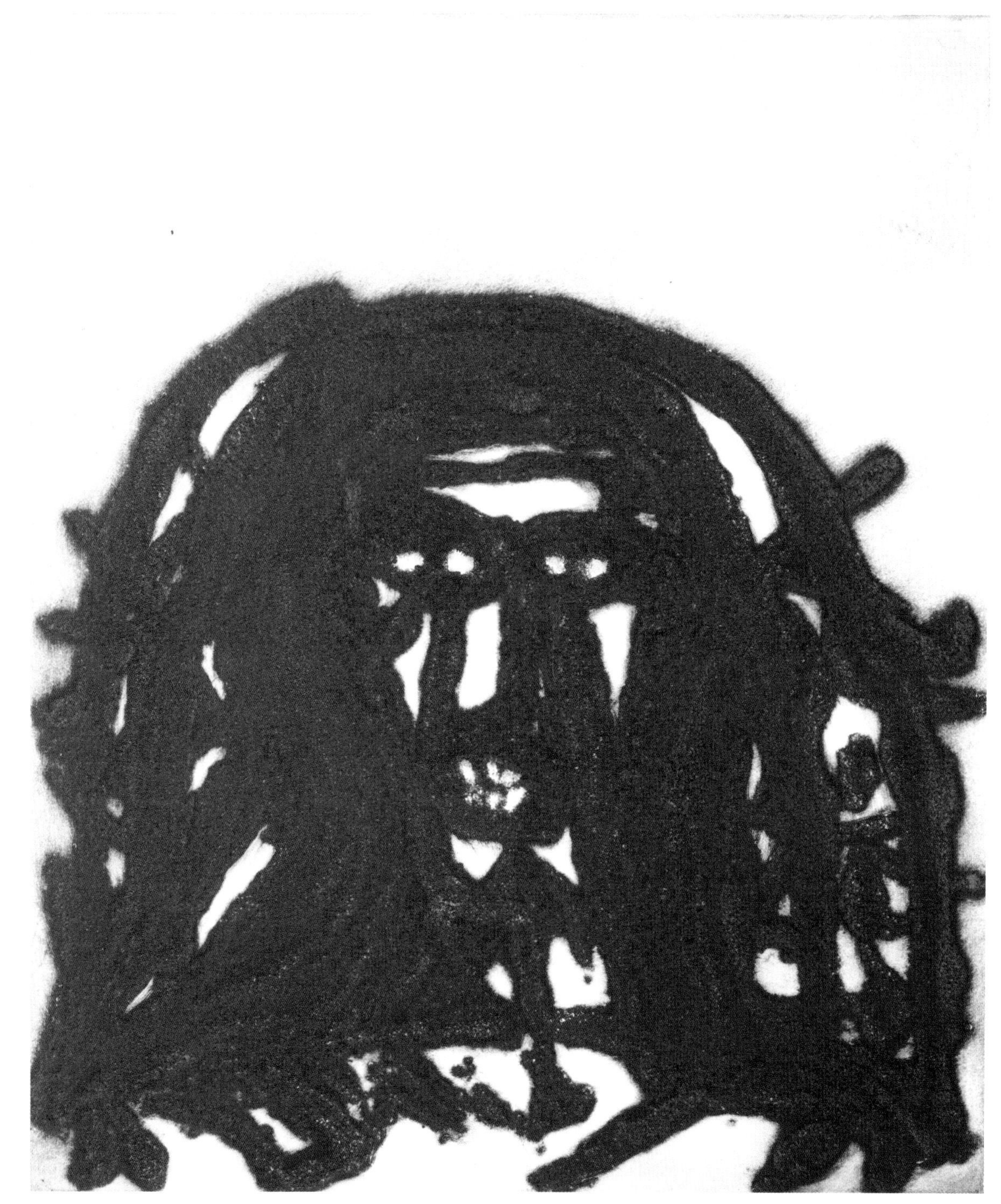

Michael Rees (born 1962): 'Bog Man', printer: Hugh Stoneman (1947–2005), signed and dated 1997, etching (printer's proof), 44.6 x 37cms. The Art Fund Hugh Stoneman Archive. Falmouth Art Gallery collection. FAMAG 2008.26.85

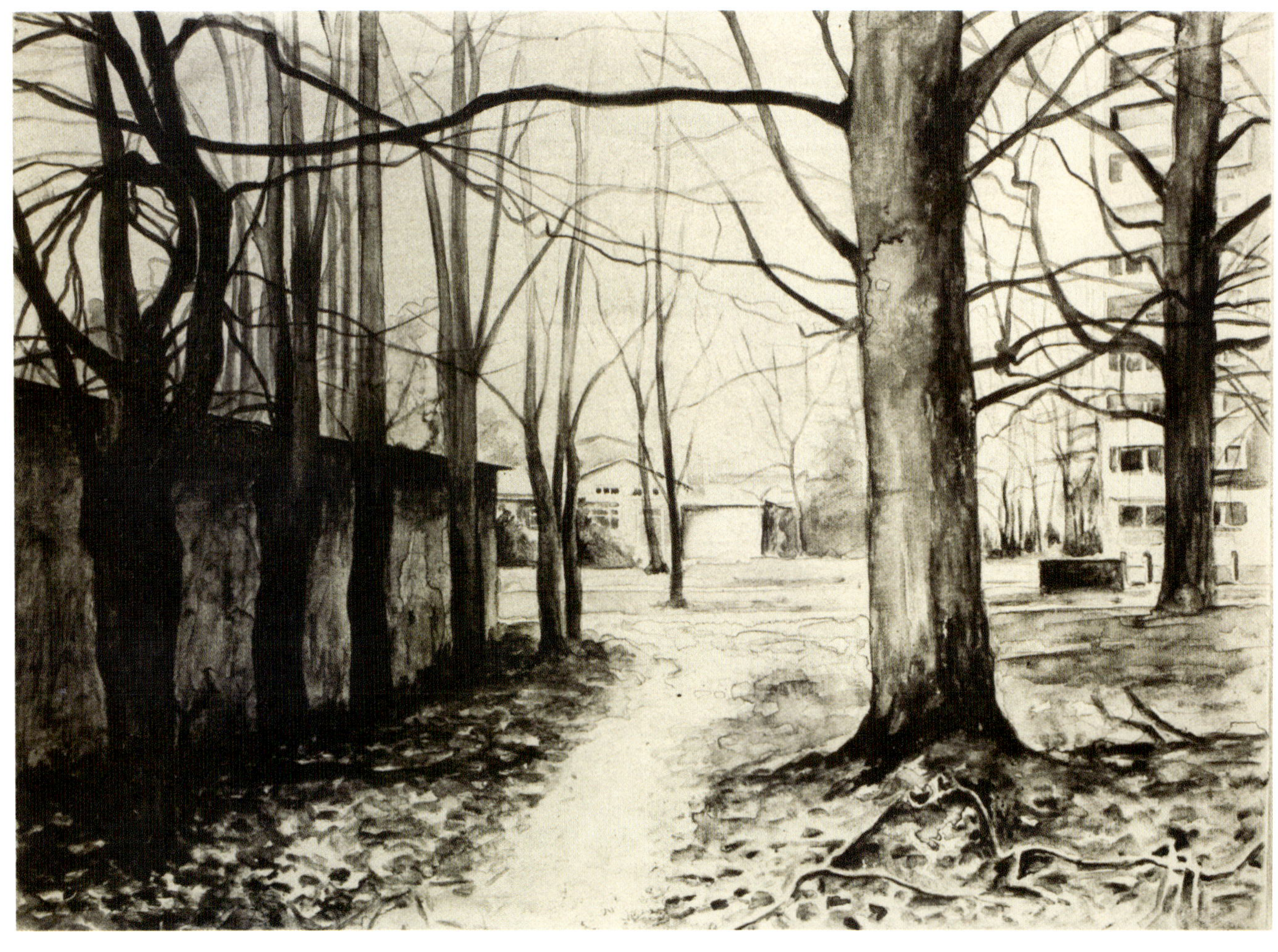

George Shaw (born 1966): 'Twelve Short Walks' (7), printer: Hugh Stoneman (1947–2005), publisher: The Paragon Press, signed and dated 2005, etching (printer's proof), 38.5 x 49.5cms. The Art Fund Hugh Stoneman Archive. Falmouth Art Gallery collection. FAMAG 2008.26.86

Kevin Sinnott (born 1947): 'Impressions', printer: Hugh Stoneman (1947–2005), publisher: Print Centre Publications, signed and dated 1990, aquatint sugarlift (number 20 of an edition of 20), 86.3 x 71.4cms. The Art Fund Hugh Stoneman Archive. Falmouth Art Gallery collection. FAMAG 2008.26. 87

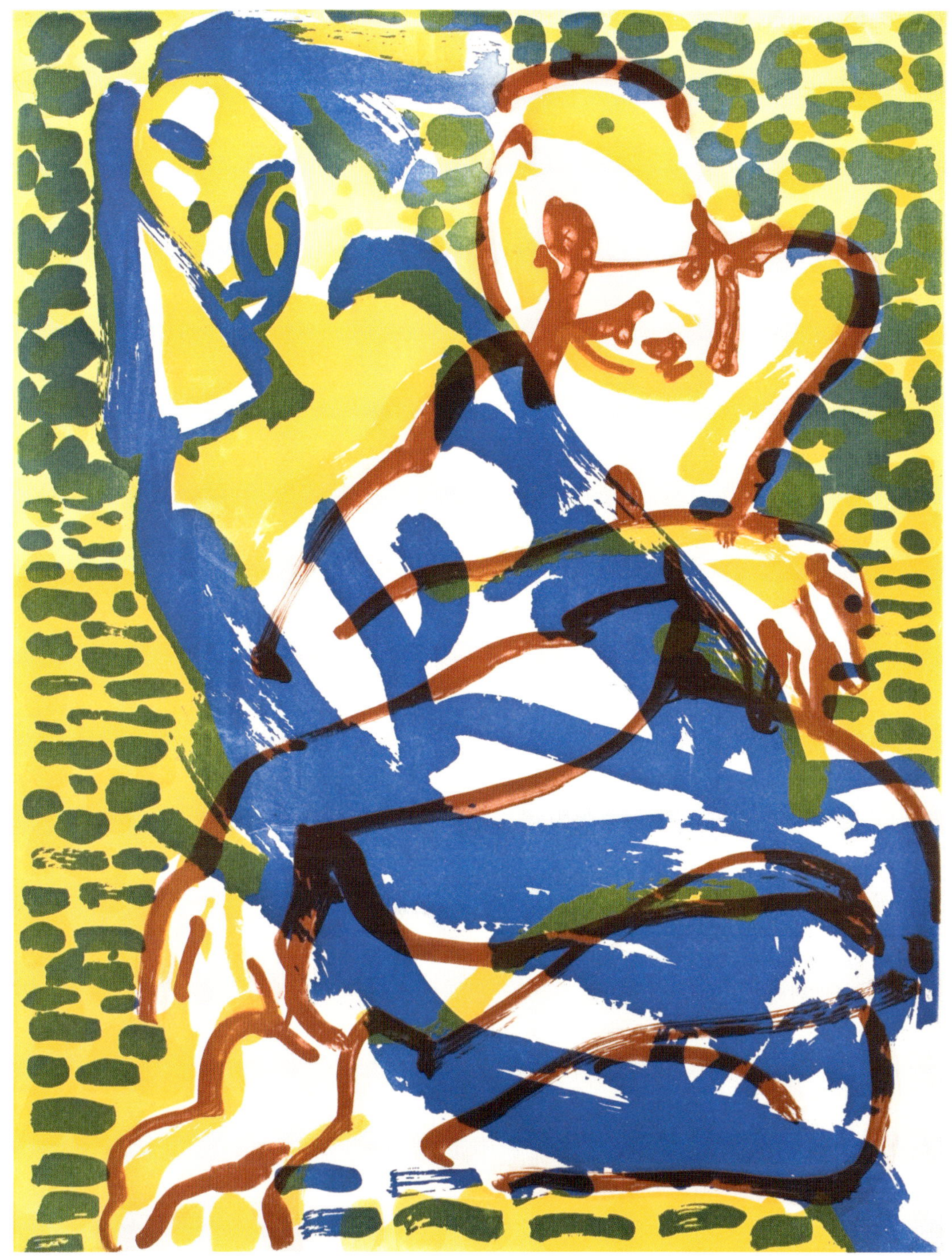

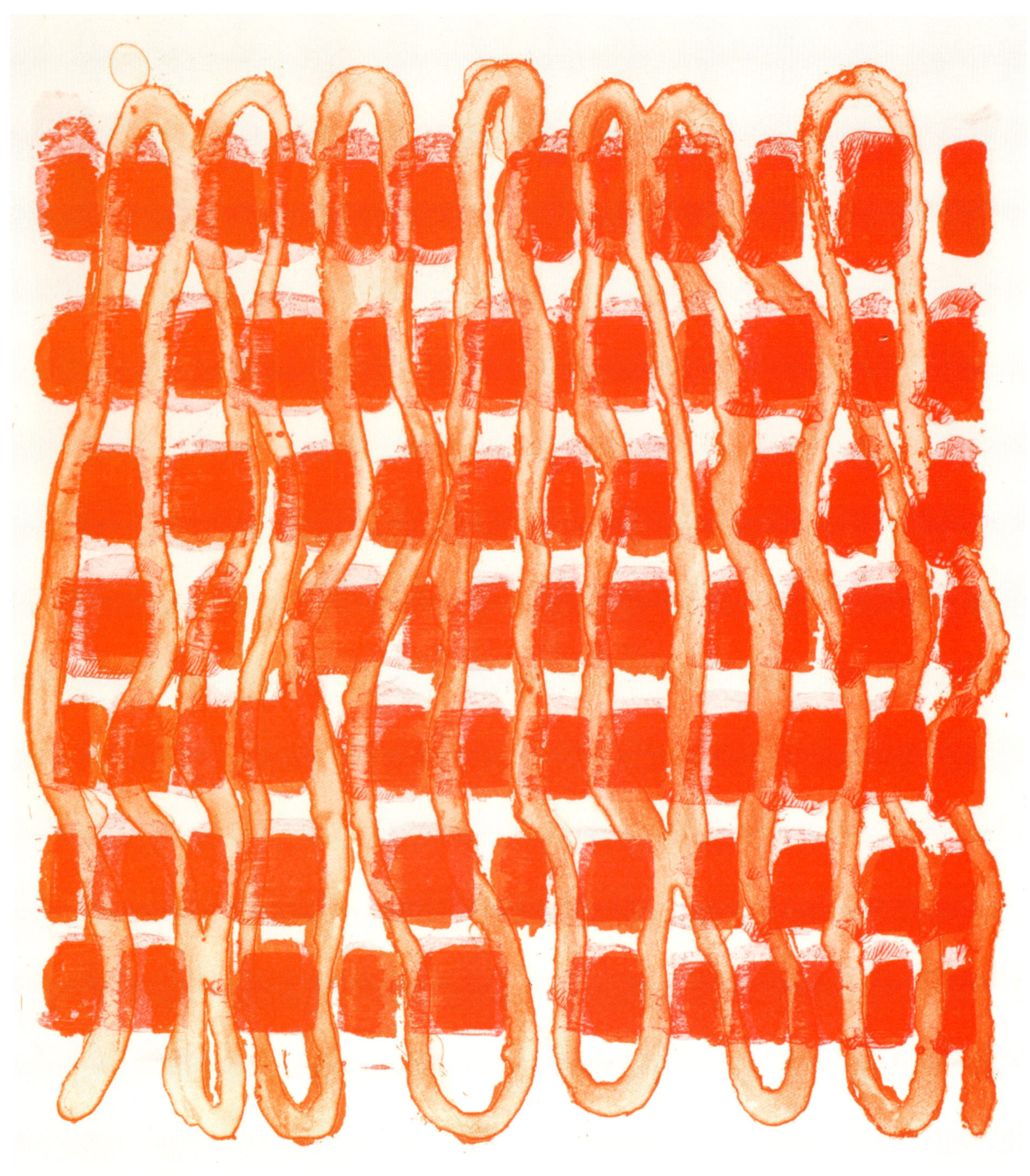

Richard Smith (born 1931): 'Warp and Weft: Signature Piece', printer: Hugh Stoneman (1947–2005), publisher: Stoneman Graphics, signed and dated 1997, aquatint (B.A.T.), 57.7 x 46cms. The Art Fund Hugh Stoneman Archive. Falmouth Art Gallery collection. FAMAG 2008.26.88

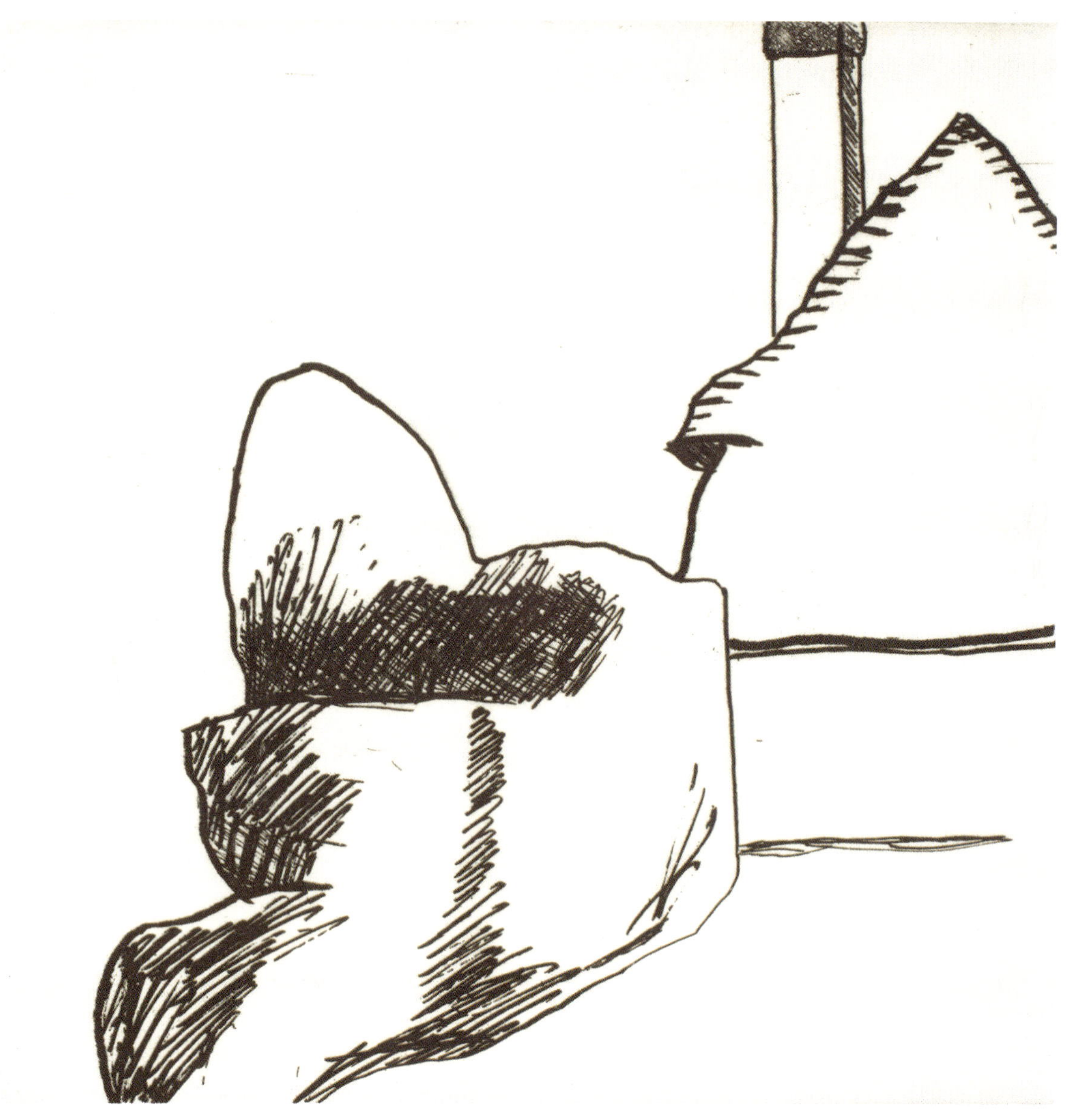

Andrew Southall (born 1947): From 'Black and White of Brick and Bark', printer: Hugh Stoneman (1947–2005), publisher: Print Centre Publications, signed and dated 1991, etching (number 24 of an edition of 35), 45.5 x 38.2cms. The Art Fund Hugh Stoneman Archive. Falmouth Art Gallery collection. FAMAG 2008.26.89

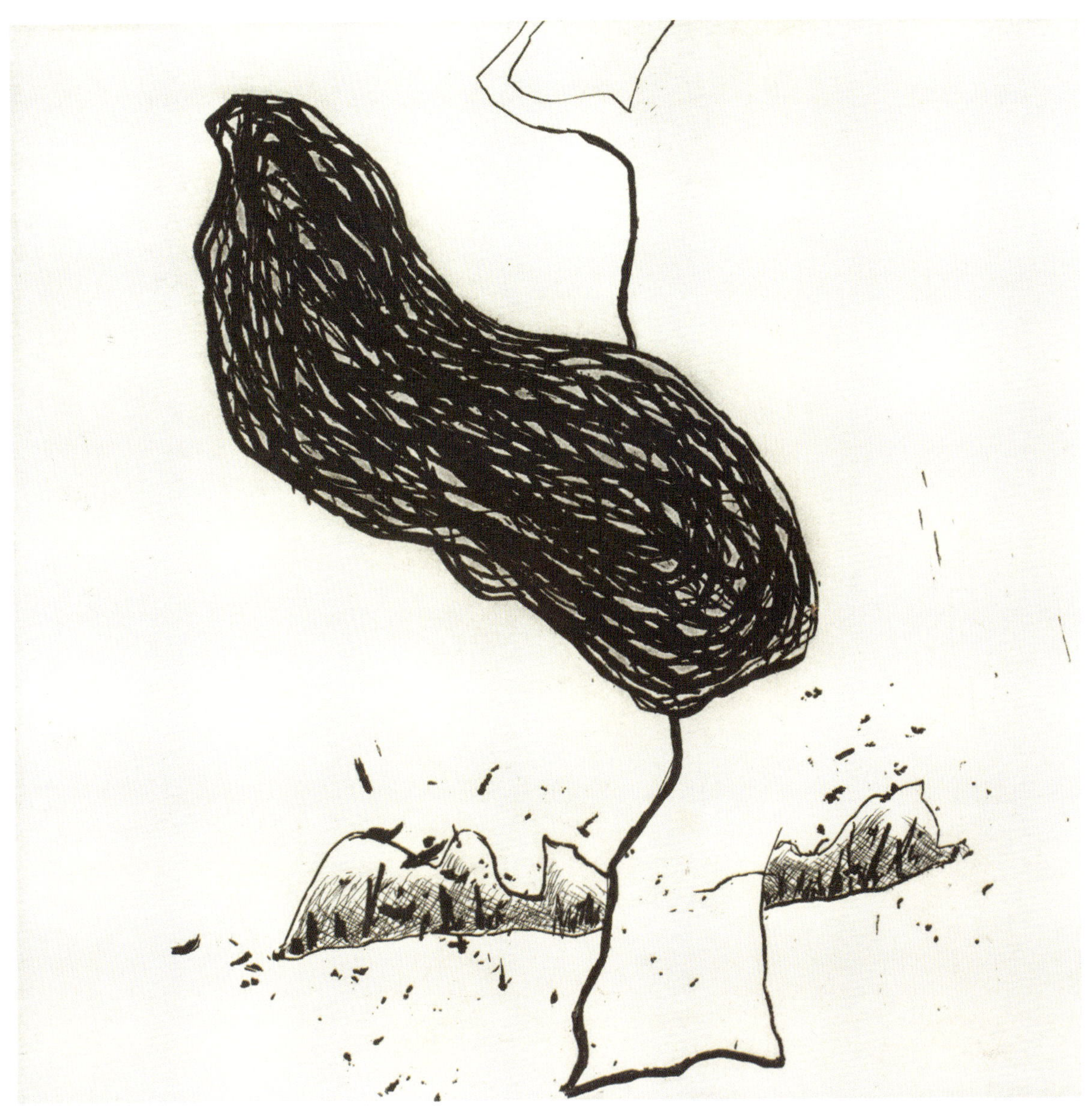

Andrew Southall (born 1947): From 'Black and White of Brick and Bark', printer: Hugh Stoneman (1947–2005), publisher: Print Centre Publications, signed and dated 1991, etching (number 23 of an edition of 35), 45.5 x 38.2cms. The Art Fund Hugh Stoneman Archive. Falmouth Art Gallery collection. FAMAG 2008.26.90

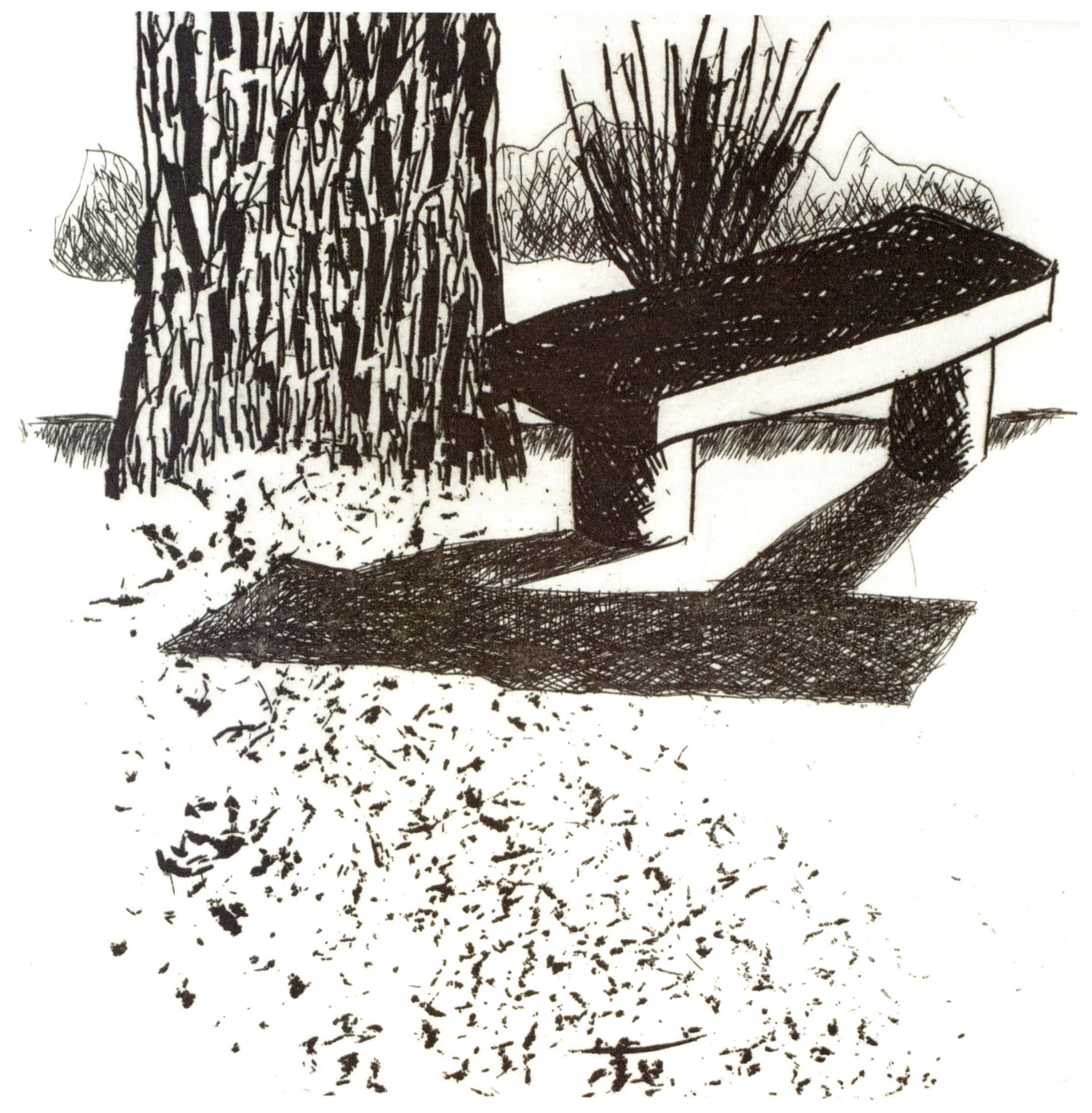

Andrew Southall (born 1947): From 'Black and White of Brick and Bark', printer: Hugh Stoneman (1947–2005), publisher: Print Centre Publications, signed and dated 1991, etching (number 23 of an edition of 35), 45.3 x 38cms. The Art Fund Hugh Stoneman Archive. Falmouth Art Gallery collection. FAMAG 2008.26.91

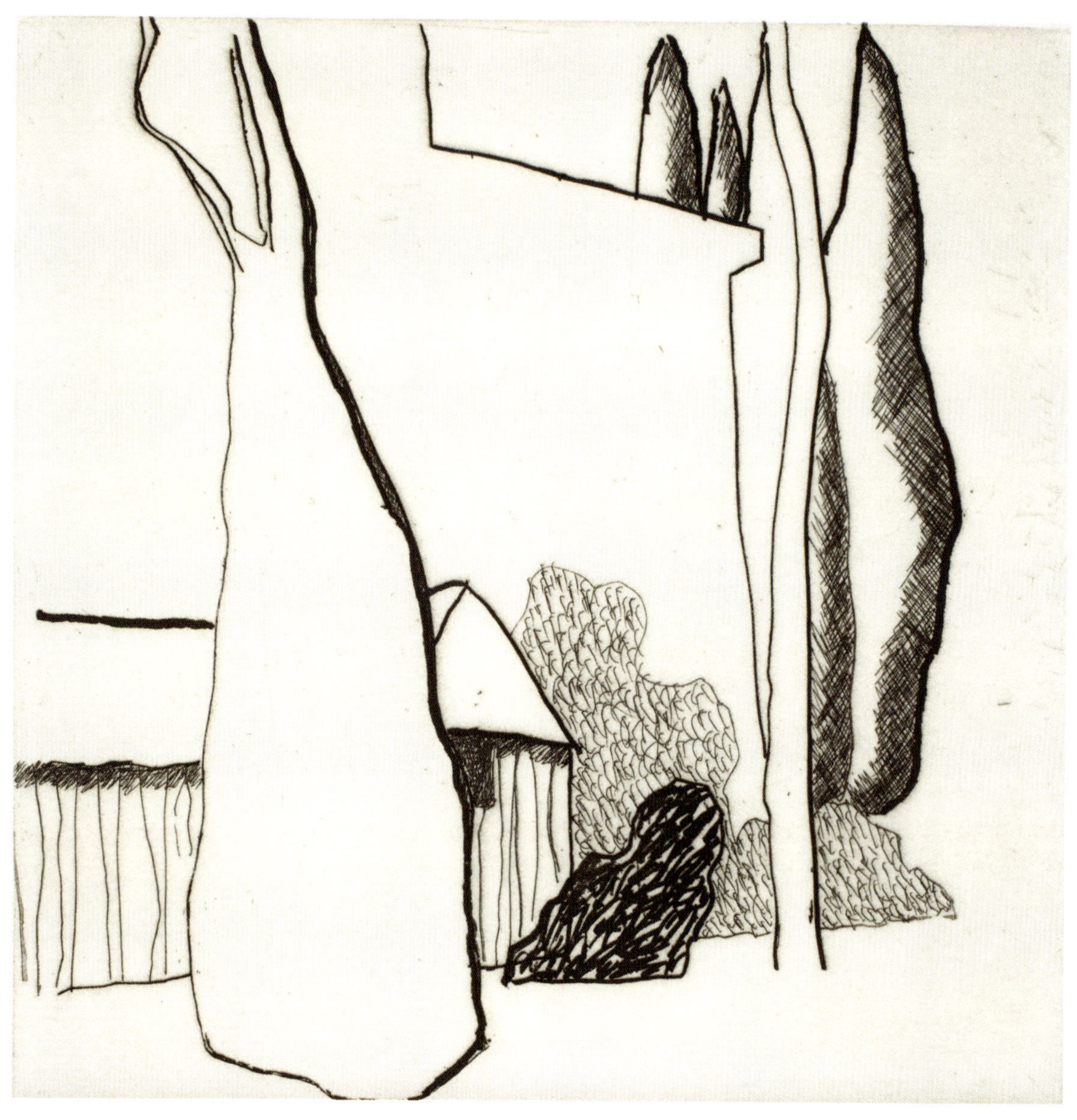

Andrew Southall (born 1947): From 'Black and White of Brick and Bark', printer: Hugh Stoneman (1947–2005), publisher: Print Centre Publications, signed and dated 1991, etching (number 23 of an edition of 35), 45.5 x 38.2cms. The Art Fund Hugh Stoneman Archive. Falmouth Art Gallery collection. FAMAG 2008.26.92

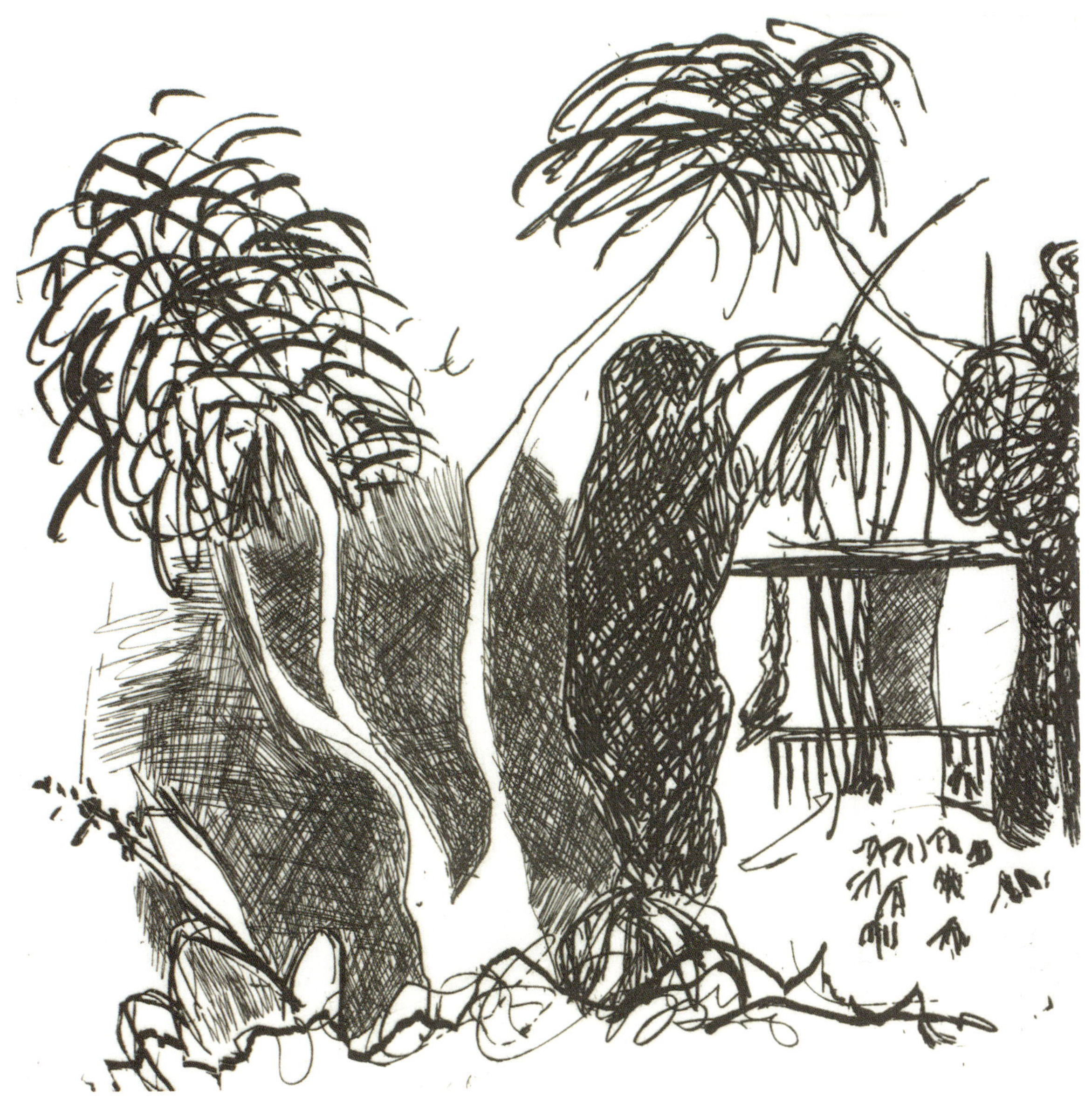

Andrew Southall (born 1947): From 'Black and White of Brick and Bark', printer: Hugh Stoneman (1947–2005), publisher: Print Centre Publications, signed and dated 1991, etching (number 23 of an edition of 35), 45.5 x 38.2cms. The Art Fund Hugh Stoneman Archive. Falmouth Art Gallery collection. FAMAG 2008.26.93

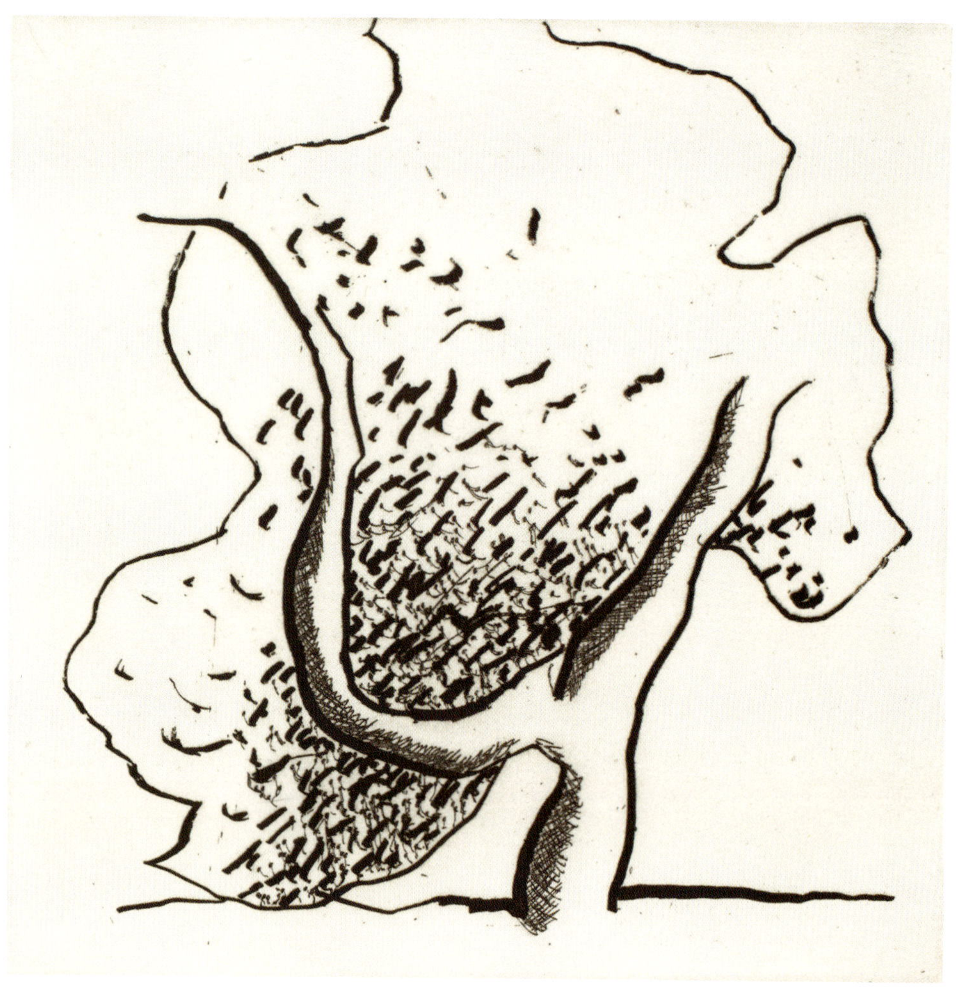

Andrew Southall (born 1947): From 'Black and White of Brick and Bark', printer: Hugh Stoneman (1947–2005), publisher: Print Centre Publications, signed and dated 1991, etching (number 23 of an edition of 35), 45.5 x 38.2cms. The Art Fund Hugh Stoneman Archive. Falmouth Art Gallery collection. FAMAG 2008.26.94

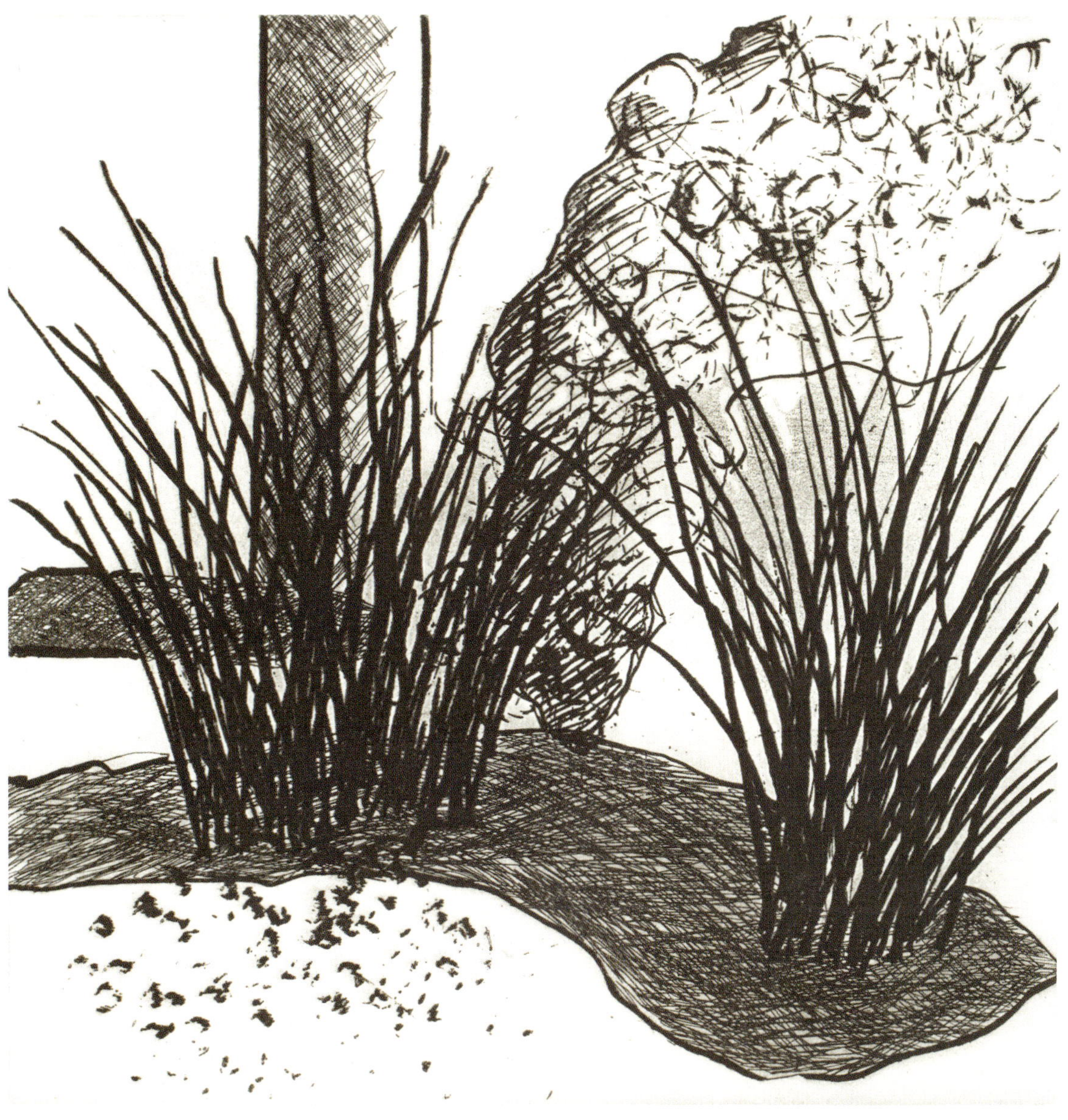

Andrew Southall (born 1947): From 'Black and White of Brick and Bark', printer: Hugh Stoneman (1947–2005), publisher: Print Centre Publications, signed and dated 1991, etching (number 23 of an edition of 35), 45.5 x 38.2cms. The Art Fund Hugh Stoneman Archive. Falmouth Art Gallery collection. FAMAG 2008.26.95

Trevor Sutton (born 1948): 'Short Stories II', 2000, printer: Hugh Stoneman (1947–2005), publisher: Flowers East, signed, etching, aquatint and drypoint (printer's proof 2/2), 45.5 x 43 cms. The Art Fund Hugh Stoneman Archive. Falmouth Art Gallery collection. FAMAG 2008.26.96

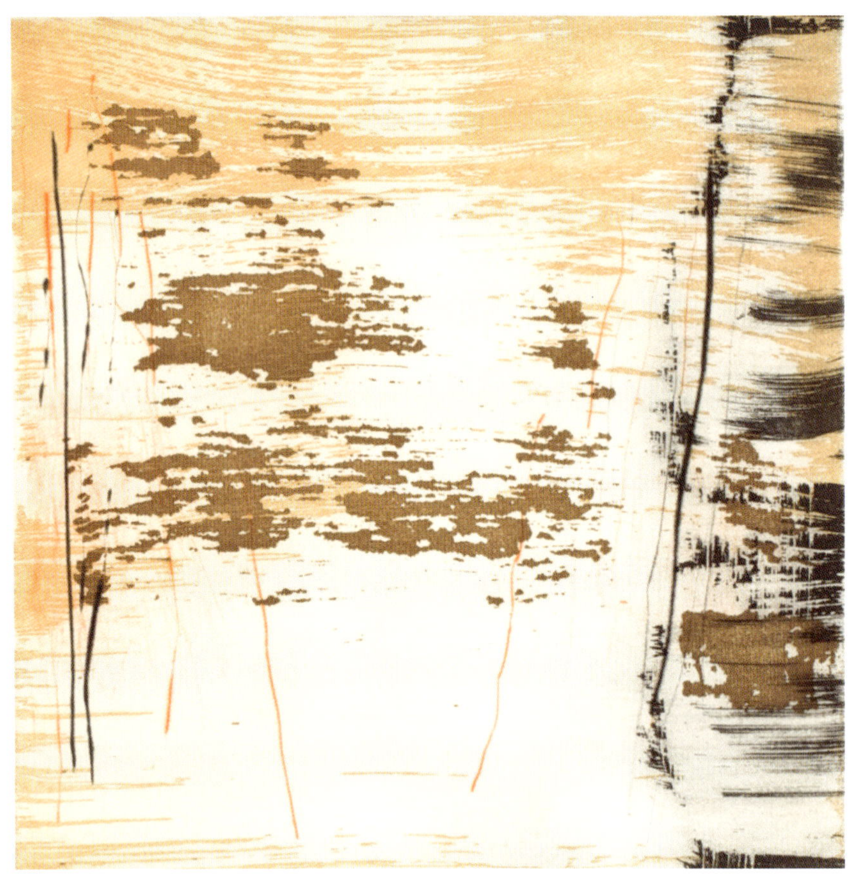

Trevor Sutton (born 1948): 'Short Stories IV', 2000, printer: Hugh Stoneman (1947–2005), publisher: Flowers East, signed, etching and aquatint (printer's proof 1/2), 45.5 x 43cms. The Art Fund Hugh Stoneman Archive. Falmouth Art Gallery collection. FAMAG 2008.26.97

Ava Vargas: 'Mexican Indian Study,' printer: Hugh Stoneman (1947–2005), publisher: Stoneman Graphics, signed and dated 1987, photogravure (B.A.T.), 40 x 59.5cms. The Art Fund Hugh Stoneman Archive. Falmouth Art Gallery collection. FAMAG 2008.26.98

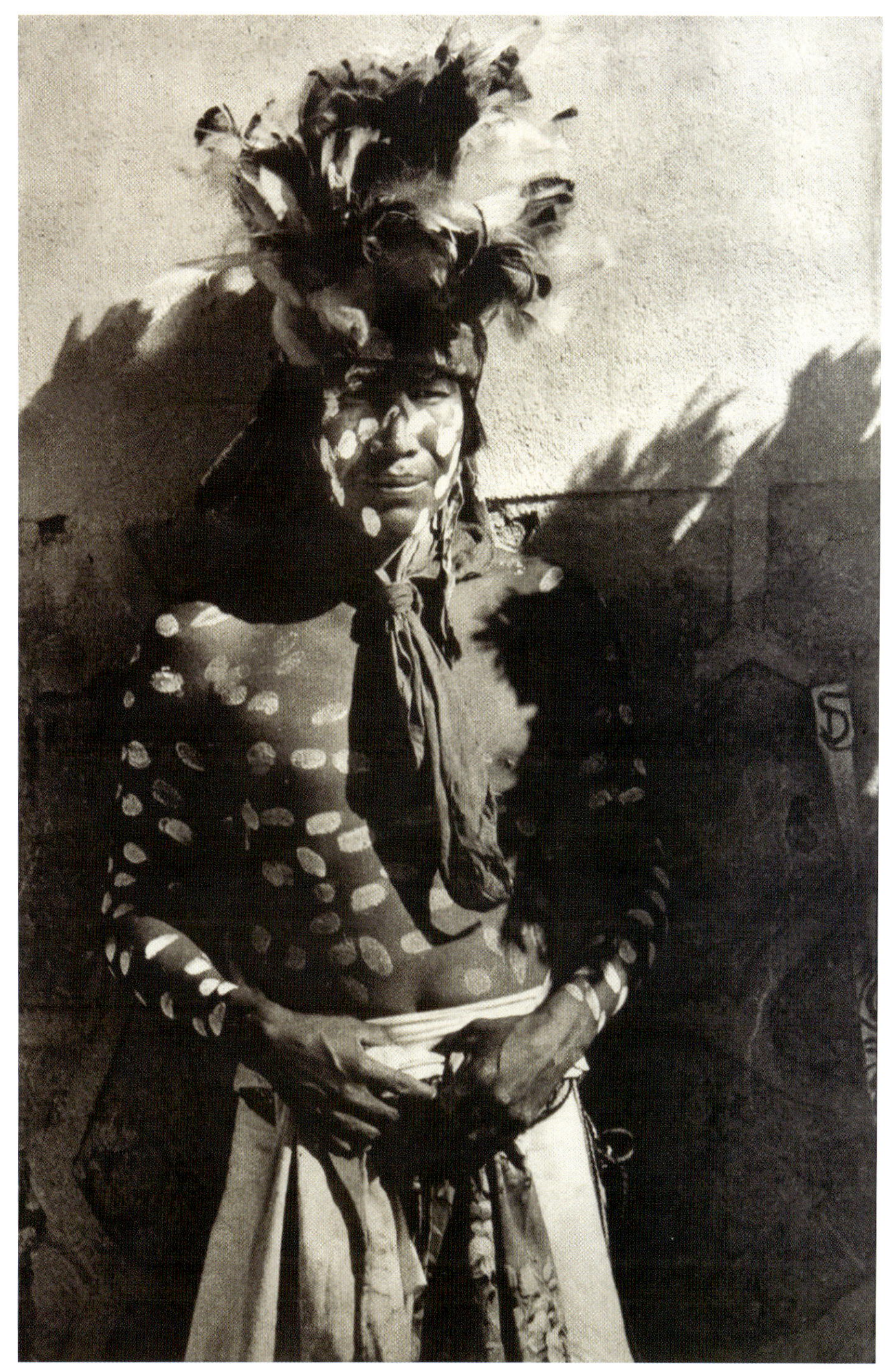

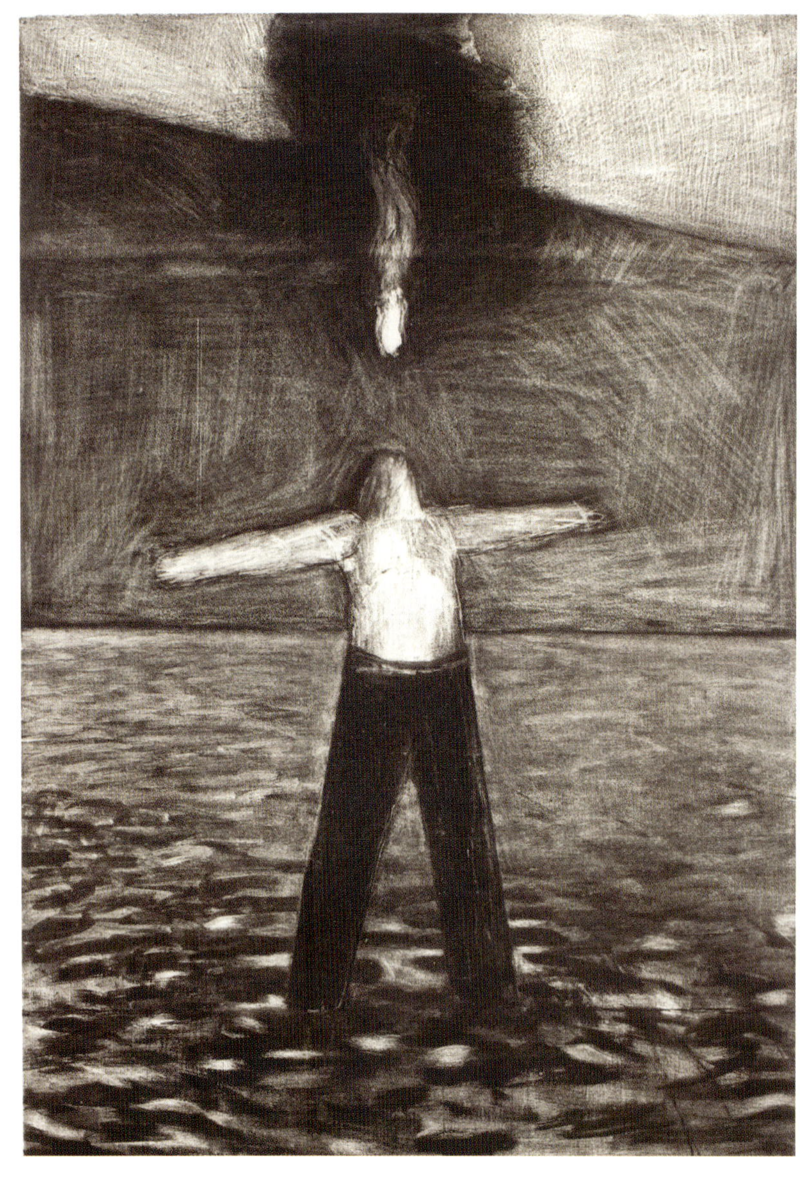

Karl Weschke (1925–2005): 'Fire-Eater', printer: Hugh Stoneman (1947–2005), signed and dated 2004, aquatint etching (B.A.T.), 56.2 x 42cms. The Art Fund Hugh Stoneman Archive. Falmouth Art Gallery collection. FAMAG 2008.26.99